THE SOUTH AFRICAN NOVEL IN ENGLISH SINCE 1950

an information and resource guide

*Bibliographies
and
Guides
in
African Studies*

James C. Armstrong
Editor

THE SOUTH AFRICAN NOVEL IN ENGLISH SINCE 1950

an information and resource guide

G. E. GORMAN

G.K.HALL&CO.
70 LINCOLN STREET, BOSTON, MASS.

Library of Congress Cataloging in Publication Data
Gorman, G E
  The South African novel in English since 1950.

  (Bibliographies and guides in African studies)
  Bibliography: p.
  Includes index.
  1. South African fiction (English) — History and criticism.
  2. South African fiction (English) — Bibliography.
  3. Bibliography — Bibliography — South Africa.   I. Title.
  II. Series.
  PR9362.5.G6   823   78-5551
  ISBN 0-8161-8178-0

This publication is printed on permanent/durable acid-free paper
MANUFACTURED IN THE UNITED STATES OF AMERICA

O

Contents

ABBREVIATIONS   vii

INTRODUCTION   ix

PART I.   SURVEY OF THE LITERATURE AND ASPECTS OF
BIBLIOGRAPHICAL CONTROL

THE SOUTH AFRICAN NOVEL: ITS EVOLUTION IN AN
ACADEMIC SETTING   3
     Growth of the Genre   3
     South African Literature in an Academic Setting   9

FORM, STYLE AND CONTENT OF THE LITERATURE   13
     Is It Literature?   13
     The Novel as Social Commentary   16
     Themes in South African Fiction   20

ACADEMIC STUDY OF THE SOUTH AFRICAN NOVEL   25
     Four Curricular Approaches   25
     Multidisciplinary Content of the Literature   30

BIBLIOGRAPHICAL PROBLEMS AND PROSPECTS   37
     Problems, Lacunae *and Incongruities*   38
     Selective Improvements and a Master Plan   42

PART II.   GUIDE TO BIBLIOGRAPHICAL RESOURCES

SOURCES OF BIOGRAPHICAL DATA   55
     Biographical Bibliographies   55
     Literary Encyclopedias and General Biographical Dictionaries   58
     Biographical Dictionaries of African Writers and Autobiographies   62

GENERAL BIBLIOGRAPHICAL GUIDES   69
     Bibliographies of Bibliographies   70
     Africana and Literary Bibliographies   71

SELECTIVE NON-SERIAL BIBLIOGRAPHIES 83
Published Library Catalogues 84
Selective Bibliographies 89

NATIONAL BIBLIOGRAPHIES AND SELECTED SERIAL
BIBLIOGRAPHIES 99
National Bibliographies and Complementary Trade Publications 100
Serial Bibliographies and Indices: Literature 103
Serial Bibliographies: Africana 104

PERIODICAL LISTS AND PERIODICAL INDICES 113
Periodical Lists 113
Periodical Indices 119
Appendix: *An Annotated List of Selected Africana and
Literary Serials* 125

DISSERTATIONS, THESES AND RESEARCH IN PROGRESS 143
Theses 143
Research in Progress 149
Appendix: *Dissertations and Theses on the South African
Novel in English Since 1950* 155

BIBLIOGRAPHIES OF AFRICAN AND SOUTH AFRICAN
LITERATURE 161
General Africana Literary Bibliographies 162
South African Literary Bibliographies 166

SELECTED PUBLISHERS AND SCHOLARLY SOCIETIES 175
Publishers 175
Scholarly and Professional Organizations 178

CONCLUSION 183

BIBLIOGRAPHY 185
General Background Literature 185
Biographical Data 195
General Bibliographical Guides 198
Selective, Non-Serial Bibliographies 200
National Bibliographies and Selected Serial Bibliographies 204
Periodical Lists and Indices 206
Dissertations, Theses and Research in Progress 209
Bibliographies of African and South African Literature 213
Selected Publishers and Scholarly Societies 218

SUBJECT INDEX 221

AUTHOR/TITLE INDEX 225

Abbreviations

ABIP	*African Books in Print*
ABPR	*African Book Publishing Record*
	American Book Publishing Record
ACLALS	Association for Commonwealth Literature and Language Studies
ALA	African Literature Association
ARD	*African Research and Documentation*
ASA	African Studies Association (U.K.)
	African Studies Association (U.S.)
AUFS	American Universities Field Staff, Inc.
AUPELF	Association des Universités Partiellement ou Entièrement de Langue Française
BHI	*British Humanities Index*
BNB	*British National Bibliography*
CACLALS	Canadian Association for Commonwealth Language and Literary Studies
CARDAN	Centre d'Analyse et de Recherche Documentaires pour l'Afrique Noire
CBCL	Conference on British Commonwealth Literature
CBI	*Cumulative Book Index*
CEDESA	Centre de Documentation Economique Sociale Africaine
CJAS	*Canadian Journal of African Studies*
ELOTBAA	English Literature Other Than British and American
ESA	*English Studies in Africa*
FESTAC	Second World Black and African Festival of Arts and Culture
FLA	Fellow of the Library Association (U. K.)

IAB	*International African Bibliography*
IAI	International African Institute
IBZ	*Internationale Bibliographie der Zeitschriftenliteratur aus allen Gebeiten des Wissens*
IDS	Institute of Development Studies at the University of Sussex
ISEA	Institute for the Study of English in Africa (Rhodes University)
JALA	*Joint Acquisitions List of Africana*
JCL	*Journal of Commonwealth Literature*
JMAS	*Journal of Modern African Studies*
JSAS	*Journal of South African Studies*
LC	Library of Congress
LIBER	Ligue des Bibliothèques Européennes de Recherche
MLA	Modern Language Association of America
NBL	National Book League (U.K.)
NUC	*National Union Catalog*
NYPL	New York Public Library
OUP	Oxford University Press
PISAL	*Periodicals in South African Libraries*
PMLA	*Publications of the Modern Language Association*
RAL	*Research in African Literatures*
RCS	Royal Commonwealth Society
RLC	*Revue de Littérature Comparée*
SANB	*South African National Bibliography*
SARA	Southern African Research Association (U.S.)
SCOLMA	Standing Conference on Library Materials on Africa (U.K.)
SOAS	School of Oriental and African Studies (University of London)
UNISA	University of South Africa
WLWE	*World Literature Written in English*

Introduction

An investigation of the South African novel in terms of its bibliographical control may seem both patently unnecessary and yet another example of the growing corpus of academic *adiaphora*. After all, some will say, South Africa is in every way atypical of the African bibliographical scene; here there is no publishing industry struggling to establish itself, no faltering attempt at national bibliography, no lack of trained librarians and bibliographers. Indeed, quite the opposite is true, for South Africa has both an established publishing industry and a mature system of bibliographical control. In fact the Republic appears every bit as advanced in these areas as countries in Europe and North America, so what point can there be in an investigation such as the present one?

As is so often the case, just below the surface are a number of flaws; in Reuben Musiker's words, "for one reason or another, the field of South African literature has been neglected by bibliographers so that . . . the area of South African English literature remains without a comprehensive bibliography."[1] In short, while overall bibliographical coverage of South African publications may be quite good, on specific subjects there is much room for improvement. The purpose of the present undertaking is to expose the bibliographical shortcomings in the area of English literature, primarily the novel, written in South Africa. This is not intended as a bibliography of the South African novel but rather as a guide to resources useful in the study and acquisition of the literature. In this attempt to provide a modicum of useful information on the South African novel, one hopes that such treatment will give librarians, scholars and students the expertise needed for effective, individual bibliographical activity.

In order to understand adequately the bibliographical problems peculiar to South African creative writing, one must not underestimate two phenomena: (1) the pervasive influence of the political situation, (2) the unprecedented growth of an indigenous literary tradition in recent years. In particular it is important for non-South Africans to realize just how powerful the government has become in its persistent efforts to control the opinions and attitudes of its citizens. This power now extends far beyond the more limited influence of most Western governments; "there is hardly an aspect of social and economic life—from the home, the school and the Church to the trade union, the factory and the political party—which has not been legislated for."[2] Indeed, Legum might well have included writing and publishing in his list, for in these areas government control through censorship is at its most effective. As one publisher who knows all too well the effects of this control has said,

> A "Publications Control Board," which recently received even wider powers, is empowered to declare any book, film or object "undesirable" (a term defined in 97 different ways), whereafter it is a serious criminal offence to distribute it or even, in some cases, merely to possess it. The Customs are empowered to place an embargo on any book arriving from abroad until the Board has given a ruling on its "desirability." In addition, the Minister of Justice has the power under the Suppression of Communism Act to ban and restrict any individual, which makes it a serious criminal offence thereafter to quote such a person or in any way reproduce, publish or disseminate anything he has ever said or written.[3]

Because of this unpleasant situation and the effective measures by successive governments to silence all forms of protest, there has resulted a massive exodus (both forced and voluntary) of South African writers to more salubrious political climates. Such authors have become scattered across the world, or at least the Western world, which has made their creative writing all but lost to bibliographical control from within the Republic. As a result of this scattering of talent, the investigator immediately finds himself requiring a multiplicity of bibliographical guides for each country in which South African writers now reside. One may think that the number of such expatriate authors is relatively insignificant, but a cursory survey of titles and publishers indicates that in fact more titles by more writers are published *outside* the Republic than within. Of course, financial considerations do play some role in this situation whereby authors come into print where the markets are most lucrative, yet this does not explain why so many works by South Africans living abroad are never noted in the various indigenous bibliographical guides. In short, we must not complacently expect that our queries about current publications can be answered by indigenous means, for the present political situation mitigates against such an expectation.

In addition there has been a totally unforeseen expansion of literary activity in South Africa, and most of us are blissfully aware of this upsurge in creative output. At best we tend only to notice that well known authors (e.g., Paton, Gordimer) continue to write at a steady pace, but what about new talent? Do such names as Sheila Fugard, Stephen Gray or Yvonne Burgess mean anything to us? Chances are they do not, for we have been caught unaware by a remarkable flowering of talent. Randall again serves as a useful reminder of such unexpected change: "there has been a remarkable upsurge of publishing activity in South Africa in the past three years, accompanied by a sustained output of work by local writers, both black and white."[4] Since the mid-1960's, an increasing number of creative writers has dared to produce readable and socially relevant fiction, and it is our task to be aware of these people and their work. Much the same picture may be painted of South African literary criticism, which after all is an essential component in our understanding of imaginative writing by South African writers. Like the work on which its existence depends, this criticism has enjoyed widespread publication and rapidly rising output. Who, for example, would care to list all the recent critical articles by the prolific Lewis Nkosi? "Peripatetic" and "prolific" are two adjectives well suited to both South African creative writing and its attendant criticism, and we must come to terms with these qualities in order to achieve effective bibliographical control.

The discussion which follows is an attempt to fulfill a two-fold function, to present a survey of the nature, condition and future prospects of South African fiction and to offer some preliminary guidance as to methods and means of exercising effective bibliographical control. Throughout the investigation our approach is entirely functional, that is, to assist in the development of that bibliographical expertise which will allow one to answer the basic "who, what, where" questions arising in the study and provision of South African literary materials. In order to achieve this practical end the study is divided into two parts, the first dealing with the literature itself and problems of definition, content and control; the second part, which arises out of this background discussion, presents a critical bibliographical survey of the various types of resource materials available to the investigator or collector of South African fiction.

In Part I the survey begins with an introductory chapter on the literature being produced, its context and content, as well as its place in academic study. Following this brief survey and general panorama of the scene, one then proceeds in Chapter Two to a more thorough investigation of several aspects characteristic of the South African novel: its nature in terms of the traditional art versus social commentary conflict, the role of commitment and propaganda in its creation, and the dominant themes which have emerged in recent years. On the basis of this discussion one has some indication of both the content and *raison d'être* of English fiction from South Africa and consequently may move into more functional areas. In Chapter Three we therefore consider precisely what place this literature might occupy in a university curriculum, either one of traditional mien or one of a slightly more innovative nature. In this chapter emphasis is largely on the relevance of South African literature to the total academic environment and the possible curricular permutations which may arise therein; in this discussion the attempt is to arouse librarians to some awareness of possibilities and prospects for the future, for it is primarily on their initiative and judgment that the availability of resources for literary studies ultimately depends.

At this juncture one moves in Chapter Four to an analysis of the bibliographical problems arising from the nature of the literature and bibliographical needs required for effective literary study and a comprehensive acquisitions policy. Chapter Four of Part I is to some extent the keystone of the entire exercise, for here one has a bridge between theory and function. In the first three chapters discussion concentrates on the literature as an art form and the place it occupies in an academic setting. In Chapter Four these background considerations are brought to bear on the practical issues of bibliographical control. A number of problems in this area are raised, and considerable discussion is devoted to possible solutions to these problems, one of the most critical being the lack of a guide to resources for the study and collection of South African fiction.

It is largely as a preliminary breaching of this particular bibliographical gap that Part II is intended to serve, for here one has a survey of the entire bibliographical apparatus now available combined with frequent discussion of the various *lacunae* and how these might be dealt with in the context of solutions proposed in Chapter Four (Part I). The first chapter of Part II surveys sources of biographical data, since many researchers frequently begin their investigations with basic questions best answered by biographical dictionaries. Chapter Two then discusses general bibliographical guides, including bibliographies of bibliographies and general Africanist/literary bibliographies. Selective non-serial bibliographies, including library catalogues, are dealt with in Chapter Three, while Chapter Four looks more specifically at serial bibliographies, including national compilations. This naturally leads one to periodical lists and indices, not to mention periodicals themselves, all of which are covered in Chapter Five. Chapter Six then examines the difficult area of theses and research in progress, and to this discussion there is appended a list of theses on the South African novel. Chapter Seven investigates those bibliographies devoted solely to African/South African literature, and the final chapter includes notes on selected publishers and associations with an interest in the South African novel.

Beginning with the most general bibliographical guides and ending with those most specifically aimed at imaginative writing in the Republic, the intention throughout Part II is to comment upon a wide range of resources having some relevance to the study of South African fiction. Most of the materials have been reviewed or dissected elsewhere, but this only rarely in terms of their usefulness to South Africa in particular; nowhere has there been an attempt to draw together in one place a selection of those publications deemed most useful in the study of South African fiction. If the present survey does this even reasonably well, then its function will have been fulfilled.

In looking at this genre it is clear that until about 1950 imaginative writing in South Africa had few notable practitioners; it was in the 1950's that authors such as Paton and Abrahams began to attract international acclaim, so it is with that period that the study begins. Every attempt has been made to bring the discussion down to 1975, with one or two excursions beyond this date for particularly noteworthy publications; however, as invariably happens in work of this sort, titles are missed or ignored, and even as these words are written one is aware of articles and book length bibliographies which have gone unnoticed. One tends to believe that these omissions often reflect the quality of the titles missed, since important works receiving wide acclaim are difficult to overlook. Even so, the occasional important title may not be included, and to the Africanist outraged by such oversight one can only apologize. So too one must be prepared for the ire of readers of "popular" fiction; throughout this investigation attention focuses unfailingly on novels of "merit" and which speak to some degree of life in South Africa, for it is this material rather than summertime bestsellers which invariably form the backbone of the novel in an academic setting.

The methodology used in collecting data has involved a three-fold approach: (1) personal experience as a student of South African fiction and the experience of present-day researchers in this field, (2) professional evaluation of the bibliographical apparatus which presently exists, and (3) a theoretical forecast of future possibilities. In each of these aspects I have been fortunate to have the advice of others either far more qualified than myself or more actively engaged in the study of South African fiction. In particular I appreciate the consideration shown by postgraduate researchers at SOAS and undergraduates at the University of Sussex in sharing their views on the present state of South African literary bibliography. It is only by considering the needs of users at these levels that one can hope to create a truly effective bibliographical apparatus.

Furthermore, in specialized areas the opinions of established scholars and other professionals cannot be ignored, for they know better than anyone the difficulties and complications which exist beyond the seeing of a less trained eye. Thus I appreciate the informal advice of librarians such as Malcolm McKee at SOAS, Reuben Musiker at Witwatersrand and Michael Rogers at IDS. Other willing sources of expertise have been James Armstrong, now with the Library of Congress office in Nairobi, Alastair Niven of Stirling University, Bernth Lindfors of the University of Texas and Hans Zell of Hans Zell (Publishers) Ltd. Most important of all has been the consistently sound and patient advice offered by John McIlwaine of University College London; without his wide bibliographical knowledge this study would be far less satisfactory than I now hope it to be. Finally, I must recognize the thankless task of typing performed by Mrs. Linda Gardiner and Mrs. Chitra Richardson, both of whom bore the burden of deciphering my writing without complaint. If there has been any attempt to maintain a reasonable standard of excellence through nearly two years of research, then it can only have been due to my wife's constant encouragement. To all of these I owe more than can be put into words, but in the end only the writer can accept responsibility for all errors and omissions, as well as for the more positive attributes!

G. E. Gorman
The Library
The Institute of Development Studies

July 1977

Notes

1. Reuben Musiker, "South African English Literature: Bibliographic and Biographical Resources and Problems," *English Studies in Africa*, 13 (1970): 265.
2. Colin Legum, "The Republic of South Africa," in *Africa: A Handbook,* edited by Colin Legum (Second edition; London: Anthony Blond, 1965), p. 338.
3. Peter Randall, " 'Minority' Publishing in South Africa," *African Book Publishing Record*, 1 (1975): 219.
4. *Ibid.*

Survey of the Literature and Aspects of Bibliographical Control

The South African Novel:
Its Evolution in an Academic Setting

Growth of the Genre

The thesis giving rise to this bibliographical excursus has originated in a three-fold assumption concerning the South African novel: first, this literature merits a heretofore largely unrecognized place in modern academic studies; second, this newly acquired respectability stems from the value of the literature both as an expression of artistic capability and as a sensitive interpretation of the present socio-political climate in South Africa; third, in order for this literature to become more readily available and thus perhaps more generally known librarians must take the lead in disseminating information about, and establishing some criteria for the acquisition of, South African fiction. The last assumption is the *raison d'être* for the present investigation, but in order to reach this primary focal point one must first present a brief analysis of the nature and function of this literature and also express some opinion as to its legitimate place in the academic world.

Concerning the Anglophone African novel as a whole, there appears to be relatively strong support for MacRae's recently expressed opinion that

> ... the novel, that great creation which spread from Spain in the late middle ages to all Europe and the Americas, now flourishes best in sub-Saharan Africa with all that means for beauty, delight and catharsis. The African novel in English ... shows prose fiction at its most alive and vital today.[1]

While this judgment may require some modification in relation to fiction from particular African countries (and more particularly from the Republic of South Africa), it nevertheless remains true that within the broader spectrum of literary activity African writing in English is achieving a level of artistic integrity which merits further attention. Part of this integrity, of which more will be said in a specifically South African context, derives from three quite specific attributes, which MacRae terms "beauty, delight and catharsis."

3

He suggests that none of these characteristics can stand alone as a justification for elevating the African novel to a new plateau of artistic achievement, and it is precisely because of this combination of factors that we will advocate the treatment of South African fiction as an especially valuable specimen of African literary effort.

At the same time, however, to suggest that the African novel is good, bad or valuable in any critical sense almost begs the question, for the fact remains that the literature exists, that it is being published in increasing quantities through a variety of outlets in the West, that it is attracting an appreciative and rapidly growing audience and that it has become the object of considerable scholarly investigation in recent years. Publishers in the United Kingdom, Germany, France, North America and in Africa itself are devoting ever larger percentages of their total output to African novels written in English; many of these novels are now appearing in one or another of the growing number of such well known series as Heinemann's African Writers Series or Longman's African Creative Writing Series. Similarly, booksellers who for years have carried a small stock of representative literary works by African novelists today are devoting more time and attention to the fiction lists of Western and African publishers. As a result, several of these booksellers are gaining the reputation of being African literature specialists, the most notable British examples being Dillon's, Heffer's and Blackwell's. Not only are the books being published and sold, but they are also being read and studied, if the number of secondary works is any guide. By the mid-1960's scholars and critics had begun to fill literary journals with studies of particular novels or novelists and also to produce more general works such as Wauthier's *Literature and Thought of Modern Africa*.[2]

By the mid-1970's all of this activity had undergone yet another massive expansion; both the number of works being produced and the amount and depth of scholarly research increased significantly. Indeed, so substantial has been this flurry of productivity that in 1977 a number of societies (including the Association for Commonwealth Literature and Language Studies, the African Literature Commission of the African Studies Association and the African Literature Group of the Modern Language Association[3]) enjoys a stable existence based on the study of African literature in its various aspects. Likewise in the area of scholarly journals one finds a growing corpus of titles devoted partially or exclusively to African literature and literary criticism (*Journal of Commonwealth Literature, Research in African Literatures, African Literature Today*[4]), while the number of "popular" literary magazines publishing original African fiction defies accurate computation due to the immense fluctuations in their fortunes. Ten years ago one easily might have encompassed most of the African literary scene in a survey such as that by Wauthier cited above; today, however, there is quite enough material for a narrowly specialized treatment as seen in Mutiso's

Socio-Political Thought in African Literature,[5] which limits itself to certain categories of fiction and still produces a substantial study.

Accompanying these changes in public awareness of African literature, in its acceptance as a legitimate field of academic inquiry, in the higher volume of output by writers and critics and in a widespread inclusion of African literature in publishers' lists has been a concomitant change in the quality of African writing. Whereas in the past what one termed "African literature" tended to be written by Western novelists such as Conrad, Cary and others who saw Africa as simply a unique and exotic background for essentially non- or extra-African themes, today one sees that the African novel is being written by native or expatriate authors intimately familiar with their settings. Furthermore, these novels no longer treat Africa or "African-ness" as a secondary theme but rather as a legitimate source of inspiration in itself and a fount of major thematic development. Commenting on Larson's recently published *More Modern African Stories*, MacRae unambiguously supports this supposition. "Mr. Larson makes a strong point. His stories are now not about Africa *vis à vis* Europe, but about African life itself. A transition has been made: African fiction, for all the strength and chastity of its prose, is now self-confident in its identity."[6]

In itself this newly discovered identity is not a startling development, for there has been an African literary tradition of sorts from at least the fourteenth century. However, in terms of modern developments the present situation is indeed a remarkable phenomenon, since only in 1947 did *Présence Africaine* appear as the first major literary endeavor undertaken by indigenous African talent with the express purpose of stating a specifically African point of view. At first this journal and the attendant creative fiction by Francophone West Africans stood alone as examples of modern creativity by African writers, but by 1950 Anglophone contributions from further south added to the gradual growth of indigenous African fiction.

In the early 1950's English fiction written within South Africa began to show similar signs of awakening and of recognition outside Africa as a valid and powerful example of this art form. In those years literary activity was sufficient to warrant the successful launching of *Drum*, the South African English equivalent of *Présence Africaine*. At the same time the work of established novelists such as Alan Paton and Peter Abrahams was attracting international attention as an unusually illuminating but solidly artistic representation of life in British Africa. In retrospect it seems difficult to believe that a work as straightforward and uncomplicated as Paton's *Cry the Beloved Country* (London, 1948) could have heralded a totally new era in South African fiction, yet we can now see that, William Plomer and Olive Schreiner notwithstanding, it did precisely that for at least three reasons. First, it expressed in strong and readily accessible language the effects of South Africa's racial and cultural policies on the inhabitants of the region. In addition it opened the way for a new protest school of South African fiction in English, and it also provided a profound influence on and impetus for similar developments among black South African writers.

That Paton could have written a work with such powerful consequences depended to a large extent on a changed political environment, for up to that time the situation was far from conducive to such outspoken activities. Indeed, in the decades prior to the Second World War the government's policy of racial discrimination had grown increasingly oppressive with the introduction of measures aimed at depriving the black populace (and liberal whites) of all political power and also at preventing the development of an indigenous cultural life. Perhaps precisely because of this policy the center of literary life naturally remained in West Africa throughout most of the 1940's; at least the long tradition of a sophisticated Francophone African culture stood no chance of being challenged by anything coming out of the claustrophobic atmosphere to the south. But the era of the Second World War introduced a hint of *aggiornamento* into this stifling environment, although in retrospect the spirit of cooperative coexistence of which many spoke so positively seems highly unrealistic.[7] Nevertheless, the belief in imminent change was widely held by large numbers of people. According to Wilson and Thompson,

> ... it did seem that the Government might begin to reverse its policy of segregation, revise pass laws and recognise African trade unions; and the war itself was seemingly being waged against precisely those principles of extreme racialism and oppression which were represented by the Nazis, but embodied also in the structure of South African rule.[8]

In spite of the fact that in reality this was very far from the truth it at least gave people the impression of change and a weakening hold by the government, and this in turn motivated individuals to become outspoken and openly join forces to foster further freedom. As Páricsy believes, "the liberation movement, which had made its start in the early thirties, was extended precisely in the post-war years, and its mass base grew considerably by the participation of industrial workers and the increasing number of intellectuals."[9]

Thus it appeared that the policies of racial discrimination and government control were being mitigated; as a consequence, more authors in South Africa felt free to work and publish in this new and freer atmosphere. Indeed, this freedom was so powerfully felt that in 1957 *Drum* sponsored its first literary competition and attracted over 1600 entries.[10] So it was that in the late 1940's and well into the next decade the activities of two separate worlds coincided in a sudden burst of literary activity. In the world of literature there was the excellent example set by *Présence Africaine* and *Drum*, the seminal work by Paton which showed the way for creative and constructive works of fiction, the growth of the *négritude* movement with its emphasis on the recognition and profession of indigenous black African socio-cultural values. As a parallel in the socio-political sphere, there was a lull in oppression and the appearance that racial discrimination and the generally negative atmosphere fostered by Calvinist attitudes were at last on the way out. While these false impressions lasted, there was a season of fruitful creativity in the literary world.

When the Nationalist government reacted to this growing sense of liberation and the attendant outspokenness of writers and intellectuals, it did so with a vengeance. In the 1950's there already were being enacted a series of measures designed to control the education, voting, labor and living conditions of the black population. This was followed by a series of laws aimed at suppressing material of a politically suspect or deviant nature, which easily encompassed works by white South Africans who continued to write in support of freedom for black South Africans.[11] For these writers, whether black or white, one of the most significant enactments came to be the 1950 Suppression of Communism Act and its 1962–1965 amendments, for this legislation effectively prohibited the printing and dissemination of all publications that could be seen as deviant in any way. As if this 1950 enactment were not enough, all possible loopholes have since been plugged by a further battery of laws: the Criminal Laws Amendment Act of 1953 lists severe penalties for those who protest against government legislation, and the General Law Amendment Act of 1962 makes it a crime ". . . to further or encourage any political aim which includes the bringing about of any social or economic change in the Republic, and no work by any 'named' person may be published or possessed without penalties."[12] As a final insurance against sedition through the written word, the government in 1963 passed the Censorship Act, which with admirable thoroughness was followed by ". . . the ruthless total banning of the written or spoken word of virtually all black South African writers. . . ."[13]

In view of these and countless other measures it is little wonder that by the mid-1960's conditions for the writer in South Africa had deteriorated to a new low, with many in the literary fraternity being banned outright, illegally imprisoned, placed under house arrest or forced into exile. Even those not silenced in these ways were unable to publish, for what editor in the country would risk the government's wrath by accepting a potentially subversive manuscript for publication? Furthermore, on a purely economic level no editor would want to take the financial risk of having a published work banned from the bookstalls, for this had happened time and again even with titles which on the surface appeared harmless enough.[14] The authors which have been banned under the Censorship Act and the Suppression of Communism Act make strange bedfellows indeed: Marx and Lenin, Hemingway and Salinger, Alex La Guma and Ezekiel Mphahlele among others. Although this situation does present its ludicrous side, there is a far more serious result which cannot be ignored; because of these oppressive policies over the last twenty-five years, nearly every South African novelist who is committed to literature as something more than a means of entertainment has been affected in some adverse way by government control. As Moore stated in 1969, the events of these years ". . . have alienated every South African writer of any compassion or sensitivity from the society developing around him. Most of them have taken refuge in exile, others are prematurely dead, banned or in prison."[15]

Yet in spite of all this, in spite of the fact that writers of the caliber of Abrahams, Mphahlele, La Guma and Rive live in exile, in spite of the fact that Jacobson and Doris Lessing have chosen to write abroad for a Western audience, the fact remains that South African fiction continues to flourish. These people are still writing, and whether like Nadine Gordimer they can manage to do so in South Africa or like Doris Lessing they must do so in other countries, there is still a South African literature which forms a large part of that sub-Saharan creative activity which MacRae believes is so significant. And this literature exists in all those manifestations which one considers essential to healthy activity—study, teaching, criticism and public acclaim. Indeed in more than one of these aspects South African literature is a major component in the totality of the continent's output. This is particularly true in the field of literary criticism, for here the South African contribution virtually overshadows all that is produced elsewhere in Africa; "without South Africa there would be almost no literary criticism and little politico-philosophical criticism. . . ."[16] So in many ways South African fiction, like its counterparts elsewhere in Africa, has gone from youth to maturity in little more than thirty years, although one must admit that this is a persecuted and therefore falsely induced adolescent maturity both in terms of content and style, as well as in terms of its impact and its acceptance as a valid field of academic inquiry. Perhaps because of the controversy surrounding it, South African literature has become subject to such inquiry before it has reached full maturity, but that is not for us to decide. What remains true is that it is written, read and studied, and this with some legitimacy, since in less than a single generation it has provided us with a full picture of the evolution of a genre of modern African literature and the society from which it emerges. In Larson's words,

> If we think of fiction as growing out of the collective experience of the society in which the author lives—out of the reservoir of ideas and experiences of the total consciousness of the society itself—then the African writer has, indeed, been the historian of his continent's increasingly widened outlook on life, moving from a virtually closed off societal view of the village and the clan to an ever-widening world view.[17]

South African Literature in an Academic Setting

This very brief overview of the evolution of South African fiction leads one to some consideration of what this rapid development implies in terms of academic study and library policy. Later chapters will deal with these topics in depth, but at this point some indication of the situation may prove beneficial. The evolution of the literature over such a brief period does in fact have direct bearing on how academics and librarians ought to treat South African fiction. In both the lecture hall and the library literature in general has long enjoyed the reputation of being slightly eccentric and certainly very broad in its coverage. In libraries English literature in particular has earned a certain notoriety for its appearance and selectivity. In the view of at least one librarian

> The very phrase "an English collection" has a vague, comfortable sound to it. It evokes a picture of haphazard assortment of volumes, variously and untidily acquired, in a spilling disorder and subject to no standards of use or selection other than distinctly personal ones.[18]

This slightly disheveled appearance is, of course, only to be expected when one considers the very long history of literary activity in the English language (not to mention far earlier literature translated into English) and its perennial attraction to large numbers of people. Accompanying this mass of primary literature is an even greater corpus of secondary material which is constantly being supplemented by the almost frenetic activity of scholars and critics.

One might expect South African fiction in English to reflect a similar pattern as a branch of the same literary tree, but this in fact need not be the case. Indeed, a later chapter will maintain that this must not be the case, but for the present less categorical statements are more in order. In any sphere of English literature which is collected by libraries "it is the proper function of a librarian to establish his custody of such a collection on a systematic basis."[19] One can see that this theoretical statement creates a number of difficulties when put into operation for a general collection of English literature. In the limited context of South African fiction in English, however, such difficulties will be less pronounced, for this literature exhibits nothing like the complexities of width, breadth and length common to its more established older cousin. In fact South African fiction may only now be reaching that point at which it is still quite manageable but large enough to deserve and warrant some sort of overall control. That is, it has existed long enough to exhibit a certain continuity; it has attracted enough attention by both writers and commentators to be of sufficient bulk; it is being sought after and read by a public large enough to warrant some sort of control in terms of acquisition, reference requirements and orderly arrangement. In short there is adequate material for the librarian who wants to develop the knowledge, skills and techniques for dealing with it logically and systematically.

The fact that this situation exists, that South African fiction and its attendant studies are not yet beyond the pale of reasonable expectations in terms of bibliographical control, in and of itself is reason enough for the librarian to undertake the development of such control. But there is yet another and perhaps more pressing reason why this must be done, and this is the recent growth, present consolidation and spreading influence of regional/area studies programs. On one side area studies traditionally have encompassed virtually all the social sciences and theoretically most of the humanities as well, yet on the other side literature (in terms of African studies at least) has been one of the more neglected areas. The fact that the arts as a whole have enjoyed less popularity than the social sciences and the even more pragmatic area of development studies need not indicate a lack of interest in this field or in literature in particular, for the academic world is now seeing yet another change in emphasis away from "practical" studies to the more traditional strongholds of art, history, philosophy, religion and literature. Yet even if this were not the trend, one could make a strong case for increasing the scope of literary studies in area programs, since literature does in fact have a direct bearing on all aspects of socio-political study (see Chapter 3).

Finally, even if some of these possibilities were not already becoming reality, the academic and the librarian both ought to be aware that the interdisciplinary approach of area studies might at any moment make demands on the literary field. Harris suggests that "since the disciplinary structure of individual area programs is subject to considerable instability, the librarians are faced with the need to maintain some basic strength in all the fields."[20] Part of the librarian's brief is both to undertake this task and be prepared for similar contingencies, so although he may not be actively collecting South African literature at a given moment, he must at least have some awareness of trends and changes in the field in order to know how and where possible demands for materials can be met.

In brief, then, there are a number of reasons underlying the need to collect South African fiction. On the most basic level there is that need common to all disciplines, the accumulation of information; for the literature in question this also means the rare chance to develop a relatively complete collection of South African novels in English. Moreover, this opportunity accompanies a growing awareness that the social sciences alone are inadequate for explaining or understanding current socio-political behavior. As a result, there is a renewed interest in the more traditional disciplines as necessary adjuncts to the social sciences, which in interdisciplinary or area programs may well place a demand on writings by South African novelists. In view of these existing and potential needs libraries must not be complacent about their policies concerning the acquisition of South African literature; what follows is an attempt to encourage librarians to engage actively in the collection of this material and to provide them with the means to develop an intelligent acquisitions policy.

Notes

1. Donald MacRae, "A World of Riches," *The Sunday Times,* 13 April 1975, p. 40.

2. Claude Wauthier, *The Literature and Thought of Modern Africa: A Survey,* translated by Shirley Key (London: Pall Mall Press, 1966). Although now ten years old, this work typifies much of what is still being published in that it distinguishes between black and white writers, of which more in Chapter 4. Otherwise it is interesting that as late as the mid-1960's such a work could deal almost exclusively with West African literature, while today such neglect of the South African contribution is inexcusable in view of the output from that country in recent years.

3. There are literally scores of associations, groups, committees, and organizations devoted to and concerned with the study of African literature in its many forms. Part II delineates the more important of these, but at this point it may be useful to note that there is not among this plethora of acronymic fixtures a single one devoted solely or even primarily to South African literature in English.

4. Again more will be said on this subject later; here it is relevant to mention that, as in the case of associations, not one scholarly or critical journal devotes itself entirely to the South African contribution. The closest attempt comes in a serial entitled *English Studies in Africa,* a South African effort which occasionally deals with indigenous output but normally includes the wider field of English literature in general.

5. G.-C. M. Mutiso, *Socio-Political Thought in African Literature: Weusi?* (New York: Barnes and Noble, 1974). Although an excellent example of how a narrow literary theme can be treated clearly and relatively thoroughly, this work again suffers from the exclusion of white South African literature, an omission which cannot be justified today on other than political grounds.

6. MacRae, *loc. cit.*

7. There are many accounts of "liberal" changes and new aspirations that developed during the war years; one of the most accessible and accurate is Monica Wilson and Leonard Thompson, eds., *The Oxford History of South Africa* (Oxford: Clarendon Press, 1971), vol. I, pp. 351 ff.

8. *Ibid.,* pp. 453–54.

9. Pál Páricsy, "A Short Survey of the History of Black African Literature," in *Studies on Modern Black African Literature,* edited by Pál Páricsy (Studies on Developing Countries, No. 43. Budapest: Center for Afro-Asian Research of the Hungarian Academy of Sciences, 1971), p. 2.

10. *Ibid.,* p. 6.

11. Government measures designed to control both the blacks and the writings which have supported their struggle for freedom are mentioned in several

studies. Two summaries which cover the measures briefly but quite adequately for our purposes may be found in Douglas H. Varley, "Trends Abroad: South Africa," *Library Trends,* 19 (1970): 139–51, which deals largely with political censorship in South Africa and its effects on writers; and in Vladimir Klima, *South African Prose Writing in English* (London: C. Hurst, 1971), pp. 12–15, 63–65, which presents a short historical resumé of South Africa's racial laws. Cf. Peter Randall, *op. cit.,* pp. 219–22.

12. Varley, *op. cit.,* p. 148.

13. Nadine Gordimer, "The Novel and the Nation in South Africa," in *African Writers on African Writing,* edited by G. D. Killam (London: Heinemann, 1973), p. 51. Cf. Nadine Gordimer, "Literature and Politics in South Africa," *Southern Review,* 7, no. 3 (1975): 206. She points out that the Censorship Act carries ninety-seven definitions of what is undesirable, including an all encompassing phrase, "the advocation of social change." In 1971 *South African Libraries,* 38, no. 4 devoted the entire issue to censorship and a discussion of the censorship system.

14. The figures for the number of banned titles, as might be expected, vary greatly. Varley (*op. cit.,* p. 143) puts the figure at 13,000 titles between 1956–1970, while Páricsy (*op. cit.,* p. 8) places it rather lower at 5,000 for "banned political and literary works. . . ."

15. Gerald Moore, *The Chosen Tongue; English Writing in the Tropical World* (London: Longman, 1969), p. xv.

16. Nadine Gordimer, *The Black Interpreters: Notes on African Writing* (Braamfontein, South Africa: Ravan Press, 1973), p. 19.

17. Charles R. Larson, *The Emergence of African Fiction* (Revised edition; Bloomington: Indiana University Press, 1972), p. 280.

18. James Thompson, *The Librarian and English Literature* (London: Association of Assistant Librarians, 1968), p. 7.

19. *Ibid.*

20. Chauncey D. Harris, "Area Studies and Library Resources," *The Library Quarterly,* 35 (1965): 210.

Form, Style and Content of the Literature

Is it Literature?

A question about the literary pretension of South African fiction must not be treated as a mere frivolity, for it is a query which arises from time to time with persuasive arguments being made for both sides of the issue. While we may readily accept the South African novel in English as literature in every sense of the term, we must accept that a strong case for rejecting its place in this art form can be based on the theory of artistic purity which maintains that any work of art must be ontologically independent and therefore has no external points of reference. Advocates of this theory tell us that the novel must be seen solely as a work of creative genius, and any attempt to regard it in a more existential and less transcendental light is not only fallacious but also detrimental to its artistic integrity. Purists of this persuasion necessarily reject the view that literature may express feelings and emotions reflecting the nature of a particular socio-cultural background and therefore can illuminate both causes and effects which we must try to discover, judge and evaluate. Instead, literature in this hypothesis of artistic purity belongs not to the world of concrete events and situations but is a state existing in and of itself. Therefore, ". . . that study which attempts to reduce the work of art to what it is not—to the search for causes, to the documentation of history and of influences, to examination of its function in rite, family and marketplace—is an irrelevant study of art."[1]

While there are no South African novelists or critics of their work who appear to subscribe to this rather extreme view, there are many who maintain that fiction in South Africa embodies none of the criteria normally associated with creative writing. One of the more outspoken representatives of this group is Lewis Nkosi, who on more than one occasion has said that

> with all the best will in the world it is impossible to detect in the fiction of black South Africans any significant and complex talent which responds with both the vigour of the imagination and sufficient technical resources to the problems posed by conditions in South Africa.[2]

13

According to Nkosi, the South African novelist is little more than a glorified storyteller operating at a very primitive level and without any reliance on the innovative techniques exhibited by literary craftsmen elsewhere in the world. The work of South African writers is nothing more than ". . . journalistic fact masquerading outrageously as imaginative literature . . . ," which simply ". . . exploits the ready-made plots of racial violence, social *apartheid, interracial* love affairs . . . without any attempt to transcend or transmute these given 'social facts' into artistically persuasive works of fiction."[3]

If one were to accept even the spirit of this criticism, might it be true primarily because of the situation in which these writers must try to create literature rather than due to an inherent inability on their part to reach a certain level of literary artistry? That is, the style and form of their writing may be simply ". . . a reflection of the ignorance in the literary society which they could only know as South Africans—one in which Symbolists, Surrealists, Imagists and alike . . . are unable to breathe any influence into literary work or thought."[4] Dennis Brutus would seem to accept this viewpoint and, while agreeing to some degree with Nkosi, is rather more charitable toward his fellow writers in saying that

> South African literature is almost entirely what one would expect
> . . . from a society which has deliberately narrowed its horizons,
> which has frightened the writer both by legislation and threat, and
> which is based on the denial of the humanity of the majority of its
> populace. . . . The general picture is that of a society in retreat from
> its own reality, taking an occasional peak outside the caprice of
> its insensitivity. . . . It is not unfair to speak of South Africa as
> having a tortoise literature.[5]

It is impossible not to agree that in terms of artistic technique South African fiction has been slow to adapt the creative styles so prevalent in the West to its own cloistered existence, but at the same time one must object to the opinion that this literature has not exhibited a growing maturity and sophistication in the last decade.

Particularly when it comes to expressing the feelings of those who live in a repressive society and evoking a strong sense of time and place, the South African novel has shown itself equal to the best that our own society can muster. Martin Tucker, writing at the same time as Nkosi, admits that in the past novelists from South Africa were rather superficial in their work, but by the mid-1960's they were beginning to exhibit a greater degree of creative ability in dealing with various issues and themes. While agreeing that the aesthetic quality found in novels from other countries was still lacking in most South African novels as late as 1967, Tucker goes on to state that ". . . white South African literary history is remarkable for its literary accomplishments no less than for its sheer profligacy."[6] He also maintains that in such works as Hilda Kuper's *Bite of Hunger* and Jack

Bennett's *The Hawk Alone* (both published in 1965) we can see the evolution of South African fiction from Nkosi's "journalistic fact" into a literary form of lasting creative value.[7] Since then, we have in writing by Nadine Gordimer (particularly *A Guest of Honour*), Sheila Fugard (*The Castaways*) and others active in the mid-1970's examples of novels which exhibit the highest literary standards and also speak powerfully of the conditions in South Africa. Likewise among black novelists Tucker sees great promise, citing Nkosi, Mphahlele and Rive as exponents of a flowering literary creativity;[8] to these names we may add those of Modikwe Dikobe, Bessie Head, Alex La Guma and Can Themba, all of whom since 1970 have written novels of great literary merit. Nadine Gordimer, who herself has contributed in no small degree to this growing maturity, agrees substantially with Tucker's analysis but looks rather more to the future for a fuller expression of creativity among black writers.

> Perhaps the best of these works are to come from those for whom that fight for social and political independence is not yet history: the black writers of South Africa may blow the breath that will bring the African novel of the political struggle with the white man to life at last. . . . In any case, it seems that the theme of the political struggle for independence, dealt with inadequately up to now, belongs more to the future of African writing than to what has already been achieved.[9]

Every critic who sees exciting developments in South African fiction refers to the literature *vis à vis* content rather than form alone, maintaining that the quality of writing results from the fusion of propaganda or social commentary with the aesthetics of literary creativity. Each of them suggests that the novels take as their inspiration some aspect of reality, whether this be political struggle, racial prejudice, social inequality or attempts to realize the values of Christian humanism. In short, literature in the eyes of these commentators is not an art form totally divorced from the realities of life but rather an outcome of the total involvement with life in all its aspects. Tucker puts this viewpoint most succinctly in speaking of ". . . the fusion necessary for literature—the heat of ideas distilled by the cold purity of form, the commingling of two elements, art and sociopolitics, in which each is servant to and in harmony with the other."[10] For the South African novelist, of course, the problem is one of balance, because in his situation it is likely that the reality of oppression impinges so heavily on his existence that the artistic urge easily takes on a secondary importance. For those seeking to do more than entertain their audience writing must be a committed activity which both reflects the turbulent socio-political atmosphere and attempts to open the way to a more equitable existence by means of artistic expression.

This is a relatively moderate view of literature, seeing it as a combination of artistic insight and social motivation, and there are those with far more radical opinions about this art form. For them all art must arise from and reflect individual experience in a concrete situation, and this is a *sine qua non* affecting anything else that literature might be or seek to achieve.

> All literature, to the extent that it deals with individuals in society, contains elements of social and political theory. Obviously the creative writer does not always write with the intention of propagating a particular idea, but he cannot create in a vacuum. When he depicts a character or an incident his judgement comes into play, thereby revealing some of the value choices he has made either consciously or unconsciously. All literature depicts the values of the people and the period. This is to say that however imaginative a writer may be, the framework of his writing must always be the society which he knows.[11]

But even this opinion does not deny the place of those elements which the purist defines as essential to art. The type of writing described by Mutiso does not merely chronicle events of the present but also extends to a vision of the future; as such it participates in the prophetic function which is inherent in true art at all levels. It may find its basis in the contemporary experience of particular individuals or societies, but from this base it attempts to see how the future may be made to reflect a new and better order.

In the West we perhaps find it difficult to understand how present reality is necessarily encompassed by artistic activity, for our own reality seems somehow less urgent, less real even, than that of a society such as exists in South Africa. Our concerns are more with intimate relationships, the interior life of dream and fantasy, psychological alienation and metaphysical despair rather than with the immediate and more obvious issues of social justice and political equality. Yet both types of concern are reality, and both realities provide the impetus for creative writing. What we must understand is not only the nature of South African reality but also how it is perceived by the novelist in South Africa and how it calls forth, tempers and controls his act of creation. We must see, in other words, how life as experienced by him is proclaimed in his novels.

The Novel as Social Commentary

The basic experience of life in South Africa for novelist and ordinary citizen alike, whether black or white, involves an oppressive discrimination in all phases of existence. Since this is the environment in which the South African author lives, one must expect it to be reflected in his writings, for as Sartre explains,

> The real business of the writer is first to come to grips with his *situation* (that is, his social environment, the place and the time

in which he lives), and then to exhort his readers to take action which will improve the conditions of life revealed by that *situation*. The writer cannot, then, be an impartial chronicler, he must take sides, in order to reveal to his readers their possibility of choice and of action, to "mettre la personne humaine en possession de sa liberté."[12]

One may question Sartre's conclusion that the writer must of necessity take sides, but it seems clearly illogical to question the basic premise of involuntary involvement with the existential situation. We accept, for example, the frequent concern of English novelists (until recently at any rate) with social class and the effects of inherent British snobbery, so why question the South African concern with race and color discrimination?

The only possible ground for disagreement lies in the frequency with which the color problem arises in South African writing, but even this is not beyond comprehension. After all, most Ghanaian and Nigerian novels of any merit deal almost exclusively with the elaborate interpersonal relations which characterize those societies, and in a similar manner South African novels frequently treat the discriminatory practices common in South Africa. Thus Doris Lessing, herself a frequent victim of Rhodesian and South African policies of discrimination, explains how the color issue pervades her writing in these words:

> I have notebooks full of stories, plots, anecdotes, which at one time or another I was impelled to write. But the impulse died in a yawn. Even if I write them well—what then? It is always the colour bar; one cannot write truthfully about Africa without describing it.[13]

Miss Lessing obviously feels that the society in which she lives and the life she is obliged to lead influence her writing, and this situation impinges on any literary theme developed or any opinion expressed in her writing. So strong and pervasive is the race issue that it cannot be avoided and frequently forces the author to be rather repetitious simply because it cannot be put aside.

> Time and time again one seizes on a theme, looks at it carefully, discovers that unless the writer is very careful it will merely repeat what has already been said in another context—and then, trying to isolate what is specifically African, what is true of Africa at this time, one comes slap up against that complex of emotions, the colour bar.[14]

In other words the South African novelist, like his counterpart anywhere else in the world, tries to tell of life; but in order to do this in South Africa he must inevitably speak of discrimination. Thus social commentary, to the extent that it involves explication or mere mention of discrimination, cannot be avoided.

If the results of *apartheid* are obvious to the ordinary South African as he goes about his daily life, this must be doubly so for the creative writer. First, by training and education the novelist tends to be of an educated elite and as such has had more opportunity to observe the inequities of the social system. As the writer's horizons widen through contact with a broad spectrum of humanity, he naturally comes face to face with other ways of living and contrasts them with his own style of life. Education, then, permits a knowledge of the possibilities of freedom that contrasts with the restricted life which he is forced to lead. Furthermore, the writer by virtue of his artistic sensitivity sees more clearly and feels more directly the inequities which others accept rather blithely or with resignation. Because of this sensitivity, the writer in most cases cannot merely accept the hatred and oppression or pretend that it does not exist; rather he must record what he sees by evaluating, judging and interpreting the social milieu out of which his themes arise. Whether he chooses to accept or criticize the values of his society, the writer must at least reflect his environment. And what does he see? Among the blacks he finds 80% of the population living below the poverty line, a high infant mortality rate and tens of thousands in prison. At the same time a majority of the whites support iniquitous social values, reactionary political attitudes and respond with apathy to the glaring socio-political problems. Because the writer sees all of these things and responds to them with feeling, what he writes as a result involves him in the South African struggle for justice; it is this involvement which is the essential quality of the social commentary in all South African fiction.

However, to maintain that these artists must absorb what they see in their society and write about issues prevalent in their environment means that one runs the risk of assuming, as Nkosi seems to do, that all South African writers speak with a single voice. An examination of their work shows that such an assumption is fallacious, for each author sees life as an individual and reflects ideas or problems from a wide range of perspectives. Some will merely record; others will interpret, and still others will judge, but always from a perspective unique to the individual writer. Thus one will see that the novels, while engaging in social commentary and reflecting to some degree the South African milieu, express a variety of socio-political opinions. There are, as Tucker terms them, novels of "the right" and "the left," novels defending or reflecting white supremacy and novels supporting the black viewpoint and destruction of the color bar.[15]

Furthermore, while every South African novelist may seem preoccupied with *apartheid,* each one treats it from a slightly different angle. For example, Paton in *Cry the Beloved Country* and Abrahams in *A Wreath for Udomo* concentrate on the resulting denial of human relationships and postulate the ultimate triumph of love over this unnatural situation. Other writers, particularly Mphahlele in *The Wanderers* and Nadine Gordimer in

A Guest of Honour, purposely reject explicit protest and prefer to let the situation speak for itself. Still others tend to be more in the tradition of "protest writers" (e.g., Rive, La Guma) and feel that the themes of love and brotherhood or rejection of violence are not enough in the present situation; they instead portray nothing but hostility between black and white and often see a violent solution as the only viable option. Practically every novel, whether popular romance or work of creative genius, will tend to reflect one viewpoint or the other, and the prevalence of these attitudes leads to yet another question: is this sort of literature socially committed or merely journalistic propaganda?

It is important not to dismiss this question too lightly, for the juxtaposition of commitment and propaganda exemplifies a basic danger in all South African writing, namely the ease with which it can slip from creativity into reportage. When this happens, when commitment and creativity give way to propaganda and reportage, the result is no longer fiction but some other form of literature. The difficulty lies in the fine line separating the two and in the fact that the author in South Africa is committed to two very different principles. On one side he opposes the present situation and sees the possibility for a better world; he wants to bring his readers to this same conviction by helping them to see both the past and the way to a better future.[16] Parallel to this social commitment, which the writer expresses through careful thematic development, is his dedication to artistry. That is, the author is also committed to the canons of his art form and to the creation of an ever better means of illuminating and elucidating life in its manifold aspects. Unfortunately, these two types of commitment are frequently incompatible, for the social or ideological concern is a powerful force which all too easily overpowers the fragile delicacy of artistic creation. When this happens, it tends to be the propagandistic thrust which acts as the unbalancing factor.

It is undoubtedly quite futile to expect South African literature to overcome the tendency toward imbalance by foregoing the use of propaganda, for this element will continue to serve a purpose in reflecting the socio-political milieu. "Propaganda is always going to be with us. There will always be the passionate outcry against injustice, war, fascism, poverty."[17] In short, it is an aspect of writing which cannot be neglected by writers unwilling to be sidetracked into peripheral issues, but it also must not become the central element in South African fiction. Here the onus is on the author to keep propaganda in and of itself from becoming the *raison d'être* of his literary activities. He must keep the creative aspects of theme and story above his political attitudes, using propaganda and social issues to inform his writing and give it a cutting edge, ". . . but they must never usurp the place of the prime motive, which is to tell a story."[18]

In fact, however, this usurpation has often occurred; time and time again one reads novels which are primarily vehicles for political protest and social theory. One can sympathize with writers who feel compelled to use literature in this way, but sympathy cannot excuse the fact that "this literature of protest, assertion and declamation has produced writing which lacks balanced sensitivity and has tended to cloud the understanding of values which, above all, society requires of an artist."[19] When this happens, it becomes difficult to see the themes which invest the writing with power and commend it to the sociologist and literary critic alike.

Themes in South African Fiction

The themes themselves have been the subject of many investigations, and it is possible here to mention the findings of only a few commentators, indicating in passing what appears to be the current state of thematic interest in South African fiction.[20] The one theme which all investigators regard as central to the literature is autobiography; indeed, so prevalent has it become that one can scarcely find a single author without an autobiographical novel to his credit.[21] Works of this type invariably have the basic elements of a "Jim-goes-to-the-city" theme: personal growth and emotional development combined with an increasing awareness of social circumstances.[22] It may well be the very simplicity and basic experience inherent in such a theme that attract so many writers; "the basic 'Jim-goes-to-the-city' theme runs so close to the actual pattern of life for most African authors that it is certain to be around for a long time and no doubt explains why autobiography is such a dominant genre in South African literature."[23] Or perhaps it enjoys such consistent popularity due to the fact that in troubled, chaotic times one tends to withdraw and romantically recall life as it used to be. Whatever reasons lie behind the recurrence of autobiographical novels in South Africa, they play a significant role in illuminating for us the personal reactions of sensitive individuals to the pressures of conflict and feelings of embitterment and loneliness.

The use of autobiography as a general theme in fiction carries within itself a number of lesser themes, which appear as the writer in the story develops into a mature individual. For example, an initial awareness of the African exposure to Western ways often opens the autobiographical novel, and this in turn is followed by feelings of isolation or alienation and then by a sense of confrontation or violent reaction to life. The more mature autobiographies often end with the theme of forgiveness and an attempt at reconciliation. These sub-themes fulfill a two-fold purpose: they illuminate the journey of one man through life and describe his reactions to a variety of situations, and they also serve to personify an entire society and its changing moods.

When one steps away from the autobiographical novel, the themes which there existed only marginally suddenly take on greater significance. For example, one of the earlier and more popular themes is that of alienation or isolation, which is often expressed by the withdrawal of the protagonist due to his inability to comprehend or cope with what he sees. This Nadine Gordimer terms the "literature of victims"; "this is by the nature of the social structure there, a considerable literature in South Africa. We are shown what people suffer under the imposition of a particular policy, a way of life, a particular morality."[24] This theme of alienation and the suffering which follows it has been well treated by Modisane in *Blame Me on History,* La Guma in *A Walk in the Night* and *A Threefold Cord,* Mphahlele in *The Living and the Dead,* to mention only a few.

As the writer matures, he begins to react, and in thematic terms this often means confrontation or violence. In the stage of alienation the author (or his character) expresses his reaction to disintegrating traditions and lost innocence through a paralytic disillusionment and shocked disbelief. Once the numbness has worn off, the writer responds with vengeance, striking out violently at the society from which he has become alienated. The result frequently is expressed in terms of open conflict and subversion, as well as spiritual and moral struggle. One sees examples of this theme in works by La Guma and Modisane and to a lesser degree in the writings of Abrahams and Rive.

When the emotional reactions have been exhausted and confrontation has ended in stalemate or death, the novelist is ready for a gentle, more hopeful theme, that of forgiveness or reconciliation. Developments in this area lie perhaps further in the future, for as yet reconciliation has not appeared with nearly the same frequency as the other themes. Nevertheless, one must not assume that all South African fiction is evolving neatly along clearly defined lines with forgiveness as the final goal, for many novelists, particularly Paton, Mphahlele and Abrahams, have treated this theme quite early in their artistic development.

Although most of these themes appear to be largely emotional or psychological, they in fact incorporate a wide variety of very real, concrete manifestations. Just as the literature cannot be separated from or treated independently of the social setting in which it is created, so the themes developed in the writing deal very directly with the social situation. Ezekiel Mphahlele has identified over a dozen situational factors common in African literature as a whole,[25] while perhaps half of them occur frequently in South African novels: racial conflict and *apartheid,* labor upheavals, oppression, urban squalor, physical violence, police terror. In short, the themes in this literature serve as vehicles for both the outer aspects and internal stresses of the South African social order in all its diversification. It is important to remember that the novels arising from this social order deal with highly relevant issues through a variety of subjects and by several means, and in this respect South African fiction does not differ in the least from its counterparts elsewhere in the English-speaking world.

It is quite clear, therefore, that here we have a literature which is a full member of its genre. It is neither glorified journalism nor hypnotically bound to a single theme; rather it is a literature which presents the reader with a strong commitment to certain ideals clothed in a variety of thematic representations. If one is to find any fault with the South African novel, it must be on two counts open to a wide spectrum of individual interpretation. First, because virtually all of the novels develop their themes through a situation that has been shared in reality by the audience, they tend not to be intimate or intensely psychological in ways that we in the West have come to expect. Second, the authors almost invariably are assertive, declarative writers, speaking with passion, conviction and a certain tactless abandon. As a result of these two traits, the novels of South Africa can lack the balanced sensitivity and carefully analyzed values which most of us regard as essential in literature. At the same time, of course, we must recognize that this particular literary tradition is of a relatively recent vintage and should continue to improve as it matures.

Notes

1. Robert P. Armstrong, "The Arts in Human Culture," in *Expanding Horizons in African Studies: Proceedings of the Twentieth Anniversary Conference, 1968, Program of African Studies, Northwestern University*, edited by Gwendolen M. Carter and Ann Paden (Evanston, Illinois: Northwestern University Press, 1969), p. 123.

2. Lewis Nkosi, "Fiction by Black South Africans: Richard Rive, Bloke Modisane, Ezekiel Mphahlele, Alex La Guma," in *Introduction to African Literature: An Anthology of Critical Writing from "Black Orpheus,"* edited by Ulli Beier (London: Longman, 1967), p. 211.

3. *Ibid.*, p. 212.

4. Dennis Brutus, "South Africa: The Tortoise Literature," in *Studies on Modern Black African Literature*, edited by Pál Páricsy (Studies on Developing Countries, No. 43. Budapest: Center for Afro-Asian Research of the Hungarian Academy of Sciences, 1971), p. 86.

5. *Ibid.*, p. 85.

6. Martin Tucker, *Africa in Modern Literature: A Survey of Contemporary Writing in English* (New York: Frederick Ungar, 1967), p. 159.

7. *Ibid.*, p. 229.

8. *Ibid.*, p. 262.

9. Nadine Gordimer, *The Black Interpreters: Notes on African Writing* (Braamfontein, South Africa: Ravan Press, 1973), p. 19.

10. Tucker, *op. cit.*, p. 16.

11. G.-C. M. Mutiso, *Socio-Political Thought in African Literature: Weusi?* (New York: Barnes and Noble, 1974), p. 3.

12. Brian Masters, *Sartre: A Study* (London: Heinemann, 1974), pp. 59–60.

13. Doris Lessing, *Going Home* (London: Panther Books, 1968), p. 17. Nadine Gordimer echoes Miss Lessing's opinion in "Nadine Gordimer: The Solitude

of a White Writer," *The Listener,* 96, no. 2480 (1976): 514, where she says, "...you close your eyes, and put your hand deep down into the world that you know around you, into your own society. And whatever is there you come up with: this is what being a writer's about. Your material, your themes, take hold of you from the life around you."

14. Lessing, *op. cit.,* p. 20.

15. Tucker, *op. cit.,* p. 207.

16. J. P. Makouta-Mboukou, *Black African Literature: An Introduction* (Washington, D.C.: Black Orpheus Press, 1972), p. 138.

17. Ezekiel Mphahlele, *Voices in the Whirlwind and Other Essays* (New York: Hill and Wang, 1972 [1967]), pp. 186–87. Varying viewpoints on the place of political protest and propaganda in the literature may be found in S. K. Panter-Brick, "Fiction and Politics: The African Writer's Abdication," *Journal of Commonwealth and Comparative Politics,* 13 (1975): 79–86; Kolawole Ogungbesan, "Politics and the African Writer," *African Studies Review,* 17, no. 1 (1974): 43–53; John Povey, "Political Protest in the African Novel in English," in *Protest and Power in Black Africa,* edited by R. Rotberg and A. Mazrui (New York: Oxford University Press, 1970), pp. 823–53.

18. Alan Paton, "Four Splendid Voices," in *Quartet: New Voices from Africa,* edited by Richard Rive (New York: Crown Publishers, 1963), pp. 12–13.

19. David Rubadiri, "Why African Literature?" in *African Writers on African Writing,* edited by G. D. Killam (London: Heinemann, 1973), p. 143.

20. Among those who have written most lucidly on this subject mention must be made of the substantial contributions by Charles R. Larson, *The Emergence of African Fiction* (Revised edition; Bloomington: Indiana University Press, 1972); Tucker, *op. cit.*; Wilfred Cartey, *Whispers from a Black Continent: The Literature of Contemporary Black Africa* (London: Heinemann, 1971 [1969]); Gordimer, *Black Interpreters*; and the interesting Unesco publication, *Apartheid: Its Effects on Education, Science, Culture and Information* (Paris: Unesco, 1967), pp. 149–60.
   Also worth reading are Mphahlele, *op. cit.,* pp. 193 ff.; Don Dodson, "The Four Modes of *Drum*: Popular Fiction and Social Control in South Africa," *African Studies Review,* 17 (1974): 317–43; Rowland Smith, "The Johannesburg Genre," in *Exile and Tradition: Studies in African and Caribbean Literature,* edited by Rowland Smith (Dalhousie African Studies Series, ed. John Flint; London: Longman, 1976), pp. 116–31; Per Wästberg, "Themes in African Literature Today," *Daedalus* (Spring 1974): 135–50. Slight variations on these works appear in D. R. Beeton, "South African English Literature from the Perspective of the Seventies," *South African Libraries,* 40 (1972): 148–57; Makouta-Mboukou, *op. cit.,* pp. 39–46 ff.; John Ramsaran, *New Approaches to African Literature: A Guide to Negro-African Writing and Other Studies* (Second edition; Ibadan: Ibadan University Press, 1970), pp. 28 ff.; Rubadiri, *op. cit.,* pp. 141 ff.

21. See Part II, Chapter 1 for mention of some of these autobiographical novels. Cf. Kolawole Ogungbesan, "Autobiographies in Africa," *Savanna* (June 1973): 1–10.

22. Wilfred Cartey, "Contemporary African Literature," in *The African Experience,* edited by John N. Paden and Edward W. Soja (Evanston, Illinois: Northwestern University Press, 1970), vol. I, pp. 582–83.

23. John F. Povey, "'Non-European' Writing in South Africa," *Review of National Literatures*, 2, no. 2 (1971): 72.

24. Nadine Gordimer, "The Novel and the Nation in South Africa," in *African Writers on African Writing*, edited by G. D. Killam (London: Heinemann, 1973), p. 43.

25. Mphahlele, *op. cit.*, p. 193.

Academic Study of the South African Novel

Four Curricular Approaches

University curricula tend to incorporate South African literature in at least one of four possible ways, although one of these is rarely encountered. Since it is the librarian's task to be aware of the circumstances in which the South African novel may become an area of special concern in an academic library, he must have some knowledge of each of these possibilities. The four ways in which this literature may be used in university education are briefly these: (1) the South African novel as one aspect of English literature or of Commonwealth (a term sometimes including South Africa) literature in English; (2) the novel of South Africa as a major facet of African literature, either in English or Western languages in general; (3) the novel as one factor in the total presentation of African cultural life; (4) the South African novel as part of an interdisciplinary approach to the humanities and social sciences. These four approaches to South African fiction derive from the function of literature as an art form which encourages aesthetic appreciation and the development of creative insights or as a vehicle for information on non-literary aspects of life and society in particular cultures.

The first of these four areas, the South African novel studied within the context of English literature, is perhaps the least popular approach; certainly it is the least frequently encountered use of this literature in university studies, and there are undoubtedly sound reasons for this exclusion. In most faculties of English literature the novel is treated as a Western or Euro-American art form exhibiting a clear historical and developmental continuity within certain well defined regional or national boundaries, particularly Britain and North America. Within these confines there is adequate scope for investigation without going too far afield in a search for possible "colonial" or regional variations. Thus one may comfortably limit a syllabus to writing by, for example, Chaucer to Durrell or Twain to Steinbeck without feeling that disregard for writing from recently established English-speaking cultures places debilitating restrictions on the width and breadth of coverage.

25

The avid Africanist may resent this situation, but on purely academic grounds little can be said in arguing for a more inclusive policy. After all, in the total output and historical breadth of English literature the South African novel is quite insignificant. Likewise in terms of creative innovation and literary sophistication the situation is South Africa has little to offer that does not already exist on a much wider scale in British or North American fiction. Therefore, one cannot react with genuine surprise to the fact that very few South African novelists (e.g., Schreiner, Paton, occasionally Abrahams and Mphahlele) appear with more than minimal frequency in syllabi for the novel in English. In this traditional academic framework the librarian will have little cause to acquire South African novels in English, and personal experience has shown that such novels rarely appear on the shelves of university libraries for the primary use of faculties of English literature. While today some of these libraries do, in fact, acquire South African fiction (Sussex and Leeds being only two examples), none of them do so for the specific purpose of supporting a syllabus in English literature.

There is, of course, one variation on the standard approach to English literature which brings the South African novel into greater prominence, and that is the whole area of Commonwealth literature in English or, in the American variation, world literature in English. In this scheme the traditional and quite legitimate limitations of an English literature syllabus purposely are expanded to treat the subject on a more international basis. In such a case there is an obvious place for fiction written in South Africa, although for a variety of reasons discussed in Chapter 4 it is often excluded or purposely proscribed.

While surface appearances may indicate that the Commonwealth or international approach to literature in English is not very popular, there has in fact been a great deal of activity throughout the 1970's to suggest otherwise. The number of universities with some reputation as centers for the supranational study of English literature is still relatively small (perhaps a dozen in America and hardly more than six in the United Kingdom[1]), but there are many individual academics actively promoting this approach in their respective institutions. Thus while one may cite the University of Leeds in Britain as one of the few universities with a syllabus devoted to the study of Commonwealth or world literature in English, there are many others in which teachers and researchers are actively engaged in the study and teaching of this literature. Just how massive this somewhat hidden interest is may be seen in the number of groups and societies which exist to promote the international study of English literature. In the United Kingdom as early as 1965 the Association for Commonwealth Literature and Language Studies (ACLALS) was established, and by 1973 there was both a European branch and a Canadian group (CACLALS). Today there are discussions under way for groups in Australia, the Caribbean and West Africa, while a South Asian branch has lately come into being. In addition the Americans have their counterparts in WLWE, World Literature Written in English, and the ALA, African Literature Association;[2] furthermore, by the end of 1975 the Modern Language Association was about to form a new subdivision, English Literature Other Than British and American (ELOTBAA).[3] While membership figures for these and similar associations generally are not available, the proliferation of such bodies suggests that the interest in Commonwealth literature is both active and growing. Further support for this claim may be taken from the fact that several British universities do collect Commonwealth literature in English, albeit on a rather small scale and with a general disregard for the South African output,[4] and that there has been a Working Party on Library Holdings of Commonwealth Literature since 1970.[5] Therefore, although in any given university there may be no more than a few individuals interested in this wider study of English literature, the potential exists for this interest to become ever more manifest in terms of formal instruction and set syllabi. This in turn may involve the librarian, so one must never assume that in even the most tradition bound institutions there is no possibility for the growth of a cosmopolitan, catholic view of English literature which includes South African fiction.

There are those who object to the inclusion of African writing in a university syllabus, whether this involves either a traditional or a Commonwealth approach, on the grounds that non-Africans neither can understand the "soul" of black African writers nor appreciate the artistry in their work.[6] However, this objection cannot be raised in a regional studies curriculum which includes African literature in English as part of a total immersion in the life and culture of Africa. This area or regional studies approach, which has been in operation for several years and which enjoys particular popularity in America,[7] places the major emphasis on the African-ness of the literature by regarding it primarily as an African creation and only incidentally as writing in English. While adherents of the Commonwealth approach often express reservations about the viability of including South Africa in their terms of reference, there has been little difficulty in seeing South African fiction within the parameters of African literary studies. Certainly there can be no objection to treating this particular national writing as part of African literature *in English*, for a language map of Africa clearly shows that the Republic is an integral part of an English-speaking belt stretching in an unbroken line from Egypt through East and Central Africa to the Cape of Good Hope.[8] Because this literature in English follows language usage in not respecting national barriers, it would be quite indefensible to exclude South African fiction from a regional approach to African literature in English.

In point of fact this general treatment of the literature ought really to be seen as a variation of the normal regional studies program, for one rarely finds African literature being studied outside an established area studies center. In such institutions as the School of Oriental and African Studies and Northwestern University, literature, whether from South Africa or any other African country, is treated as an essential component in the full explication of African cultural life and intellectual heritage. In this situation both teacher and pupil fully understand that one cannot begin to comprehend a culture without some knowledge of its literature, so they are as much interested in creative writing as in history, art or anthropology. Very often national or regional boundaries do play some part in this approach, for academic work of this sort tends to focus on particular countries within a given area. Thus while the immediately preceding treatment of African literature normally regards this subject as a single, unfragmented entity, in the traditional area studies program the emphasis is less on literature *qua* literature and more on its place as an expression of the cultural life in a given country or region within Africa.

In either of these approaches to African literature within an area studies curriculum, creative writing has tended to be a poor relation when compared with other of the humanities or the social sciences.[9] Hence even such a highly respected regional studies center as SOAS only recently has begun to express a clear interest in African fiction, particularly from Southern Africa. To a large extent this negligence merely reflects the pragmatic, functional approach of area studies, a view which regards a region in purely sociological, anthropological, political and economic terms. Certainly for a developing country the issues raised by the scientist may have greater urgency than those raised by the humanist, yet many of us agree with Fanon that poetry and other forms of literature may be as important as the more practical issues of economics or social structure,

> ...for the poets (and writers in general) are the ones skilled in communication. They can speak in universal forms which will be understood by people whatever color or nationality. They speak the language of consciousness, of dignity, regardless of race or color; they can cultivate the integrity of the blacks and the other characteristics that are essential to being human. For they know that communication makes community, and community is the possibility of human beings living together for their mutual psychological, physical and spiritual nourishment.[10]

Perhaps the time is now ripe for these more humanistic concerns, for as a country like South Africa moves beyond the immediate needs of food, housing and employment (but not political freedom), it becomes more feasible to undertake a more leisurely study of its cultural achievements. Thus while some may still bemoan the relative neglect of African or South African literature in regional studies, the void is gradually being filled with both researchers and university programs in African literature. The growth in this direction may be seen by comparing the opportunities for studying

African literature in America in 1974–75 with what had become available in 1976; in that short space of time some twenty-eight additional centers reported a formal interest in African and Afro-American creative writing.[11]

It is only natural to expect African literature to have its widest popularity in regional studies programs, for this approach always treats the area in question as an integrated socio-cultural entity, the purpose being to present ". . . a synthesis or integration of multidisciplinary specialized knowledge about an area . . . , and the scientific objective of this attempt is the understanding of the area as a functioning socio-cultural whole."[12] This comparative or multidisciplinary approach, however, in practice often reverts to more traditional disciplinary divisions under the aegis of regional studies. As a consequence, the Africanist trained in such a system has tended to be either an historian *or* a literary critic, a sociologist *or* an anthropologist, the only common ground among them being an area rather than a genuinely interdisciplinary interest. This, of course, cannot be defended on any logical grounds, for as Gwendolen Carter said in 1966, "the vitality and usefulness of all area studies are dependent on the interaction maintained at all times with new disciplinary interests and techniques, and the infusion of insights drawn from investigations in other parts of the world."[13] This in fact comes close to what one might term a cross-disciplinary approach in which the social scientist relies on the humanities in much the same way as the technologist relies on the natural sciences; the humanities, and literature in particular, have a direct relevance to the more pragmatic aspects of regional studies and therefore merit closer attention from all sides.

John Povey has been particularly eloquent on this subject and more than once has spoken of the potential value of African literature in illuminating other disciplines. In the introduction to Barbara Abrash's *Black African Literature in English Since 1952* he stated that

> Many interdisciplinary programs are being constructed and presented around an area focal point and for these the discovery of such a literature is all important. These writers can open the world of Africa directly to the eyes of American students. They become the window through which we see the new Africa in the words of the most able and responsive of its young men. Not by the explanations of the anthropologists, but from the directly conceived experiences, we learn of the nature of change in modern Africa.[14]

Like all of African literature, South African fiction in English shares this potential value in a cross-disciplinary situation, for it partakes of many areas of academic interest; broadly political, it provides insights into the mood and temper of the present socio-political situation and into historical aspects of the recent past, and it also presents the philosopher, the literary historian, the social anthropologist and the educator with living examples of various theories or ideas. In other words this literature ". . . provides a vivid image of Africa seen through African eyes. As such, it is a unique instrument for enlarging our perception and our understanding of the experiences, the problems, and the tragedies of modern Africa."[15] In Chapter 2 it was stated that the South African novelist must reflect upon and write about the social situation in which he finds himself, and it is because of this that his novels have ramifications in disciplines far removed from traditional literary studies. South African novelists, like their counterparts throughout Africa, engage in polemics and persuasion, narration and introspection, description and dissection, as well as in diatribe and invective;[16] in every case the material around which these literary forms are constructed holds interest for the Africanist in several disciplines.

While this viewpoint is particularly important in the context of African studies, its value must not be limited in this way. Indeed, it seems quite clear that this interdisciplinary approach has its place throughout the academic spectrum, and it is just this aspect which has been least investigated in terms of African literature and which we see as the approach with the greatest potential growth, namely the use of South African fiction as part of virtually every discipline in the humanities and social sciences, whether in regional studies, interdisciplinary education or traditional curricula.

Multidisciplinary Content of the Literature

Literature embraces many areas and cannot be understood without considering the history, philosophy, politics and social context in which it arises. In other words literature itself demands an interdisciplinary approach, and there is no reason why this situation cannot be reversed. In fact it is not too polemical to maintain that African literature in particular virtually cries out for this wider application, for it is what followers of Sartre call "functional" in that it advocates a particular cause and instructs its audience. In other words as an author seeks to stir people, so he will vindicate a viewpoint, assert a belief, support one group or another.

Perhaps the strongest adherent of this viewpoint is Gideon-Cyrus Mutiso, who believes that we must be able legitimately to derive socio-political and cultural theory from literature. He makes a powerful case indeed for valuing literary works because of the manner in which they exemplify the nature of a society from within, delineate its problems and particular characteristics, describe human reactions to that society and express the most desirable choices among competing values. In discussing the derivation of social theory from literature he states quite plainly that from the literary production of any group ". . . we should be able to extrapolate the major social and political concepts that will be used for the socialization of present and future generations."[17] Such extrapolation does not depend on literature being written for propagandistic or polemical reasons, for in every case the writer goes beyond the limitations of these literary forms.

The artist—the novelist or poet in particular—also plays a crucial role in a society in explaining and interpreting the nuances of that society to those without. Enlightenment concerning the values and activities of a society can thus be facilitated by studying its literature.[18]

Such explaining and interpreting is precisely the task of the sociologist and the political theorist; as the writer uses a particular topic, be it class consciousness or color discrimination, to provide a local setting for motives or desires common to all men, so the sociologist may extrapolate from such work examples to illustrate particular issues in social theory. The novel is thus not a competitor of any of the social sciences; as Bantock sees it, the novel instead bears witness to influences of a certain social environment and thereby provides the sort of evidence about the nature of society which is of interest to the social scientist.[19] On the surface it may appear that the two types of investigators have little in common, for whereas the social scientist is concerned with general classes of events, social processes and groups, the novelist tries to weave a coherent story, using for this purpose threads of highly magnified description and specific details. The writer therefore uses an individual or an event as the microcosm of an entire situation, while the social scientist tends to lose the individual in examining an entire group.

Yet in dealing with either microcosm or macrocosm both men in their own particular fashions are moving within a world of daily life that is at once commonplace, commonsensical and relatively unspecialized in the technical or scientific sense. Within this movement both attempt to construct independent worlds of interrelating human beings, which in some way are abstractions out of the "real" world, abstractions containing nothing except that which is relevant to the actions or patterns under observation. In so observing, creating and extrapolating, the writer and his more methodical counterpart share one essential element which binds their work so closely together. "A concern for social meaning within a common sense world has been found to be the common factor in the activities of both the literary artist and the social scientist. Both rely, in their investigations into this social meaning, on some element of typicality. . . ."[20] From this point of typicality the writer moves toward particularity in both telling the tale and displaying the social phenomenon, and in doing this he naturally indicates characteristics which may be attributed to this phenomenon, thereby affording insights of interest to the social scientist, who in his turn is moving from the typicality to generalizations about the phenomenon.

It is in this manner that the writer and the social scientist complement one another, and for our purpose the effects of the former on the latter are most significant; as the novelist uses a model to give a particular experience an immediacy lacking in general analysis, so ". . . the story of his model . . . will be enriched by truths . . . which simply cannot emerge with the same force and paradigmatic clarity from scientific data and analysis."[21] It is this enrichment, we believe, which gives the African novel a place of importance in a variety of analytical disciplines. By now it is obvious that this literature has some relevance to the social sciences, and there are any number of novels which may be used to support this claim. To cite only two examples, Ezekiel Mphahlele in *Down Second Avenue* says a great deal about the urban South African which is of interest to the sociologist; likewise Doris Lessing in *Martha Quest* and *A Proper Marriage* includes much of value to the social anthropologist interested in comparing present social networks with those of late colonial British Africa.

But it is not only sociology and social anthropology which can benefit from the work of novelists; the political scientist and even the economist to some degree can learn from creative writing. "Creative writers can often provide a key that is not to be found, or may be found only with great difficulty, in the more rebarbative writings of political philosophers or men of affairs."[22] It is perhaps in this area that South African fiction has the greatest potential impact, for the nature of the political system in South Africa means that politics is never far from the central concern of writers in the Republic, many of whom have been affected quite directly by various political factors or enactments. As one outspoken critic has commented,

> A writer is not just an artist. He is also a citizen of his country and he belongs to the time in which he is living. While he cannot be expected to create according to command, he must certainly love his people and manifest his solidarity with them in their struggle for total liberation.[23]

While this statement is somewhat biased and not altogether accurate in terms of the writing by all South African novelists (e.g., Wilbur Smith[24]), it does reflect the viewpoint and approach of the majority of these writers. Thus their writing can be extremely useful in putting flesh on the bones of political theory or the study of modern political systems. A prime example of this correlation between fiction and political studies may be seen in Miss Gordimer's *A Guest of Honour*, which deals both directly and indirectly with a variety of political themes relevant to post-colonial Southern Africa.

Indeed, this particular novel goes beyond politics to cast light on postcolonial history as well, which brings us to yet another subject often treated in South African fiction. History plays a large part in this writing, for novels from South Africa tend to exemplify much that has changed (and continues to change) in Africa. Thus Miss Gordimer's novel, while dealing with political themes, also indicates many factors in recent African history; the same is true of most other South African novels, whether they purposely choose a particular historical setting or indirectly reflect the history of their own time.

It has proved virtually impossible for the contemporary African writer to avoid reflecting, nor has he sought to do so, the fundamental transformation taking place in the Africa of his generation. ... The transformation has, after all, affected society as well, and here one is involved by one's very existence.[25]

As a result, novels by Paton, Abrahams or almost any other South African cannot help but reflect the historico-political or historico-social realities of their time. A prime example of the historical continuity which one may observe in South African fiction lies in Doris Lessing's often cited series, Children of Violence. Through the eyes of Martha Quest, the main character in each sequel, one sees how the fabric of history in Southern Africa has changed between 1939 and the present day. In a similar way one can select novels to represent almost any historical period or event of the postwar era either in South Africa or the wider African scene.

And one could continue to cite examples of novels that are relevant to any of the humanities, but this will not seem unusual to anyone with even the most elementary acquaintance with literature. Perhaps both librarians and their teaching colleagues have overlooked this relationship because it has not always seemed so obvious, but there are in fact very few situations in which literature has no role whatever. Whether the librarian wishes to accept this as justification for collecting South African fiction remains for him to decide. Should the challenge be accepted, we can assist by outlining not only some of the problems likely to be encountered but also the essential tools for a balanced acquisitions policy.

Notes

1. The six listed in 1970 included East Anglia, Edinburgh, Exeter, Hull, Kent and Leeds; of these only East Anglia, Exeter and Leeds had African Commonwealth collections of an adequate size (400+) to support a teaching program. A. J. Horne, "An Outline of U.K. Library Holdings of Commonwealth Imaginative Literature: Statistics," unpublished paper presented at the Conference on Library Holdings of Commonwealth Literature, Commonwealth Institute, London, 5 June 1970. Mimeographed.

2. "Commonwealth Literature: Its Study and Sources," *The Royal Commonwealth Society Library Notes*, n.s. 204 (1974): 1; Richard K. Priebe, "African Literature and the American University," *Issue*, 4, no. 4 (1974): 21.

3. "Minutes of the 1975 Annual General Meeting of the Canadian Association for Commonwealth Literature and Language Studies on Tuesday, May 27, 1975 at the University of Alberta," Supplement to *Moko*, 6 (1975): 4.

4. Horne, *op. cit.*; cf. Gail Wilson, comp., *A Handbook of Library Holdings of Commonwealth Literature in the United Kingdom* (Reprint; London: Commonwealth Institute Working Party on Library Holdings of Commonwealth Literature, 1974 [1971]).

5. Donald H. Simpson, "The Working Party on Library Holdings of Commonwealth Literature," *Education Libraries Bulletin*, 18 (1), no. 52 (1975): 13–17.

6. Dorothy Blair, "African Literature in University Education," in *African Literature and the Universities*, edited by Gerald Moore (Ibadan: Ibadan University Press, 1965), pp. 74–76.

7. There are currently some 115 centers of higher education in the United States offering courses on African and Afro-American literature, and many of these fall within a general African studies curriculum. Mitsue Frey and Michael Sims, compilers, *Directory of African and Afro-American Studies in the United States* (Fifth edition; Waltham, Massachusetts: African Studies Association, 1976). However, Richard Priebe, *op. cit.*, pp. 19–22, maintains that this apparent popularity obscures the genuinely tenuous position of African literature in these universities. Nevertheless, one cannot help but feel that this unsettled existence is better than the minimal formal British interest in African literature. In the U.K. there are no more than five centers for the study of African creative writing (Lancaster, Leeds, SOAS, Sussex and York). International African Institute, *International Guide to African Studies Research* (London: International African Institute, 1975). "Most UK research on Africa is carried out by staff and senior students within teaching departments of the universities. Interdisciplinary degrees on *African studies* are available only at Birmingham and . . . SOAS in London; African studies courses may be taken as part of a first degree in Edinburgh, Oxford, Sussex and York. Edinburgh, SOAS, Birmingham, Cambridge, Leeds and York have African Studies Centres with coordinating functions, and several other universities have more informal groupings of faculty members with African interests." *Ibid.*, p. 53.

8. Rede Perry-Widstrand, "Publishing in Africa: A Paper for the Seminar on African Literature Organised by the Finnish Unesco Commission, Helsinki, September 13–15, 1974," unpublished mimeo. Between pp. 12–13 the author includes a map from *Africa Report*, July–August 1973, p. 19, which illustrates the contiguous spread of English-speaking Africa.

9. Gwendolen M. Carter, "African Studies in the United States: 1955–1975," *Issue*, 6, no. 2/3 (1976): 3. Cf. John F. Povey, "African Literature and American Universities," *African Studies Bulletin*, 11, no. 2 (1966): 13–19 for an interesting view of the potential for this literature from the perspective of the mid-1960's.

10. Rollo May, *Power and Innocence: A Search for the Sources of Violence* (London: Fontana, 1976 [1972]), p. 246.

11. Frey and Sims, *op. cit.*; cf. Gail von Hahmann, ed., *Directory of African Studies in the United States 1974–1975* (Fourth edition; Waltham, Massachusetts: Research Liaison Committee, African Studies Association, 1975).

12. C. K. Yang, "A Conceptual Review of Area and Comparative Studies," in *The Comparative Approach in Area Studies and the Disciplines: Problems of Teaching and Research on Asia: Selected Papers Presented at the Conference on Asian Studies and Comparative Approaches Sponsored by the Comparative Studies Center, Dartmouth College, September 13–17, 1965*, edited by Ward Morehouse (Occasional Publication no. 4; New York: Foreign Area Materials Center, University of the State of New York, State Education Department, 1966), p. 46; cf. Donald Wilhelm, "The Crisis in

Area Programs: A Time for Innovation," *African Studies Review*, 14 (1971): 171–78, which argues for a restructuring of area programs to include comparative and cross-disciplinary studies.

13. Gwendolen M. Carter, "African Studies in the United States," in *Proceedings of a Conference on African Languages and Literatures Held at Northwestern University, April 28–30, 1966*, edited by Jack Berry, Robert P. Armstrong and John Povey (Evanston, Illinois: Northwestern University, 1966), p. 4.

14. John Povey, "Introduction," in *Black African Literature in English Since 1952, Works and Criticism*, compiled by Barbara Abrash (New York: Johnson Reprint, 1967), pp. ix–x; cf. A. Norman Jeffares, "The Study of Commonwealth Literature," *The Journal of the Royal Society of Arts*, no. 5149 (1968): 16–33, especially p. 23.

15. Albert Gérard, "Bibliographical Problems in Creative African Literature," *Journal of General Education*, 19, 1 (1965): 26.

16. John A. Ramsaran, *New Approaches to African Literature: A Guide to Negro-African Writing and Related Studies* (Second edition; Ibadan: Ibadan University Press, 1970), pp. 25–26.

17. G.-C. M. Mutiso, *Socio-Political Thought in African Literature: Weusi?* (New York: Barnes and Noble, 1974), p. 5; cf. G.-C. M. Mutiso, "African Socio-Political Process: A Model from Literature," in *Black Aesthetics: Papers from a Colloquim Held at the University of Nairobi, June 1971*, edited by Andrew Gurr and Pio Zirimu (Nairobi: East African Literature Bureau, 1973), pp. 104–74.

18. Mutiso, *Socio-Political Thought*, p. 3; cf. pp. 15–16 and note 10 above.

19. G. H. Bantock, "Literature and the Social Sciences," *Critical Quarterly*, 17 (1975): 99. Bantock's article is an excellent introduction to the topic under discussion, providing much material of value to one interested in the interdisciplinary uses of literature. One good example of the way in which literature may be used in other fields is found in A. Shorter, *African Culture and the Christian Church: An Introduction to Social and Pastoral Anthropology* (London: Geoffrey Chapman, 1973), which contains an extensive bibliography of African creative writing used to elucidate ideas in a chapter entitled "African Values in Christian Catechesis."

20. Bantock, *op. cit.*, p. 124.

21. Joseph Blotner, *The Modern American Political Novel, 1900–1960* (Austin: University of Texas Press, 1966), p. 6; cf. Mercer Cook and Stephen E. Henderson, *The Militant Black Writer in Africa and the United States* (Madison: University of Wisconsin Press, 1969), p. 9.

22. Renee Winegarten, *Writers and Revolution: The Fatal Lure of Action* (New York: Franklin Watts, 1974), p. xxiii.

23. W. Jeanpierre, "Negritude and Its Enemies," in *African Literature and the Universities*, edited by Gerald Moore (Ibadan: Ibadan University Press, 1965), p. 20.

24. Insight into the purely commercial aspects and entertainment value of some South African fiction may be gained from Denis Herbstein, "The Man with the Golden Typewriter," *The Sunday Times Magazine*, 11 April 1976,

pp. 55–60. This article concerns Wilbur Smith, who has written numerous bestsellers and who says of himself, " 'Some of my critics say I have no literary merit. . . . I know I'm no Solzhenitsyn. But I also know I'm a successful author.' " *Ibid.*, p. 60.

25. Clive Wake, "The Political and Cultural Revolution," in *Protest and Conflict in African Literature,* edited by Cosmo Pieterse and Donald Munro (London: Heinemann, 1969), pp. 45–46.

Bibliographical Problems and Prospects

When a librarian with no detailed knowledge of African literature in English is asked either to establish or expand a collection of South African fiction, how precisely ought he to proceed? To begin with he will want to acquaint himself with the nature of this literature, particularly those aspects outlined in the preceding three chapters; this will provide one with a basic background without which there cannot be a sensible acquisitions policy. The librarian then must turn to the general bibliographical coverage of South African documentation as a whole in order to determine what is available for his use, and one's first impression undoubtedly will be that the position is a relatively strong one in comparison with bibliographical tools for other African countries. Superficially this evaluation cannot be faulted, for in bibliographical terms South Africa is rather highly developed, having as an impetus one of the largest book trades in Africa, which includes both healthy indigenous firms and several well established expatriate publishing houses. Coupled with this thriving industry is a system of bibliographical control second to none in Africa and comparable to that in many European countries, a system which includes numerous trade publications and catalogues recording current output, an established national bibliography, a handful of bibliographical journals and a group of professionally trained librarians with a desire to maintain adequate facilities for the dissemination of information about South African publishing. One is faced, in other words, with a situation which appears to warrant the opinion that ". . . coverage of this area presents no immediate difficulties from the point of view either of up-to-date bibliographical information or of source of supply."[1]

Unfortunately, such an evaluation is simply too complacent and self-satisfied in view of the very real problems which beset the librarian/bibliographer working in this area. How, for example, does one cope with late or faulty coverage by major subject or national bibliographies? By what means does one deal successfully with the scarcity of bibliographical data which results from the banning and censorship of much internally produced writing or overcome the difficulty of locating titles from small African or

37

European publishers who may be politically committed but bibliographically haphazard? And then there are difficulties posed by the Diaspora of South African novelists to most parts of the English-speaking world, one consequence of which is an individual author's appearance in print in several countries or with a number of publishers; furthermore, there is the problem of creative works within South Africa which, because of government opposition, must become quasi-ephemeral underground publications. These are but a few of the many issues neglected by those who write so optimistically about the South African scene; in contrast to their views it seems more reasonable to say that ". . . we are far too confident about our acquisitions coverage of South Africa."[2]

Problems, Lacunae and Incongruities

In the area of South African fiction this over-confidence is particularly noticeable. Where, for example, are assessments of publishing, bibliographical tools and acquisitions procedures by librarians experienced in these matters? With two exceptions[3] such surveys for South African literature simply do not exist at any thoughtful or incisive level, and even these two attempts are rather superficial in their conclusions and by now somewhat dated. With similar neglect no one has undertaken a thorough analysis or evaluation of the bibliographical resources available for the study of South African literature. There is also in the provision of comprehensive retrospective or current bibliographies of creative writing a marked dearth of useful compilations, although this may be changing with the imminent appearance of such a guide under the joint editorship of Reuben Musiker and André de Villiers.[4] There is, of course, a handful of more general bibliographies, most notably the compilation by Jahn and Dressler with a forthcoming supplement by Bernth Lindfors, but even these are inadequate for South African fiction either because of the dates which they cover or their limitation to works by black/colored writers.[5] Still, should any of these publications prove useful as retrospective guides, there is no ongoing publication devoted specifically to the recording of current South African fiction; the closest approximation to this ideal is the frequently out-of-date and less than complete annual listing in the *Journal of Commonwealth Literature*.[6]

Looking beyond the strictly bibliographical requirements of librarians and the existing guides to South African fiction, one finds that information on publishing in the Republic is also very limited. Recent lists by Philip Altbach, Maduka Anyakoha and Hans Zell mention very few sources of information either about South African publishing in general or of value to the librarian attempting to come to grips with problems of literary production in the Republic.[7] In order to acquire material efficiently one must have some guidance to the types of publishers and dealers, the breadth of their interests and their response to overseas orders; it would also help to have practical advice on possible means of dealing with the smaller, less internationally oriented firms, as well as some indication of actual problems encountered in relations with South African publishers and successfully employed means of overcoming such problems. Ideally one would like to see surveys similar to Downey's evaluation of the African Imprint Library Services as a supplier of publications relevant to development studies,[8] but as yet such reports relevant to South African literature simply do not exist.

Just as there are no guides aimed at the collector of South African fiction and no practical surveys of attempts to deal comprehensively with the South African book trade, so there is also no European center to which one can turn for advice in dealing with literature from South Africa. In the United Kingdom SCOLMA certainly has never touched on this area, and no other body or institution with an interest in Africana either appears to have adequate expertise in South African literature or seems willing to share its experience with a wider audience. Assuming that this regrettable gap may be due to current financial restraints or a very recently developed interest in the field, one might have expected the wealthier and larger North American libraries to have expressed an active interest in this area, but such is not the case. Thus on every front the librarian meets with silence and a lack of concern, and this state of affairs demands a remedy.

Before proposing solutions, however, one must first tackle two basic incongruities in the treatment of South African literature; one of these concerns the place of South African studies as a whole, and the other relates to the novel or creative writing of South Africa in particular. In the general area of African studies one might assume that there is no possibility of excluding South Africa from the field of inquiry, since it is clearly part of the African region in terms of its cultural development and historical influence. Yet one finds that in a high percentage of cases there is a strong reluctance to admit South Africa to its legitimate place in African studies because of the political status of the Republic or because of its socio-political policies. In his introduction to *South African Studies*, for example, Moss reports that

> A number of members of the African Studies Association, in company with a not inconsiderable body within the thinking public in Britain, feel...that, in view of the current political and social situation in the Republic of South Africa ... ties of all kinds, including the academic ... should be broken. It is fair to say that ... the majority of members do not share this view. Nevertheless, the minority view is very important....[9]

While one may sympathize with the rejection of all that South Africa stands for, it is clearly illogical to exclude the country from academic study because of this. In doing so scholars are only spiting themselves by ignoring a country with an undeniably powerful influence on the African sub-continent, if indeed not on the developing world in general. South Africa is facing many of the same problems that plague her more liberal and less developed neighbors, and there is much to be learned from studying the issues and their solutions in the Republic, as well as their possible ramifications for the rest of Africa. Not to admit this leaves a rather large vacuum in our understanding of Africa's culture, history, society and politics. Therefore, it seems clear that the only sensible policy must be one that treats South Africa as a legitimate and integral facet of African studies. In fact SCOLMA has always included the Republic within its terms of reference, but in general this policy has not been the norm. Now, however, this inclusive coverage appears to be taking on greater respectability, since the Working Party on Library Holdings of Commonwealth Literature is compiling a union list of Commonwealth literary periodicals which will include South African publications.[10]

Within the field of African literary studies one finds that South Africa very often receives some coverage, but with an important qualification. Black or colored writing tends to be granted the seal of legitimacy, while the white contribution is not. Again one can understand how scholars, particularly those with connections or special interests in black Africa, might feel a kinship with outspoken black writers in the Republic coupled with a total rejection of the white establishment and its supporters. However, there is no legitimate reason for extending this policy into the academic world, for to admit only black literature into one's field of inquiry tells only half the story. As one scholar, himself a practitioner of this black exclusiveness, admits in the introduction to a recent bibliography,

> ... it can be argued that such arbitrary classification is unjust and unrealistic since writers such as Alan Paton, Nadine Gordimer, Harry Bloom, Dan Jacobson, David Lytton and, from Rhodesia, Doris Lessing address themselves in their work to the same problems as Alex La Guma, Ezekiel Mphahlele, Richard Rive, Dennis Brutus and others listed here.[11]

Killam then goes on to qualify this argument by stating that 1) the writing of white South African authors is part of "... a continuing tradition of writing in English which began before the turn of the century..."[12] and that 2) writing by white South African novelists is better known and more readily available, implying that because of this it can be ignored in bibliographical surveys.

If one considers these last two points rationally, they exhibit a clear lack of coherence and therefore may be easily discarded. In the first place the fact that white South African writing derives from a long tradition makes it no less a part of the entire corpus of South African fiction, and to exclude it implies that black South Africans have been writing in a vacuum without the cross-fertilization which many of them admit having derived from their white colleagues. Furthermore, to ignore the white contribution in any survey, bibliographical or otherwise, gives a highly unbalanced view of the situation. To say that white writers are covered by other resources is not sufficient, for what one requires is a single compilation which includes and evaluates all the output of the genre, thereby providing the basis for comparative analysis.

As with so many controversial topics of this sort, the problem revolves in part around a semantic differentiation. The issue here is most clearly highlighted in a recent interview with Kole Omotoso concerning the newly established Union of Writers of African Peoples. Having stated that the Union would include all writers using any of the languages within the continent, Omotoso was then asked whether this would encompass South African writers.

> Omotoso: "Oh, yes . . ."
> ABPR: "And white South African wrtiers?"
> Omotoso: "No! The name of the Union is Union of Writers of *African* Peoples. White South African writers are not Africans."[13]

In other words the terms "African" and "South African" are sometimes defined in such a way as to necessitate the exclusion of white writers.

Several researchers have attempted to come to grips with this issue by offering their more rational and less exclusive definitions. These attempts run the gamut from the fairly narrow view of "South African" as meaning a native-born citizen of the country to the more moderate view of Musiker, which includes residents as well as citizens who write about the South African setting; beyond this is the completely open-ended viewpoint expressed at the Congress of Africanists in Accra, which sees "African" as being any work which treats an African setting or experience.[14] In our view this very loose definition makes the literary boundaries so vague that it becomes impossible to study South African literature in any thorough or comprehensive fashion, while the narrow view of Omotoso is far too crippling and myopic to permit any investigation involving solid conclusions or adequate coverage of the field. Therefore, one is left with a more moderate definition based on viewpoints expressed by Astrinsky and Musiker: South African English literature is that which is written by citizens (expatriate or otherwise) and residents of the country and which includes to some degree themes and issues arising from the South African milieu. This definition has the virtue of including in theory *all* South African writers regardless of color, and this is the most important factor. There is nothing to be gained by arbitrarily separating authors according to their shade of skin, for the significance in what they say lies not in this difference but rather in a comparison of their themes, aims and artistic development.

Much the same point can be made about exclusion based on language, for this also introduces an arbitrary and false differentiation into the literature of a country. As Achebe sees it, "a national literature is one that takes the whole nation for its province, and has a realised or potential audience throughout its territory. In other words, a literature that is written in the national language."[15] As in so many African countries, South Africa has more than one nationally recognized language, in this case English and Afrikaans, unless one also wishes to include Xhosa and other indigenous tongues as well, which would increase the number substantially. Without devaluing the importance of these languages, particularly Afrikaans, as vehicles for literary expression, one may justifiably exclude them in the present context for two reasons: 1) they are spoken by a small percentage of the total population and 2) are not part of an internationally recognized literary tradition. While this may fracture any homogeneity which exists when considering South African literature as a whole, it is a widely accepted policy in literary studies. Thus one studies Commonwealth English literature on the basis of language rather than national boundaries, extracting the relevant writing from India, Canada and elsewhere, leaving behind works in Tamil, French and other national languages. Within the Republic this is also the norm, since there is the National English Documentation Centre as well as an Afrikaans counterpart. Therefore, it is fair to focus attention on South African writing in English as part of a universal literary tradition.

Selective Improvements and a Master Plan

Having at least made a case for including South Africa as part of African literary studies and for treating South African writers as a single group without regard for color, it is now possible to suggest solutions to the less emotive problems of bibliographical control. It is in a way perhaps easier merely to plead the case for a redefinition of terms than to offer concrete proposals for improving bibliographical coverage, for the latter involve not only good will but also practical cooperation and concrete results. Nevertheless, one can at least attempt to indicate likely directions which the soluions might take.

Looking first at South African publishing, there is unfortunately little of practical value that can be suggested for improving the situation described on pages 37–39. As already stated, an essential ingredient in any work of this sort, namely the publication by librarians and others experienced in the field of their own findings and attempted solutions, simply does not exist on any noticeable scale. One can but hope that professional journals will begin to encourage contributions of this sort in the not too distant future. A useful, if limited, beginning along these lines has been made with a series of company profiles in the *African Book Publishing Record,* which includes both publishers and prominent bookshops.[16] In addition *ABPR* recently has carried two articles which discuss different aspects of African and South African publishing at greater length.[17] One trusts that these examples will be followed and enlarged upon in other relevant publications;

in particular it would be extremely useful to see articles of the caliber of Keith Smith's "Who Controls Book Publishing in Anglophone Middle Africa?" or those appearing from time to time in *Scholarly Publishing* being written specifically on the South African situation.[18] These along with purely practical reports of library experiences in dealing with publishers based in the Republic would do much to encourage current thinking and innovation.[19]

In the provision of a comprehensive bibliography of South African literature the situation appears rather brighter than is the case for data on South African publishers and booksellers. This more positive state of affairs is due largely to the already mentioned (see page 38 and note 4) undertaking by Reuben Musiker and André de Villiers, which is scheduled for publication in 1978. Advertised as a comprehensive retrospective guide to South African English literature from its earliest days up to the mid-1970's, one may expect the work to be a reasonably complete and accurate record of all published literary material. The project relies both on Musiker's considerable knowledge of the South African scene and also on the combined expertise of a team of qualified bibliographers supported by the considerable resources of the Institute for the Study of English in Africa. However, the one major drawback is that this multi-volume compilation will be only retrospective and will not continue beyond coverage of the mid-1970's. Thus, while it will be a most welcome attempt to record past publications, it will in no way further the equally important listing of current titles. To exercise adequate control over his collection and acquisitions program the librarian must know not only what has been published but also what is coming onto the market at the present time. Such current information can be gleaned only from an ongoing bibliography of both primary and secondary literary publications, and a project providing this service for South African English literature remains to be undertaken.

There are, of course, a number of scattered resources which together form an acceptable bibliography of current creative writing and literary criticism; these are discussed in Part II. Yet to rely on these variable and somewhat disparate bibliographical resources is no substitute for a single ongoing compilation devoted to South African literature. Because the number of titles, both primary and secondary, in this field has not yet reached unmanageable proportions, it is still possible for a guide of this type to be established without undue strain and pessimism from the outset. The ideal for such a project would be an international cooperative effort operating under the aegis of a bibliographical committee sponsored by one of the major African studies or African literature societies in conjunction with SCOLMA or some other body concerned with Africana library materials. This committee ought to consist of approximately three members, each one based in a country known to be a major producer of titles by or about South African writers—South Africa, Britain and America. The committee member in the Republic would be responsible for reporting the titles of all primary and secondary works published there and in the rest of Africa, perhaps with the assistance of an East African colleague. The British bibliographer could cover the United Kingdom and other European countries with some interest in South African literature, namely France, Germany, Switzerland and possibly Sweden. Similarly, the North American compiler would oversee the collection of data about the important and rapidly growing output from that continent.

While this suggestion for a bibliography by committee may seem unnecessarily bureaucratic and subject to all the vagaries which traditionally plague efforts at international cooperation in librarianship, such a program in fact embodies a number of advantages which more than outweigh the administrative difficulties. In the first place the gathering of data and compilation of lists would tend to be faster and more efficient due to the division of labor. Furthermore, each regional expert might be expected to understand the peculiarities of his own area and therefore know how to avoid the *lacunae* and pitfalls of bibliographical control attempted from outside the given region. As a result, the project should allow a pooling of knowledge and expertise, which in turn ought to insure a thorough and accurate compilation of relevant data. All of these factors would enhance, although not insure, the possibility of producing an annual or semi-annual bibliography on a regular and up-to-date basis; such a production could not help but be a great advance on the present situation in which bibliographies of this sort consistently appear up to three years later than the date of coverage. In terms of administration and continuity this proposal would tend to create a self-perpetuating organism quite unlike the faltering efforts of singlehanded compilations. Where several researchers are involved, the loss of a single member need not mean the suspension or termination of the project, since the committee as a whole would be expected to carry on by appointing a successor to fill the void. With a sponsoring association or institution in the background, continuity of this sort would be even more certain, since the administrative machinery necessary to maintain the committee's activity would already exist. Furthermore, the reliance on a supporting agency also should mean that administrative costs would be far lower than in a comparable but independently organized scheme with its separate administrative framework.

In fact it seems quite clear that not to rely on already existing bibliographical and literary associations would be a major error in the present atmosphere of financial strain and cooperative effort in other areas. Such organizational support would involve both academic associations and research centers, one for manpower and the other for finance or housing facilities. For example, such groups as the African Literature Association, Association for Commonwealth Literature and Language Studies, African Studies Association and SCOLMA could be asked to suggest individuals from their membership who would be qualified and willing to undertake certain aspects of the research. At the same time one of the many African studies centers or libraries could be asked to house the project, make its collection available to the committee or provide space for a coordinating bibliographer in much the same way that SOAS provides facilities for the compiler of the *International African Bibliography*. Among possible centers of this sort which both appear sympathetic to bibliographical activity and contain substantial resources to support the project one need mention only a handful: the University of Texas at Austin, Northwestern University, Yale University, Boston University, the School of Oriental and African Studies, Royal Commonwealth Society, University of Leeds and the Institute for the Study of English in Africa.

Ideally this type of cooperation would extend to the actual publication of the bibliography as well, since to rely on an already established outlet would obviate the heavy expense of starting a new serial with very limited circulation. At present there are a number of journals which seem ideal candidates to serve as vehicles for an annual bibliography of South African literature; *Research in African Literatures, Africana Journal, Journal of Commonwealth Literature, African Research and Documentation, English Studies in Africa* are but five possible candidates. The most suitable would be the first two serials, one of them devoted specifically to African literature and the other with a strong bibliographical orientation. The remaining three journals would be less acceptable because of their rather slow coverage of material in general, and the bibliography of South African literature is something which ought to appear every spring for the preceding year. In addition to these established publications one cannot rule out the possibility of starting a new bibliographical newsletter, particularly if it were issued as an annual occasional guide by the sponsoring association or institute. With camera-ready copy and other inexpensive reprographic techniques it is possible to produce an aesthetically acceptable document at a price well within the range of most budgets; for example, at current prices two hundred copies of a twenty-page document produced in A4 format from camera-ready copy would cost approximately £100, and mimeograph reproduction is far less expensive. While cost is not a prohibitive factor, it would be preferable not to add yet another title to the range of Africana publications but rather to rely on one of the better known and more widely read journals in this area.

Assuming that a committee were established along the lines suggested above, how might it take shape in a British setting? First, the committee would have to decide whether the actual compilation of data could be handled by one of its members or should be entrusted to a bibliographer engaged for this purpose. If it were decided to appoint a bibliographer, SCOLMA could be asked to find a suitable candidate, who would then be given a place in SOAS. This individual could then coordinate information supplied to him by the committee members and on the basis of this data would compile a semi-annual or annual list for publication in *African Research and Documentation* or one of the other serials noted above. If, on the other hand, a committee member himself were able to undertake the actual coordination and compilation of data, he would do this from his own home base, the end result being the same.

A possible corollary to this scheme stems from a proposal made by Bernth Lindfors in 1968 for the establishment of an American archive for African literature.

> ... If an official American archive of African literature were to be established at one of the major universities and a professional librarian appointed to acquire such books, the opportunities for American scholars to do serious research in African literature would be greatly increased.[20]

Although not suggested in the context of international African literary studies, the Lindfors proposal has an obvious application at this level as well. Such a center would be ideally suited to meet the needs of the proposed bibliographical committee, particularly if it were able to maintain a brief for collecting international documentation on African literature. Of course, this would require the closest collaboration with agents and libraries in South Africa, Britain and America both in terms of funding and providing copies of titles published in the various countries, particularly since it would serve as an international center open to researchers throughout the world. Although difficult to imagine in the present economic situation, there certainly is a need for such a center, when one considers the total lack of any institution which collects comprehensively in the field of African literature, let alone the more restricted area of South African creative writing. If such a collaborative venture could be established, it would be of inestimable value for the international bibliography of South African literature, since the committee or its bibliographer would have at hand in the center nearly all current publications on the subject.

Perhaps for some time to come it will not be possible to consider in practical terms the foundation of an international center for African literary documentation both for financial reasons and because of the massive problems certain to attend an undertaking of this sort. However, by limiting coverage to South African literature in English the scope would be narrowed considerably, thereby making it financially possible and economically feasible. But there are also more compelling reasons to concentrate on this particular type of African literature. First, South African creative writing in English, although indisputably part of the wider African culture, is different enough to warrant a separate acquisitions effort; as a clearly defined entity in its own right, this literature can easily stand alone without detriment either to other African literatures or itself. In much the same way one can envisage individual collections of East, West and North African literature, each one of which is a well defined subdivision within the world of creative writing. Furthermore, the output of titles for African literature as a whole has reached such proportions that practical considerations in terms of finance, space and personnel virtually dictate some division of labor in collecting efforts, and there is no reason why it cannot be done along regional lines. Furthermore, because South African writing in English can, as we have seen, be considered as part of Commonwealth or world literature in this language, there is the possibility of including South Africa within an acquisitions policy devoted to literary activity of this sort, which again makes it possible to see specifically South African writing separated from African literature as a whole.

Assuming that both of these proposals for an international archive are beyond the realm of possibility at the present, there is yet a more limited possibility, again suggested by Lindfors, that is worth considering.

> An alternative to such an archive might be a formal system of regional or national cooperation among research libraries which are actively collecting African literature. Such a system could be modelled on the Farmington Plan, with each library specializing in a particular area or language group in its acquisition of literary works from abroad . . .[21]

In Britain this alternative has obvious application in terms of South African literature within the already existing SCOLMA framework, which is our answer to the Farmington Plan; it is in fact at this level that an archive or documentation center for South African creative writing in English has the greatest chance of success. There are already libraries specializing in South African publications as part of the SCOLMA venture; in addition there are various centers which on their own have developed collections of African literature.[22] To date, however, there has not been a concerted effort to combine these two special interests into the building of a collection of specifically South African literature. Within the already existing structure a marriage of this sort is far from unthinkable, and it has far more chance of success than either an international or national center of African literary documentation. As already suggested, these last two proposals would require the development of a totally new framework for bibliographical cooperation, and this in itself would tend to negate the possible success of either venture from the outset. Within SCOLMA, however, we already have the impetus for and interest in more localized cooperation. It should not be overwhelmingly difficult for SCOLMA to encourage a library already collecting South African documentation or one with a strong interest in literature to take on the additional area of English literaure from the Republic; certainly the annual output of primary and secondary documentation in this area is neither so copious nor so disparate as to impose impossible financial or logistical burdens on a prospective collecting center. One's preference, of course, is for a more international effort along these lines, since it would undoubtedly assure better coverage of the output, but even a less ambitious national effort within SCOLMA would do much to improve the extremely limited attention presently given to South African literature. While some attempt along these lines would provide an ideal setting for compiling the bibliography envisaged, it by no means is a necessity, and one can imagine the proposal functioning quite adequately without benefit of such a center.

The final, and perhaps crucial, element in a scheme for developing adequate bibliographical control of South African literature does not in the end depend on any of the foregoing suggestions. This *sine qua non* is, of course, the preparation of a bibliographical guide to assist all librarians, libraries and scholars interested in the acquisition and study of English literature from South Africa.[23] Such a guide requires neither international cooperation nor financial support of any sort, yet it is an indispensable tool for providing information on the various resources available to those working in the discipline. An important element in this compilation would be a brief discussion of the South African literary tradition to assist those with little knowledge of the subject; on a more practical level it should outline the form and content of the material, the bibliographical control available from various types of publications and institutions, as well as production and distribution patterns. In the discussion of available resource material, coverage should include everything from the most general to the most specific Africana and literary publications: bibliographies of bibliographies, selected general bibliographies, guides to African studies and literature, African and South African literary bibliographies, theses, bibliographical and scholarly periodicals. This comprehensive treatment of relevant types of publications would enable the librarian to evaluate the various materials and help him to decide which titles belong in a collection of South African literature. In order to fulfill its function as thoroughly as possible the guide also ought to contain a brief outline of the publishers and booksellers with an interest in the field, as this will enable one to develop a thorough acquisitions network with greater ease and less frustration than is presently the case.

Since the proposed guide would be extensively annotated and essentially comparative in its approach, it would also serve the needs of researchers by pointing out which materials warrant consultation and which ones ought to be avoided. In addition the commentary should direct one to relevant resources for specific types of information—bibliographical inquiries, biographical data, theses, periodical literature, literary criticism and the like. Also of interest to the researcher would be the frequent indications of *lacunae* in the field, for these could well encourage others to undertake a project aimed at filling one or more of the gaps; librarians in particular should be motivated by these hints, for it ought to be preeminently their task to provide fuller bibliographical coverage of the subject.

It is just this type of guide which the present project seeks to develop, although on a more modest level than the ideal outlined above and within the limitations imposed by a relatively brief time available for research. Thus one finds in the preceding three chapters a general overview of the South African literary tradition, which is aimed at providing readers with some basic acquaintance with the literature. Part II then presents a practical, comparative analysis of the types of materials noted in the preceding two paragraphs and includes a discussion of selected publishers and academic associations relevant to the field. One trusts that by attempting in this way to equip investigators with at least the basic knowledge required for an intelligent manipulation of data, the future acquisition and study of South African literature will be somewhat easier than it hitherto has been.

Notes

1. D. A. Clarke, "South Africa: Politics and Economics," in *Conference on the Acquisition of Material from Africa, University of Birmingham, 25th April 1969*, edited by Valerie Bloomfield (Zug, Switzerland: Interdocumentation, 1969), p. 116.

2. Susan Knoke, "Report on a Library Acquisitions Trip to Africa, December 1969–March 1970," *Africana Library Journal*, 1, no. 4 (1970): 14.

3. Albert Gérard, "Bibliographical Problems in Creative African Literature," *Journal of General Education*, 19, no. 1 (1965): 25–34. Although covering the entire field of African literature from the perspective of the mid-1960's, Gérard's analysis continues to hold some truth for the present South African situation, particularly in terms of possible solutions to the problems. Cf. Reuben Musiker, "South African English Literature: Bibliographic and Biographical Resources and Problems," *English Studies in Africa*, 13 (1970): 265–73. While Musiker provides little more than a bibliographical guide to resources available in 1970, he also offers some incidental, constructive criticism of activities up to that time.

4. Reuben Musiker and André de Villiers, eds., *Bibliography of South African Literature in English* (provisional title). This project is based at the Institute for the Study of English in Africa (Rhodes University) and is described by Irina Winterbottom in "Towards a Bibliography of South African Literature in English," *English in Africa*, 3, no. 1 (1976): 49–52. It is intended to cover material published up to 1974, including secondary material on the authors, and will contain some 8,000 monograph titles falling within a wide definition of "South African." The author, however, does not indicate the project's policy regarding the black/white distinction common to other works, nor does she clearly state the degree of exhaustivity at which the bibliography aims.

5. Janheinz Jahn and Claus Peter Dressler, *Bibliography of Creative African Writing* (Nedeln, Liechtenstein: Kraus-Thomson, 1971). Since its publication, this has become a classic reference tool for African literature. Cf. Bernth Lindfors, *Bibliography of Criticism on African Literature in English* (provisional title) (Detroit: Gale Research, c. 1978). Lindfors maintains that this will update and complement Jahn's compilation by including

material not noted in that work, as well as by attempting to cover all criticism by and about black African writers. "Jahn and Dressler included only a selection of bibliographical references to critical material; my bibliography will attempt to be as comprehensive as possible, so it will supplement Jahn and Dressler's listings considerably. Since the bibliography covers only 'black' African literature, no coverage of white South African writers will be attempted. Furthermore, only those black and colored South African writers who write in English will be treated." Bernth Lindfors: "Letter to G. E. Gorman, September 10, 1976."

6. The *Journal of Commonwealth Literature*, published originally by Heinemann (no. 1–no. 8) and now by Oxford University Press, began to cover South African literature in an appendix to no. 10 (1970). This listing now appears as part of the annual bibliographical issue (no. 2) in each volume. Cf. John F. Povey, "African Literature and American Universities," *African Studies Bulletin*, 11, no. 2 (1966): 18 for a comment on the necessity for a continuing bibliography of African literature.

7. Philip G. Altbach, "Publishing in Developing Countries: A Select Bibliography," *Scholarly Publishing*, 6 (1975): 267–79; Maduka W. Anyakoha, "Publishing in Africa: A Bibliography," *A Current Bibliography on African Affairs*, 8 (1975): 296–319; Hans M. Zell, "Publishing and Book Development in Africa: A Bibliography," *African Book Publishing Record*, 2 (1976): 95–103. Zell does, however, include some two dozen references under the heading, "The Acquisition of African Published Materials," but of these only four were written as recently as 1975, which is somewhat disheartening for one seeking current information. On the Editor's Page of the same issue Zell notes the purposely obstructive policies adopted by some South African publishers: "One South African publisher [Perskor-Boeke], in fact, blatantly *refuses* to supply information. . . . A few others, notably again from South Africa, are not apparently willing to take the trouble to supply complete bibliographic data . . ." (p. 155). It is precisely this type of information which librarians need to have in a single guide to South African publishers.

8. J. A. Downey, "A Blanket Order Supplier: A Resumé of the Work of the African Imprint Library Services," *Africana Libraries Newsletter*, no. 5 (May 1976): 1–8.

9. M. R. Kettle and R. P. Moss, eds., *Southern African Studies: Report of a Symposium Held at the School of Oriental and African Studies in the University of London on 24th September 1969, by the African Studies Association of the U.K.* (Birmingham: University of Birmingham, Centre of West African Studies, 1970), pp. i–ii.

10. The *List of Commonwealth Periodicals of Literary Interest*, as the project is provisionally titled, will be a finding list of British holdings of 1) Commonwealth magazines of general interest but with some literary content, 2) scholarly journals concerned at least in part with literature, 3) smaller press publications, 4) school and university literary magazines. Thus one can expect it to include a widely representative selection of South African periodical literature.

11. G. D. Killam, "Modern Black African Writing in English: A Selected Bibliography," *Canadian Journal of African Studies*, 9 (1975): 537.

12. *Ibid.*

13. Kole Omotoso, "Interview," *African Book Publishing Record*, 2 (1976): 12; cf. "Declaration of African Writers," *Issue*, 4, no. 4 (1974): 8.

14. A number of writers has tried to define "African" and "South African" *vis à vis* creative writing; the following is a representative selection of their definitions: Emile Snyder, "The Teaching of Modern African Literature Written in a Western Language," in *Proceedings of a Conference on African Languages and Literature Held at Northwestern University, April 28–30, 1966*, edited by Jack Berry, Robert P. Armstrong and John Povey (Evanston, Illinois: Northwestern University Press, 1966) refers to the Congress of Africanists' definition of African literature as ". . . any work in which an African setting is authentically handled, or to which the experience which originates in Africa is essential" (p. 100). Aviva Astrinsky, comp., *A Bibliography of South African English Novels 1930–1960* (Cape Town: University of Cape Town, School of Librarianship, 1965) defines South African writers as those who have spent ". . . a considerable part of their lives in South Africa and wrote at least some of their novels by being its citizens or residents" (p. 1). Reuben Musiker, "South African English Literature: Bibliographic and Biographical Resources and Problems," *English Studies in Africa*, 13 (1970), largely agrees with Miss Astrinsky in regarding South African English literature as something written by residents or citizens of the Republic without any regard for color (p. 265).

15. Chinua Achebe, "English and the African Writer," *Transition*, 18 (1965): 27.

16. "Company Profiles" has appeared in every issue of the *African Book Publishing Record* to date (see Zell, *op. cit.*, p. 100), but the only references relevant to South Africa and its creative writing (i.e., profiles of Oxford University Press Southern Africa, Longman Rhodesia Ltd., Longman Penguin Southern Africa Ltd. and Evans Brothers) are found in vol. 2, no. 1 (1976): 15, 21–23. "Prominent Bookshops in Africa" has only begun to appear with vol. 2, no. 3 (1976) and as yet has not dealt with the South African scene.

17. Julian Rea, "Aspects of African Publishing 1945–74," *African Book Publishing Record*, 1 (1975): 145–49. This article, in addition to its historical interest, contains useful general insights into the problems of publishing developments and provocative remarks on future possibilities. Cf. Peter Randall, " 'Minority' Publishing in South Africa," *African Book Publishing Record*, 1 (1975): 219–22. This report paints a clear picture of publishing difficulties in the Republic and also outlines possible developments within the current political situation.

18. Keith Smith, "Who Controls Book Publishing in Anglophone Middle Africa?" *The Annals of the American Academy of Political and Social Science*, 421 (1975): 140–50; Philip G. Altbach, " 'Third World' Publishing: Problems and Prospects," *Scholarly Publishing*, 5 (1973): 247–53; Robert P. Armstrong, "The University Press in a Developing Country," *Scholarly Publishing*, 5 (1973): 35–40; Alden H. Clark, "Publishing in Sub-Saharan Africa," *Scholarly Publishing*, 2 (1970): 67–74; cf. Datus C. Smith, Jr., "The Bright Promise of Publishing in Developing Countries," *The Annals of the American Academy of Political and Social Science*, 421 (1975): 130–39.

19. Examples of the type of survey which would be useful for South Africa are Julian W. Witherell, *Africana Acquisitions: Report of a Publication Survey Trip to Nigeria, Southern Africa and Europe, 1972* (Washington,

D.C.: Library of Congress, African Section, 1973) and Eugene de Benko, "Books and Publishing in Selected African Countries: Excerpts from a Report on a Library Acquisitions and Publications Survey Tour in Africa, November 1970–May 1971," *Africana Library Journal*, 3, no. 2 (1972): 3–14; cf. James C. Armstrong, "African Acquisitions Trip Report—1975," *Africana Libraries Newsletter*, no. 2 (1975): 13–23; D. A. Clarke, ed., *Acquisitions from the Third World: Papers of the LIBER Seminar, 17–19 September 1973* (London: Mansell Publishing, 1975).

20. Bernth Lindfors, "American University and Research Library Holdings in African Literature," *African Studies Bulletin*, 11 (1968): 310.

21. *Ibid.*

22. Both types of collections are outlined in Robert Collison, comp., *The SCOLMA Directory of Libraries and Special Collections on Africa*, rev. by John Roe (Third edition; London: Crosby Lockwood Staples, 1973) and in Gail Wilson, comp., *A Handbook of Library Holdings of Commonwealth Literature in the United Kingdom* (Reprint; London: Commonwealth Institute Working Party on Library Holdings of Commonwealth Literature, 1974 [1971]).

23. Something of this sort has been suggested in relation to Commonwealth literature: "there is a need for a handbook (or listing of basic texts) as guidance for teachers conducting courses in Commonwealth writing. This is something different from normal bibliographies. This would be a series of lists from various Commonwealth areas indicating the basic texts that would be needed for the study of any particular area. It would be a guide to the selection of texts for study, a guide to library ordering, and a guide for general reading (for those staff and students not involved in formal course work)." "Report of Working Party on the Teaching of Commonwealth Literature," in *National Identity: Papers Delivered at the Commonwealth Literature Conference, University of Queensland, Brisbane, 9th–15th August, 1968*, edited by K. L. Goodwin (London: Heinemann, 1970), p. 204.

Guide to
Bibliographical Resources

Sources of Biographical Data

Individuals interested in the South African novel often find that their research begins with a need for biographical information on a particular author as a background to effective evaluation of the writer's work. In addition investigators frequently wish to have a brief overview of several currently active authors in the Republic, and in both cases the ideal source of information is the comprehensive biographical dictionary. However, as is so often the case with other categories of reference material for South African fiction, there is not a single biographical compendium geared specifically to the provision of such data on writers from the Republic.

Nevertheless, there are a number of alternative sources of information which together go some way toward forming an adequate corpus of biographical resource material, and it is to these publications that the librarian and researcher alike must turn. These alternative guides take several forms, including national biographical dictionaries, monograph biographies of individual writers, semi-autobiographical novels and more comprehensive bio-bibliographies. Some are intended specifically to serve as biographical directories, while others fulfill the function of this genre only incidentally; *in toto* this group provides less than complete coverage of all currently active South African novelists, which is what one might expect from such an *ad hoc* conglomeration of material. The following survey attempts to cover the most readily available items of a biographical nature, but one must remember that sources discussed in other chapters may also warrant consultation, as they frequently provide access to information on individual authors as well. This is particularly true of the titles mentioned in the sections specifically devoted to African and South African literature.

Biographical Bibliographies

The first step in seeking biographical data must be to consult bibliographies which will guide one to the relevant sources, and here the inquirer is rather badly served. In fact there is as yet no bibliography specifically for this purpose, as Chapter Two will indicate, and even such likely substitutes

55

as published library catalogues have little to offer. Twice the Royal Commonwealth Society has published its library catalogues, which ostensibly have some relevant biographical content. The first of these, edited by Donald Simpson in 1961, intimates that artistic and literary figures are included, yet for South Africa there is not a single reference to modern literary figures among the several historico-political personalities.[1] A decade later the multivolume supplement to the 1930–1937 subject catalogue was published, but even here the section devoted primarily to biography treats South African writers only marginally better than the Simpson effort.[2] In the 1971 compilation there are a few relevant entries, but by and large the citations do not refer to strictly biographical sources. The fact that such library catalogues generally provide little bibliographical data on South African literary biographies is not surprising, for on the one hand not many biographies exist, while on the other a single library in 1961 or even in 1971 would be unlikely to have a comprehensive collection of biographical material relevant to a literature of comparatively recent vintage.

Of far greater potential value are two ongoing attempts by the Wilson Company to provide current indices to biographical material on figures in a variety of professions.[3] The quarterly *Biography Index* is issued in a triennial cumulation and currently covers biographical information found in some 1,900 periodicals which are covered in other Wilson indices. It includes current books of biography and periodicals, as well as incidental biographical data in non-biographical books and even obituaries. It provides a useful index by profession in each volume, so one can easily find which literary figures have been covered in the past year. Although the *Biography Index* to date has included only the better known South African writers (e.g., Cope, Gordimer, Jacobson), there is no reason why it should not in time encompass a wider range of such personalities. This depends, of course, on what those publications scanned in the course of compiling the *Index* themselves choose to cover, but here one may assume that these primary sources will incorporate information on other South Africans as they become more prominent. Therefore, one will want to scan future cumulations of the *Biography Index* for relevant bibliographical citations. Much the same comment may be made of *Current Biography,* which provides biographical information on people currently in the news; because South African novelists, due to their frequent opposition to the political regime, are often unwillingly cast into the limelight, one may expect other writers to join such personalities as Abrahams, Gordimer and Paton, who already have been covered. The entries in *Current Biography* often include sketches of writers' work and bibliographical citations for further study. These tools will, of course, require supplementing by reference to such literary periodicals as the *Journal of Commonwealth Literature,* since in their bibliographical coverage they frequently list biographical sources under a given author's name.

In addition these ongoing indices of biographical data are themselves indexed in a very useful Gale publication, *Biographical Dictionaries Master Index*.[4] Appearing for the first time in 1975, the *Index* contains some 725,000 entries based on the coverage of more than fifty biographical serials. The entries are arranged alphabetically by the names of individuals and exhibit at least a partial interest in South African novelists (Abrahams, Cope, Gordimer). While the serials thus indexed have extremely wide fields of interest, at least two of them are more than marginally attentive to the literary world (i.e., *Current Biography* and *Contemporary Authors*). Because of this, one will certainly want to scan the *Index* for references to South African authors, and it may well be that future editions will include a larger number of these novelists. As an index to current biography, this Gale publication is unique in its field, but it must be used in conjunction with the large number of non-serial biographical guides which it does not attempt to cover.

In the mid-1960's the Hoover Institution began compiling a list of biographies written for *West Africa,* one result of which was an article by Karen Fung in the *African Studies Bulletin*.[5] This was intended in 1966 to be the first phase of an ongoing bio-bibliographical project based at the Institution; according to Duignan's description, it was to provide thorough and inclusive coverage of biographical data on figures throughout Africa,[6] but this ideal was never achieved. Beyond Miss Fung's article the only concrete result of the project has been Virginia Adloff's biographical compilation on francophone West African personalities.[7] One must regret the demise of this potentially useful undertaking in view of the generally high quality of the Hoover Institution's bibliographical work; however, the idea of a similar ongoing project including South African writers is a very real possibility worth considering.

Because the Hoover Institution's work remains an unfulfilled hope, one must consult other resources, among them two bibliographies of South African autobiographies. The contribution by Ushpol must be seen for what it is, a bibliography compiled as part of a librarianship course at the University of Cape Town.[8] In any work of this sort the compiler tends to lack detailed knowledge of the subject, is limited to a very brief time for data gathering and works within the restriction of readily available libraries and other sources of information. While Ushpol suffers from all these drawbacks as well from the dated coverage of a mid-1950's compilation, this is still the only bibliography of its kind for the early autobiographies of modern South African fiction; for this reason alone it deserves consultation, albeit with the care which must be given to any guide of this type and date. Slightly more colorful and topical is Susan Anderson's 1970 bibliographical essay on selected South African literary autobiographies.[9] Because so many South African writers are outspoken in their opposition to the government and consequently suffer various types of repression, they find it both helpful and motivating to record their stories as autobiographies; it is as a guide to writings such as these that we require more articles of the caliber of Miss Anderson's.

Since there are no adequate bibliographies of biographical literature, anyone studying individual authors must begin with the very general reference works for Southern Africa. A very brief guide of this sort is the *African Encyclopedia*,[10] which contains limited entries for such well known authors as Nkosi and Mphahlele. These entries are little more than *curricula vitae,* yet coverage includes black authors frequently excluded from the more compendious resources. A similar encyclopedia in one volume is the geographically more limited *Encyclopaedia of Southern Africa*,[11] which is now in its sixth edition and again covers the better known writers (Paton, Gordimer, Cope). It does not include details of any of their publications and suffers from an apparent exclusion of black writers, as well as the inadequacy of extremely short entries. However, either of these works is more acceptable than the much larger *Standard Encyclopaedia of Southern Africa*,[12] which in its ten volumes entirely ignores the literary figures in whom we are interested. Similar in size to the *Standard Encyclopaedia*, but with a wider geographical coverage, will be the long-awaited *Encyclopaedia Africana*. The first volumes in this project are entitled *Dictionary of African Biography,* but they will not include living authors and so will be of limited use to researchers in modern South African literature.[13]

Literary Encyclopedias and General Biographical Dictionaries

From these general encyclopedias it is possible to begin focusing on more specialized reference sources of two types, the literary encyclopedia and the biographical dictionary. Of these two reference sources the latter has a slight edge in terms of numbers and percentage of entries relevant to South African literature. At the same time, however, the fact that there are so many publications to consult is clearly a major drawback to efficient use of these materials. Among the encyclopedias the best known are those by Steinberg[14] and Fleischmann,[15] but neither of them will do as sources of information on South African writers. *Cassell's Encyclopaedia*, for example, contains only very brief sketches on prominent figures from the Republic; for Alex La Guma one learns in eight lines merely that his work was banned and that he was placed under house arrest for his activities, leaving the country in 1966. One is also told that by 1967 he had written three novels, and none of this data is substantial enough to justify the time spent in seeking it.[16]

The wider choice one finds in biographical dictionaries may be divided into two types of selections, general biographical dictionaries and specifically African or South African oriented materials. The general biographical dictionaries, of which Webster's[17] and Chambers[18] may be regarded as the best examples, are both outdated and quite oblivious to South African writers.

More limited in scope are the biographical compilations dealing with either Africa or, more specifically, South Africa. Friedrich-Ebert-Stiftung issues *African Biographies*,[19] a constantly updated listing which is limited to political and government figures who fall within the category of "African leaders." In this respect it is very like Taylor's *The New Africans*[20] (which excludes South Africans) or Dickie and Rake's *Who's Who in Africa*.[21] One must always take care with biographical compilations which are essentially political in nature, for they often prefer to ignore South Africa; even when including the Republic, however, one will find that only the most prominent South African *political* figures are covered. Some of these dictionaries specify precisely what they include on a clearly socio-political basis; thus the *Dictionary of African Biography*[22] states that it limits coverage to members of the Organisation of African Unity, that it is concerned with free Africa and will never countenance racism by putting the names of citizens from racialist regimes in its pages.

The specifically South African biographical dictionaries tend to be primarily historical in content and include for the most part deceased individuals of some prominence. For example, de Kock's *Dictionary of South African Biography*[23] closely resembles the British *Dictionary of National Biography* in being more complete for the past than for the present and includes only such writers as Olive Schreiner and Rider Haggard. The single volume compilation by Rosenthal[24] is little better, being largely historical and now a decade out of date, while the annual *Who's Who of Southern Africa*[25] includes brief details on the lives and writings of a few prominent white South African novelists.

Since these two categories of reference material (encyclopedias and biographical dictionaries), whether general or specifically South African in content, tend to ignore literary figures from the Republic, the inquirer must turn to resources with a specific interest in literature. These publications include dictionaries and directories of literary biography, which, due to the perennial attraction of English literature and its personalities, exist in vast numbers. South Africa has tended to bask in the reflected glory of its parent genre, so it is only incidentally that South African novelists are mentioned in these guides. Nevertheless, the degree of their inclusion is significant in comparison with the negligible coverage in the materials surveyed so far. As an example, one need only compare *The International Who's Who* with either *The Author's and Writer's Who's Who* or *The Writer's Directory 1974–76*.[26] The first of these mentions only Gordimer and Paton, which is about what one might expect in an international compendium covering most professions. *The Writer's Directory,* on the other hand, provides in its biennial volumes the biographical details on more than 18,000 authors writing in English in a variety of disciplines. The fact that it is not limited to literature but covers all of the arts, the humanities and the sciences detracts from its usefulness, although in its 939 pages there are occasional entries for South African novelists (Cope, La Guma, Jacobson, Gordimer, Modisane). Of far greater value is the sixth edition of *The Author's and Writer's Who's Who*, which focuses clearly on the literary world. Its brief entries include data on the author's date of birth, education and family background, as well as basic bibliographies. While this compilation incorporates information on some of the lesser known writers (e.g., Jabavu), it also excludes some of the more widely known individuals (e.g., La Guma, Modisane, Mphahlele). This may be due to the fact that the wish of those who do not want to be included is honored, but whatever the reason, this compilation exemplifies perfectly the uneven coverage of South African novelists in these general literary guides.

Other biographical compilations which the researcher may want to consult include Richardson's *Twentieth Century Writing*, Kinsman's *Contemporary Authors*, Wakeman's *World Authors* and *The Penguin Companion to Literature*.[27] Richardson's guide relies heavily on the assistance of Cosmo Pieterse for many of the South African entries, which cover the usual names along with some of the less frequently mentioned individuals (e.g., Hutchinson). To be more useful the data could be somewhat fuller, but the information provided does have a high degree of accuracy. Kinsman's bio-bibliographical guide has been issued since 1962 in four annual volumes in one cumulation, and there is a cumulative index to volumes 1–48. The entries are of a uniformly high standard and are usefully divided into personal, critical and bibliographical sections (including works in progress). The one drawback is that all the volumes contain a very low proportion of black writers. *World Authors* also includes brief bibliographies for each author and some comment on the works cited; it is limited to individuals who came to prominence in the two decades following 1950, which means that South African coverage is weak for the fairly large number of newly recognized authors. *The Penguin Companion to Literature* provides a great deal of additional data but in a rather confusing fashion, since South Africa appears in two separate volumes, one for the Commonwealth and one for the Orient and Africa. Nevertheless, these two books together form a useful addition to the corpus of biographical reference materials. The volume by Daiches on the Commonwealth provides in its 575 pages details on 7,500 writers from the English-speaking world (excluding the U.S.).The entry for each writer contains a short biographical description and a brief bibliography, and the same is true of the entries in the Dudley and Lang volume. Although South Africa receives rather uneven coverage (Jabavu, Matshikiza and Modisane are included, while such writers as Cope and Hutchinson are not), *The Penguin Companion* contains adequate information on most black writers and many whites of note in the 1960's and therefore is not to be neglected. However, when consulting the two volumes one must note that while the Daiches compilation is arranged in a straight alphabetical sequence by author, the other volume is arranged first by region and then alphabetically by author.

Three additional publications which by virtue of their titles might appear to be relevant are *Brief Lives: A Biographical Guide to the Arts, Webster's New World Companion to English and American Literature* and *Who's Who in Twentieth Century Literature.*[28] Although often used as reference sources in English literary studies, in terms of South African fiction none of these works is particularly relevant. Kronenberger's *Brief Lives* was originally published in 1965 and because of this relatively early date does not include any of the many South Africans who have come to prominence since the mid-1960's. Pollard's *New World Companion* is not really a biographical compilation at all, containing only a single paragraph on South African literature and its thematic emphasis on racial conflict. Seymour-Smith's *Who's Who* also fails to cover South African writers and so need not be consulted.

At the other end of the spectrum is the extensive and, although not invaluable, certainly best of the general biographies of literary figures so far considered: James Vinson's *Contemporary Novelists.*[29] Contributors to this publication include Bernth Lindfors, Gerald Moore and A. Norman Jeffares, all of whom are highly respected scholars of African literature. These men have been responsible for the brief critical statements on most of the South African writers included, and each entry also contains a biographcial sketch, a bibliography and often a paragraph by the writer himself on his development and interests. The excellent coverage afforded the twelve or so South Africans in the present edition[30] makes *Contemporary Novelists* something of a *sine qua non* among the general biographical guides discussed so far. One trusts that there will be future editions listing still more personalities from the Republic.

Before turning to those publications intended specifically as biographical dictionaries of African writers, mention must be made of another type of material not intended primarily as a source of biographical data, namely surveys and anthologies of literature; good examples of these compilations are the works by Tibble and Rutherfoord.[31] Tibble's *African-English Literature* contains in pages 44–55 bio-bibliographical sketches of several prominent novelists, among them Abrahams, Mphahlele, La Guma, Modisane, Hutchinson, Nkosi and Jabavu. This was only an interim attempt in 1965 to provide biographical data, and after twelve years it can hardly be regarded as up-to-date. Much the same comment applies to Rutherfoord's *African Voices,* which contains a section entitled "About the Authors" on pages 197–203. Coverage is afforded only to the writers anthologized in the book, yet among the well known names are several not included in more current compilations. The coverage given to these often neglected authors (e.g., Ontepetse, Sentso, Themba) may make Rutherfoord's volume a useful source of information for some time to come.

Biographical Dictionaries of African Writers and Autobiographies

Having analyzed only a highly selective number of general bibliographical guides, one may now turn to three resources which are both specifically African in content and partly biographical in intent; when taken together, they provide the inquirer with details on more writers than all of the preceding resources combined, yet these three still omit certain individuals which can be found only in the other guides. The earliest of these more relevant texts is Hans Zell's *Reader's Guide to African Literature*, which was published in 1971 in America and in 1972 in Britain.[32] While the book as a whole contains valuable material to be analyzed in following chapters, pages 114–99 include biographies of prominent African authors, which makes the work relevant to the present discussion. Although Zell mentions a number of writers, only seven of them are South African novelists, all of them quite predictable names. This is a very small proportion of the total number of possible entries, yet Zell's approach gives his work a special interest. His intention is to provide a more "committed" perspective than one normally finds in the purely factual entries, so there is a particular emphasis on personalities, personal attitudes and values of those writers listed. This can be a most useful viewpoint, considering the "committed" nature of most South African fiction, and it is for this reason that Zell and Silver provide a valuable source of information.

Far more comprehensive is a work which tends to be given a class of its own, namely Jahn's *Who's Who in African Literature*,[33] which appeared a year after Zell's selective, interpretive compilation. The 411 pages of Jahn's more thorough guide consist basically of an alphabetical sequence of authors but include useful appendices of writers by language and country (pp. 393, 401). Coverage extends to individuals past and present from sub-Saharan Africa who write in African or European languages. Under each name there are biographical details, titles of works and some critical evaluation. The volume as a whole is thorough, although Jahn suffers from that black exclusiveness which, as we have seen, is endemic to much Africana scholarship. He thus excludes all white South Africans, and the entries for the black writers from South Africa exhibit a certain lack of organization and content which detracts from the overall usefulness of the work. For example, the data on La Guma includes what can only be described as "dust jacket blurbs" by five critics without any connecting statements by Jahn. The same is true for Abrahams; no attempt has been made to place his works in their biographical context. The whole exercise would have been improved greatly by a more judicious use of quotations and more attention to where particular works fall in an author's life. Thus, although Jahn's scholarship is generally well regarded in academic circles, in terms of South African interest and in comparison with the third compilation in this group his work cannot be said to have the same indispensable quality which other researchers attribute to it. Nevertheless, *Who's Who in African Literature* is still more comprehensive than any of the preceding volumes.

Most useful of all, however, is the more recent attempt by Herdeck entitled *African Authors.*[34] This is the first volume of a series which, according to the Gale Research Company's recent notice, will be published as regularly revised editions. These future volumes Herdeck sees as consisting of corrections, additions and new critical essays, and there are to be cumulative editions every six years. It is as an ongoing project that this undertaking has the most potential, since it undoubtedly will expand to cover more South Africans than are found in the present volume. However, like Jahn's work this one suffers from the exclusion of South African whites, and this will continue to be a major drawback for our interests.

African Authors consists in the main of an alphabetical sequence of bio-bibliographical entries followed by a series of critical essays. In the second part a group of appendices lists the authors according to the following categories: chronology, genre, country of origin, African languages, European languages, sex. A third part, and one which follows Jahn's example, covers the publishers, journals and dealers specializing in African literature. The final section lists many of the more important bibliographies, critical essays and anthologies. While the biographical section includes a rather high percentage of entries for South Africa, in the final analysis only a dozen of them fall within the limitations of the present study, namely modern and in English. Nevertheless, these entries provide a fairly complete summary of the work and history of each novelist and are to be recommended for their lucidity and accuracy. In terms of the South African writers falling within the present investigation it seems clear that Herdeck has achieved his goal, which he describes as follows:

> My major effort . . . beyond remedying, where possible, the factual, interpretive, or critical inadequacies, of previous scholarship, is to furnish a panoramic overview of each of the more important authors and to give a reasonably complete summary of his achievements both in and outside of literature.[35]

Nevertheless, errors do occur, as in the entry on page 236 which suggests that the two novels by Mopeli-Paulus (*Blanket Boy's Moon* and *Turn to the Dark*) are one and the same. In spite of such minor irritations, the 605 pages contain data which is consistently full, factual and helpfully interpretive; the only major failing is the limitation to black authors, but when this is balanced against Jahn's comparable policy, one must in the final analysis agree with Larson's preference for the work by Herdeck.[36] Particularly worth watching for will be the proposed 1978 revision, which one may expect to contain many more entries for the newer South African novelists.

Taking these three volumes of bio-bibliographical data for African authors together with all the other available resources discussed above, one will find that some of the lesser known South African novelists are not mentioned at all. This means that in the final analysis the researcher may well have to rely on individual monographs of a biographical or autobiographical nature for information. In terms of full biographies there is not yet much to offer, although there is bound to be more material of this type as individual writers continue to grow into artistic maturity. Twayne's World Authors Series deals primarily with prominent Western writers, but at least three works in this series are about South Africans and contain a fair amount of incidental biographical data.[37] Unfortunately, all of the individuals so far dealt with in this series are more briefly treated in the general biographical guides. The same is true of Wade's book on Peter Abrahams, which on pages 1–7 and 98–131 presents a rather full sketch of the author's life.[38] Nevertheless, researchers will have to watch both Twayne's World Authors Series and Evans' Modern African Writers for future South African biographies, as works in such series inevitably contain more detailed information on selected individuals than can be found elsewhere.

The sphere of autobiographies proves to be much more useful, since very many South African novelists (particularly non-whites) exhibit a penchant for the autobiographical novel. Among those who have been active in this genre one may mention Abrahams, Hutchinson, Jabavu, Matshikiza, Modisane and Mphahlele;[39] although such works are not straightforward factual pieces, they do contain much valuable interpretive material about the writers. More factual are the stories by a few novelists which deal with specific incidents in their lives; these pieces take the form of either brief articles, such as the piece by Jacobson,[40] or full length books, such as Doris Lessing's *Going Home*.[41] The importance of such works may be seen in the latter volume, which casts significant light not only on Miss Lessing but also on the background out of which the Children of Violence series has arisen. Indeed, without *Going Home* one might well miss the full characterization of Martha Quest, the main protagonist in Children of Violence. So while it is unfortunate that researchers requiring quick reference to the lives of South African writers may have to rely on autobiographies and similar full length material, it can be most beneficial to be forced to turn to such writings.

Although all of these biographical resources taken together may provide a passable body of material for biographical reference, it is unlikely that a single library either will have all the titles mentioned or will be able to afford the cost of acquiring all of these publications. Many larger, more general collections will, of course, already possess some of these books for a variety of other needs, but what of the specialist Africana library or the institution wishing to build up a collection of materials for South African literary studies? In such cases one must be highly selective in acquiring titles, and it seems appropriate to offer some suggestions to assist in the selection process.

Certainly any library collecting South African literature will want to have the works by Herdeck and Jahn, and probably Zell's compilation as well. In terms of the more general publications one may safely exercise a greater degree of selectivity, although Vinson definitely warrants a place among the biographical reference materials. Much the same may be said of *Current Biography* and Kinsman's *Contemporary Authors* because of their ongoing, cumulative nature and reasonable proportion of South African names. Of the larger encyclopedic volumes Oxford's *African Encyclopedia* is as adequate as any of the more voluminous and more expensive works, while virtually none of the literary encyclopedias contains enough additional information to warrant its purchase for this specific subject. The *Author's and Writer's Who's Who* and the two volumes of *The Penguin Companion to Literature*, on the other hand, are quite useful and may well deserve a place in a collection on South African literary biography. Finally, librarians will want to watch for new studies and anthologies similar to those by Tibble and Rutherfoord, which may provide needed biographical data.

The small library which acquires this handful of titles will have the minimum amount of resource material for biographical information on South African novelists; the larger, more general collection will undoubtedly have most or all of the other titles mentioned earlier, since most of them are integral parts of general reference collections or holdings in English literature. Even in this case, however, the researcher is not well served, since it is unlikely that all the documents will be housed in one location for his convenience. And even if they were, the large number of titles through which one might search with only a limited chance of finding data on a given author is both time consuming and frustrating. It is here that the proposed South African literary bibliography project/center might play a role by compiling from all available literary resource material a comprehensive dictionary or directory of South African literary biography. This is only a limited variation of the mid-1960's project mooted by the Hoover Institution (see page 57 and note 6), but because it has a narrower scope than this earlier undertaking, it may well be easier and less expensive to complete. Barring this, an alternative proposal might be to have an individual bibliographer compile a roster of all South African novelists active since 1950 and then prepare an exhaustive finding list of biographical data in the currently available resources discussed in the preceding pages. If this were then published in one of the more widely circulated scholarly journals or by one of the African literature societies, it would be of inestimable value to other workers in the field. Until this is done libraries will have to continue picking their way carefully through the dross, and investigators will have to be prepared for long and frequently fruitless searches for biographical data.

Notes

1. Donald H. Simpson, ed., *Biography Catalogue of the Library of the Royal Commonwealth Society* (London: Royal Commonwealth Society, 1961).

2. *Biography* (Vol. 7 of *Subject Catalogue of the Royal Commonwealth Society*. Boston: G. K. Hall, 1971).

3. *Biography Index: A Cumulative Index to Biographical Material in Books and Magazines* (New York: H. W. Wilson, 1946– ; quarterly with triennial cumulations); *Current Biography* (New York: H. W. Wilson, 1940– ; monthly, with annual cumulations and indices for 1940–1970 and 1971–1974).

4. Dennis Le Beau and Gary C. Tarbert, eds., *Biographical Dictionaries Master Index; First Edition, 1975–1976* (3 vols.; Detroit, Michigan: Gale, 1975).

5. Karen Fung, comp., "Index to 'Portraits' in *West Africa*, 1948–1966," *African Studies Bulletin*, 9, no. 3 (1966): 103–20. "Portrait: Ezekiel Mphahlele," *West Africa*, no. 2390 (March 23, 1963): 317 is an example of the type of article with which Miss Fung deals.

6. "The Hoover Institution has started a program to collect African biographical data in all forms. The need for the systematic gathering of such material is obvious to all. The plan is to locate and film biographical information in much the same way that the political ephemera project is operated, i.e., individuals or institutions are requested to provide copies of their collections. As a start the 'Portraits' which appear in *West Africa* have been xeroxed and indexed." Introductory remarks by Peter Duignan in Fung, *op. cit.*, p. 103.

7. Karen Fung, "Letter to G. E. Gorman, 24 February 1977."

8. R. Ushpol, *A Select Bibliography of South African Autobiographies* (Bibliographic Series. Cape Town: University of Cape Town, School of Librarianship, 1958).

9. Susan Anderson, "Something in Me Died: Autobiographies of South African Writers in Exile," *Books Abroad*, 44 (1970): 398–403.

10. *African Encyclopedia* (London: Oxford University Press, 1974).

11. Eric Rosenthal, ed., *Encyclopaedia of Southern Africa* (Sixth edition; London: Frederick Warne, 1973).

12. *Standard Encyclopaedia of Southern Africa* (10 vols.; Cape Town: Nasionale Opvoedkundige Uitgewery, 1970–1974).

13. *African Book Publishing Record*, 2 (1976): 157. This is now to be published by Reference Publications, 551 Fifth Avenue, New York, N.Y. 10017. The project headquarters remain in Accra, where L. H. Ofuso-Appiah serves as general editor. Cf. *African Book Publishing Record*, 1 (1975): 289–91.

14. S. H. Steinberg, ed., *Cassell's Encyclopaedia of World Literature* (Revised edition by J. Buchanan-Brown, 3 vols.; London: Cassell, 1973).

15. W. Bernard Fleischmann, *Encyclopaedia of World Literature in the Twentieth Century* (New York: Frederick Ungar, 1967–1968).

16. Steinberg, *op. cit.*, vol. 3, p. 6.

17. *Webster's Biographical Dictionary* (Springfield, Massachusetts: G. and C. Merriam, 1972).

18. J. O. Thorne and T. C. Collocott, eds., *Chambers Biographical Dictionary* (Revised edition; London: W. and R. Chambers, 1974).

19. Friedrich-Ebert-Stiftung, *African Biographies* (Bonn-Bad Godesburg: Verlag Neue Gesellschaft, 1971– , regularly updated).

20. Sidney Taylor, ed., *The New Africans; A Guide to the Contemporary History of Emergent Africa and Its Leaders* (London: Paul Hamlyn, 1967).

21. John Dickie and Alan Rake, *Who's Who in Africa: The Political, Military and Business Leaders of Africa* (London: African Development, 1973).

22. Ernest Kay, comp., *Dictionary of African Biography* (Second edition; London: Melrose Press, 1971).

23. W. J. de Kock, ed., *Dictionary of South African Biography* (Cape Town: Nasionale Boekhandel for the National Council for Social Research, Department of Higher Education, 1968–).

24. Eric Rosenthal, ed., *Southern African Dictionary of National Biography* (London: Frederick Warne, 1966).

25. *Who's Who of Southern Africa; Including Mauritius and Incorporating South African Who's Who* (Johannesburg: Combined Publishers [Pty.], 1907–). Cf. *African Who's Who* (Fourth edition; Johannesburg: Central News Agency, 1969), which is reported to include both living and dead non-whites, although the third edition's subtitle (". . . in the Transvaal") suggests a very limited geographical coverage.

26. *The International Who's Who* (38th edition; London: Europa, 1974, annual); *The Author's and Writer's Who's Who* (Sixth edition; London: Burke's Peerage, 1972); *The Writer's Directory* (London: St. James Press, 1973).

27. Kenneth Richardson, ed., *Twentieth Century Writing: A Reader's Guide to Contemporary Literature* (London: Newnes Books, 1969); Clare D. Kinsman, ed., *Contemporary Authors: A Bio-Bibliographical Guide to Current Authors and Their Works* (Detroit: Gale Research, 1962–); John Wakeman, ed., *World Authors 1950–1970* (Wilson Authors Series. New York: H. W. Wilson, 1975); David Daiches, ed., *The Penguin Companion to Literature: Britain and the Commonwealth* (Harmondsworth: Penguin, 1971); D. R. Dudley and D. M. Lang, eds., *The Penguin Companion to Literature: Classical and Byzantine; Oriental and African* (Harmondsworth: Penguin, 1969).

28. Louis Kronenberger, ed., *Brief Lives: A Biographical Guide to the Arts* (London: Allen Lane, 1972 [1965]); Arthur Pollard, ed., *Webster's New World Companion to English and American Literature* (London: Compton Russell, 1973); Martin Seymour-Smith, *Who's Who in Twentieth Century Literature* (London: Weidenfeld and Nicholson, 1976). Seymour-Smith has also written the *Guide to Modern World Literature* (London: Wolfe, 1973), which contains a few pages on South African literature that are of virtually no value for biographical information.

29. James Vinson, ed., *Contemporary Novelists* (Second edition; Contemporary Writers of the English Language. London: St. James Press, 1976).

30. *Ibid.*; the authors include Abrahams, Cloete, Gordimer, Head, Jacobson, Krige, La Guma, Lessing, Mphahlele, Paton, van der Post.

31. Anne Tibble, ed., *African-English Literature: A Short Survey and Anthology of Prose and Poetry Up to 1965* (London: Peter Owen, 1965); Peggy

Rutherfoord, *African Voices: An Anthology of Native African Writing* (New York: Vanguard Press, 1961).

32. Hans M. Zell and Helene Silver, eds., *A Reader's Guide to African Literature* (New York: Africana, 1971; London: Heinemann, 1972).

33. Janheinz Jahn, Ulla Schild and Almut Nordmann, eds., *Who's Who in African Literature: Biographies, Works, Commentaries* (Tübingen: Horst Erdman Verlag for the German Africa Society, 1972).

34. Donald E. Herdeck, *African Authors: A Companion to Black African Writing. Vol. 1, 1300–1973* (Washington, D.C.: Black Orpheus Press, 1973).

35. *Ibid.*, p. 5.

36. Charles R. Larson, "Review of Jahn, *Who's Who in African Literature,*" *Africana Library Journal,* 4, no. 4 (1973): 23.

37. Edward Callan, *Alan Paton* (Twayne's World Authors Series, no. 40. New York: Twayne Publishers, 1968); F. I. Carpenter, *Laurens van der Post* (Twayne's World Authors Series, no. 68. New York: Twayne Publishers, 1970?); C. van Heyningen and J. A. Berthoud, *Uys Krige* (Twayne's World Authors Series, no. 2. New York: Twayne Publishers, 1967?). Callan's volume has been the basis for a bibliography of the same title and by the same author, which on pages 11–16 and 68–74 includes relevant biographical data. Edward Callan, *Alan Paton,* trans. Rolf Italiaander (Hamburger Bibliographien Band II; Hamburg: Hans Christian Verlag, 1970).

38. Michael Wade, *Peter Abrahams* (Modern African Writers, ed. Gerald Moore. London: Evans Brothers, 1972).

39. Peter Abrahams, *Tell Freedom; Memories of Africa* (London: Faber and Faber, 1954); Alfred Hutchinson, *Road to Ghana* (London: Victor Gollancz, 1960); Noni Jabavu, *Drawn in Colour; African Contrasts* (London: John Murray, 1960) and *The Ochre People; Scenes from a South African Life* (London: John Murray, 1963); Todd Matshikiza, *Chocolates for My Wife; Slices from My Life* (London: Hodder and Stoughton, 1961); Bloke Modisane, *Blame Me on History* (London: Thames and Hudson, 1963); Ezekiel Mphahlele, *Down Second Avenue* (London: Faber and Faber, 1959). Cf. Anderson, *op. cit.*, who points out both the factual data and personality insights to be gained from reading such works, all of which (except Javabu) are mentioned in her article.

40. Dan Jacobson, "Settling in England," *Commentary,* 29 (1960): 23–24.

41. Doris Lessing, *Going Home* (St. Albans, Herts.: Panther Books, 1968 [1957]).

General Bibliographical Guides

As a general rule of thumb it is safe to say that most researchers rarely consult bibliographies of bibliographies; the reasons for this lack of consultation are probably as numerous as the various approaches to African literary studies. Some may ignore bibliographies because their contents are assumed to be far too general to bother with or because the individuals feel that their personal expertise surpasses anything that a general bibliographical guide can provide. Others may fail to consider bibliographies of bibliographies as possible reference tools simply because their existence is unknown, and this is far too often due to the failure of librarians to point out the mere availability of such resources, let alone to provide some evaluation of their contents.

Whatever the reason for this failure to consult the available bibliographies, it is a situation not to be encouraged, for even in the field of South African literature they play some role in research and basic information retrieval. The beginning researcher by consulting bibliographies of bibliographies will save much time in determining what is available in his field, while the established scholar on occasion will come across new sources of information. Having said this, one must not expect to find in these resources much that is relevant to South African literature, yet this fact in itself means that the material warrants some comment, if only to serve the purpose of warning prospective users what to avoid.

The poor coverage afforded to South African literature in general bibliographical guides is further aggravated by a number of other factors, primarily the fact that this writing is not yet a widely established area of study outside South Africa. As a result, it tends to straddle, in bibliographical terms, the more traditional fields of literature and African studies; this means that one will have to consult bibliographies of bibliographies for both disciplines. In addition those guides in this genre which do cover Africa very often fail to include the Republic beyond a very basic level. Furthermore, there is as yet no bibliography of South African literary bibliographies, of which there are more than a handful either in monograph form or as serial articles.

Because of this combination of factors mitigating against easy access to bibliographical information about South African literature, the researcher once again is forced to rely on a variety of resources in his search for relevant bibliographies. This chapter attempts to assist in easing the complexities of the search by covering general bibliographies of bibliographies, bibliographies of African bibliographies and bibliographies of literary bibliographies. In view of the fact that this type of material in its narrowest sense is inadequate for South African literature, bibliographies of bibliographies as a genre has been extended to include both literary research guides and African studies guides, which serve a bibliographical function in indicating the availability of other bibliographies and general sources of information.

Bibliographies of Bibliographies

The most widely respected bibliographies of bibliographies are very few in number and generally not worth consulting for information either on African studies as a whole or on South African literature in particular. Paramount among these is Besterman's *World Bibliography of Bibliographies*,[1] which in volume 1 (columns 166–90) covers Africa in general. It includes very few bibliographies of interest for African studies, South Africa or South African literature and, as a consequence, is of very limited use for the literature of our period. On its own, Besterman need not be consulted except in the form of Professor Pearson's revision (see below, pages 72–73 and note 14). Of equally little value are the three volumes published to date by Unesco;[2] each edition of *Bibliographical Services throughout the World* totally ignores South Africa's contribution to the field and need not be consulted at all. This is not, however, a particularly telling loss, since Reuben Musiker has compiled a similar guide specifically for the South African scene.[3]

Of rather more use are three very different types of bibliographical guides, two of which are serial publications and the other a guide to serial publications. The Wilson Company's *Bibliographic Index*[4] is perhaps the single most useful tool among the general bibliographies, since in its trimestral parts and annual cumulations it attempts to note currently appearing bibliographical material. In the several volumes already published there is the occasional reference to information relevant to South African literature, and most researchers will want to check at least the annual cumulations for useful citations. The *Index* itself is a subject listing of bibliographies published either separately or appearing as part of books and periodicals and which contain a minimum of fifty citations. Each issue examines some 2,200 periodicals for bibliographical content, and although few are of specifically South African interest, the breadth of coverage warrants consultation for the occasional entry concerning South African literature. Similar to the Wilson publication is *Bibliographische Bericht,* a semi-annual serial edited by the Staatsbibliothek Preussischer Kulturbesitz.[5] It too concentrates on recent bibliographies and with its strong European emphasis nicely complements the *Bibliographic Index*. There is an index for each issue and cumulative indices for 1959–66 and 1966–70 with another cumulation about to appear.

A somewhat complementary compilation is Gray's monograph on serial bibliographies;[6] this is a guide to selected bibliographies in the humanities and social sciences and contains some entries for African literature. Arranged according to the Dewey Decimal Classification, it includes under 896 (African literature) some five items which the researcher will find of value.[7] However, the fact that it was published in 1969 and devotes comparatively little space to Africa in relation to the coverage of, for example, Australia means that it is becoming increasingly less useful as publications in this field continue to expand. Finally among the general bibliographies of bibliographies one may be attracted to Collison's *Bibliographies Subject and National*[8] simply on the basis of its title. Personal experience has shown this to be useful only in a very general way as an explication of the value and use of bibliographical tools, and in the present context it adds little to the meager knowledge to be gleaned from the foregoing publications. Indeed, with the possible exception of the *Bibliographic Index* and *Bibliographische Bericht* one is probably best advised to avoid wasting time in consulting any of these general bibliographical guides.

Africana and Literary Bibliographies

When one turns to bibliographical guides specifically limited to Africana, the resources become much more valuable for the student of South African literature. Indeed, the field of Africana bibliography has a very long tradition going back at least to the mid-nineteenth century with the seminal works by Ternaux-Compans and Gay,[9] but for the present study the titles of interest are necessarily of more recent vintage. Within South Africa there have been modern bibliographical guides since 1942, and these efforts have been complemented, and usually surpassed, by the excellent Western output beginning in the early 1960's. The field has attracted such highly respected scholars as Pearson and Duignan, as well as numerous less widely known researchers, among them Panofsky and Musiker. At the same time one must hasten to point out that many of these individuals have not produced bibliographies of bibliographies but guides to Africana research, which also serve as resources of the former type.

One of the earlier modern bibliographies from within the Republic is Freer and Varley's *Bibliography of African Bibliographies*, which was last revised by Lewin Robinson in 1961.[10] Arranged according to the Universal Decimal Classification, it contains sections for English language and literature, individual South African authors and English literature by form. It is particularly helpful in listing the bibliographical contents of the South African P.E.N. yearbooks for 1954, 1955 and 1956–57. In terms of literature the concentration is heavily on South African writing, which, but for the primary emphasis on Afrikaans literature, would be a useful compendium for our purposes. However, this emphasis plus its date make the currently available revision of little value for more current references. A work with the same title but produced in 1968 as a mimeographed document presents its information by geographical classification and has far too many inaccuracies and misleading citations.[11] Although Miss Garling appears to have relied heavily on Besterman and has failed to notice inconsistencies in her references, she does cover a much wider and more recent range of material than do Freer and Varley. Nevertheless, both Garling and the earlier South African publication contain nothing which is not also included in the more accurate and later bibliographical compilations. The other general Africana bibliography from the mid-1960's is Bogaert's CEDESA publication, *Sciences Humaines en Afrique Noire: Guide Bibliographique (1945–1965)*.[12] It consists of a classified arrangement divided into two main sections, Bibliographies Générales and Bibliographies Spécialisées, and the breadth of coverage is much wider than the title suggests; within the section on Ouvrages Généraux it contains many entries relevant to literature, and parts 1 and 2 both contain several items of interest for South African studies. Bogaert's bibliography has been generally ignored by other scholars, but in terms of South African literature it may be regarded as an indispensable guide with extremely accurate citations. For the period covered this guide is an excellent source of information which generously complements Duignan's more inclusive scholarship.

Another extremely useful French language publication is the catalogue of the First International Exhibition of African Books edited by Fontvieille.[13] Although limited to items displayed at the exhibition, it includes a rather surprising range of titles from several African, European and American publishers. Arrangement is rather confusing for a bibliography, since the first part is organized by the country of exhibitors and then by topic (history, literature, ethnology); the second part contains the "Bibliographie Complementaire," and it is in this section that a number of relevant titles are found. Pages 865–67 and 907–16 cover general and literary bibliographies, including standard guides (e.g., South African Public Library's *Bibliography of African Bibliographies*) along with some of the less well known compilations (e.g., Taylor's *African Studies Research*). In the "Bibliographies Littéraires" section one also finds the most commonly mentioned literary guides (e.g., Abrash and Ramsaran) and some cited only in this compilation (e.g., Gérard's "Bibliographical Problems"). Coverage is widely representative, although for South African titles there again is much to be desired.

A much newer general bibliography than any of those yet discussed is Besterman's *World Bibliography of African Bibliographies,* which has been revised under the careful eye of J. D. Pearson.[14] It includes 1,634 publications available down to 1973 and is arranged both geographically and by subject. The two sections, "Africa: General" and "Africa: Literature," contain most general resources of recent vintage and are very up-to-date for South Africa, including literature in English. Particularly beneficial is the listing of bibliographical guides produced by the library schools at the universities of Cape Town and Witwatersrand (although these must be consulted with the care advised in the preceding chapter). It is in short a useful and thorough bibliographical guide which reflects Professor Pearson's wide knowledge of Africana bibliography and current scholarship.

A specifically South African guide which the researcher will want to consult was prepared by Reuben Musiker in 1971 with a supplement covering relevant publications through 1974.[15] Musiker is certainly the most active bibliographer in the Republic, and these two publications indicate his first-hand acquaintance with bibliographical production and research within South Africa. They are in fact revised consolidations of his frequent reports appearing in *South African Libraries*, the *South African Library Association Newsletter* and elsewhere,[16] and it is quite useful to have these articles collected together in this way. The 1971 compilation, which would be slightly dated without the recent supplement, is a very adequate survey of the field with useful evaluative annotations for most of the citations. Its 104 pages cover current national bibliographies, subject bibliographies, periodicals (indices and lists) and theses; much of this material is pertinent to South African fiction, as are Musiker's general comments on the state of bibliographical studies in the Republic. It is interesting to see in the subject bibliography section the high percentage of citations from the student bibliographies at Cape Town and Witwatersrand, which may be indicative of the level of bibliographical scholarship up to 1971.

The 32-page supplement to *South African Bibliography* forms an indispensable adjunct to the original compilation and again draws upon Musiker's serial articles on bibliographical progress in the Republic. It is rather more thorough in its literary coverage, which shows to what degree the situation has improved of late. Particularly useful are Musiker's notes on current bibliographical projects, which give some indication of the output one may expect to see in the near future. Musiker continues to be active in bibliographical affairs, and one will want to consult future reports for evaluations of relevant materials; unfortunately, these articles frequently appear in journals other than *South African Libraries* and the *South African Library Association Newsletter*, which may make their location slightly difficult to trace.[17] The other relevant publication by Musiker is a guide to South African reference books which covers literature on pages 82–83, the only useful citations being his own bibliography and the South African P.E.N. yearbooks.[18]

The remaining bibliographies of African or South African bibliographies are much less substantial and rather older than most of the foregoing publications and may be mentioned very briefly. These include compilations by Helen Conover, Matthews, Reitz and Taylor.[19] The earliest and least successful of these is Miss Conover's 1961 publication, which is merely a seven-page introductory listing of 29 annotated entries of no real interest to the literary researcher. The guide by Matthews, which covers materials for 1967–1968, contains some useful general bibliographies which may assist one in locating literary publications, but there is not a single reference to bibliographies of South African literature. The compilation by Reitz, a course term paper completed during a program in library studies, is based on earlier bibliographical work by Musiker and the South African Public Library. Nearly one half of the discussion is devoted to current (1967) bibliographical tools and contains helpful comments on national bibliographies and theses, two areas which often confound the researcher. Reitz's comments are balanced and well founded, as on pages 9–10, where he discusses the comparative merits of thesis bibliographies by Lewin Robinson and Potchefstroom University. Nevertheless, Reitz covers such a limited number of resources that one will not need to make a particular effort to consult his work.

The compilation by Taylor, which is a highly selective list of bibliographies and other materials for undergraduates, may serve as a useful introduction to the wide range of materials available up to 1964. Because Taylor does not assume that the user possesses a great deal of background knowledge in African studies, his work serves as a very useful introduction to African bibliographies and thereby complements the later more specialized guides by other scholars. Indeed, an updated version of this type of bibliography would be well received by present undergraduates overawed by Duignan or frustrated by Panofsky. In fact Panofsky does mention two other works prepared by Taylor, one appearing in 1965 and the other compiled in 1972 but as yet unpublished.[20] Since neither has been available for this investigation, little can be said about them, but they may be well worth consulting for references to African or South African bibliographies.

The closest approximation to an updating of Taylor is *The Student Africanist's Handbook*,[21] which is geared to the needs of undergraduates seeking some initial acquaintance with materials for African studies as a whole. Hartwig and O'Barr begin their work with two slightly naïve and extremely elementary chapters, one on the nature of African studies and the other a background to an understanding of the continent; while these sections are rather too basic for most researchers (even undergraduates), the remaining four chapters do contain references to a respectable number of basic bibliographical tools. The authors survey the field first by discipline and then by region, with two additional chapters on aids for "intensive" research and special topics (including biography). The section on general references and disciplinary sources (pp. 39–48) mentions several general bibliographies, as well as a number of reference books and multidisciplinary periodicals, and the literature section (pp. 78–81) includes bibliographies along with a few reference books and periodicals. Of the bibliographies only a few are relevant to South African fiction; two drawbacks are the total lack of annotation and the somewhat eclectic choice of materials for inclusion. Surely the students for whom Hartwig and O'Barr ostensibly write would profit from a comparison of the resources and some indication of the relative merits of each publication. Another serious flaw is the failure to provide an index, which is a major defect in any work of this sort. Nevertheless, the *Handbook* does fill a gap left by Taylor's unrevised contribution and should be consulted by those who feel themselves to be true neophytes in African bibliography.

The final compilation in this group of shorter bibliographical guides may appear slightly anomolous, since it is ostensibly an anthroplogical bibliography.[22] Nevertheless, Gibson's coverage extends in nearly 900 entries to both literature and South Africa, and the literary researcher will find the occasional useful entry for both areas of study. Gibson is particularly worth mentioning as an example of what could be done quite easily for South African literature. Indeed, the suggestion for something of this sort to be found below on page 78 is based in part on an idea derived from Gibson's work.

For the present, however, this handful of bibliographies, with the possible exception of Taylor and Hartwig and O'Barr, deserves only minimal consultation when compared with two relative giants in the field, Peter Duignan and Hans Panofsky. Strictly speaking, neither of these men has produced what can be called a bibliography of bibliographies, for each of them attempts to provide the user with a bibliographical guide to the entire range of Africana publications. Nevertheless, both works contain reference to a substantial number of bibliographies and for this reason deserve analysis here as well as in the chapter on general bibliographies.[23] Duignan must, of course, take pride of place primarily because of his excellent scholarship, sound judgment and extensive coverage of all material available through 1970. The researcher interested in South African literature, therefore, will use Duignan's *Guide* as a basic source of information for bibliographies and will find it unsurpassed as an indicator of the best tools and resources available in all areas of African studies. Particularly relevant for literature are the entries on pages 351–64, which divide creative writing into bibliographies (entries 1027–36) and reference works (entries 1037–71). These sections fall within Part III, Subject Guide in General, and there are also some useful titles to be found in Part IV, Area Guide, which under South Africa is again subdivided into bibliographies (entries 2857–72) and reference works (entries 2880–2962). Most of the items for Southern Africa in Part IV were contributed by Reuben Musiker, whose own work on South African bibliography appeared also in 1971; this common date correctly suggests that there is a significant overlapping in the coverage provided by these two rather different guides.

Duignan has not tried to provide a full subject guide to bibliographies, and for this reason his seminal work must be used in conjunction with some of the other publications already indicated, particularly Musiker's supplement to his own 1971 publication. In fact the date of Duignan's *Guide* means that it is gradually losing value for the more recent bibliographical output, and it is party for this reason that Panofsky has prepared his *Bibliography of Africana,* which carries the reporting of bibliographical activity forward to 1973. Many will realize that Panofsky's effort has had a particularly adverse reception, and this not least by Duignan himself in a 1975 review.[24] One must agree with the reviewer's general conclusion that this work is not of an admirably high standard, that it fails to include many relevant materials and incorporates a number of errors and unsound judgments. A particular shortcoming for our interests is the brief three paragraph discussion of South African literature (pp. 300–301), which lists only a single recent bibliography. Much more useful is the subject bibliography for literature, which on pages 97–103 cites several titles not recorded in either Duignan or Musiker. However, these too have limited value for the student of South African literature, and this fact plus the entirely inadequate index mean that Panofsky is a guide only marginally worth consulting as a means of locating the titles of a few useful publications.

A much shorter but more up-to-date compilation than Panofsky's effort has been prepared by Easterbrook.[25] Coverage is based on entries gleaned from the *National Union Catalog* (U.S.), *Joint Acquisitions List of Africana, International African Bibliography, Africana Journal, Current Bibliography on African Affairs, African Studies Newsletter* and *Research in Education.* Out of a total of 664 entries there are 21 for literature, which include all of the key general literary bibliographies but without reference to those limited to South African literature. In spite of this shortcoming and the occasional incorrect citation (e.g., the title of Margaret Amosu's guide) one will want to use this bibliography as a convenient updating of both Duignan and Panofsky. The subject index provides quick access to the relevant literary bibliographies.

Thus far the discussion has focused solely on the bibliographical resources devoted specifically to African studies, but to understand fully the scope of material available for South African literature one must also delve into bibliographies of literary studies. Because literature as an academic discipline enjoys a wide and continuing popularity, there has developed an admirable corpus of titles geared to the bibliographical and research needs of those working in this field. To attempt a complete survey of this ancillary material would require another work altogether, and we are fortunate in having Miss Patterson's *Literary Research Guide* to perform that very service.[26] This volume does for English literature what Duignan's publication has done for Africana; in fact Patterson supersedes, from the perspective of African literature, all predecessors in the field and thus presents in a single volume information on most bibliographies of literature likely to be of use to the Africanist. The *Guide* aims to satisfy the requirements of both students and researchers by providing data on a very wide range of resources, which are arranged according to function within the various genres. Miss Patterson covers general guides, bibliographies of bibliographies, biographies and abstracting and indexing services, all of which have some bearing on the search for bibliographies of Africana bibliography. The materials are arranged not only by type but also by literary categories, many of which the Africanist will find useful: English literature, national literatures, Commonwealth literature, world literature. Because of the wide scope of South African English literature and the consequent impossibility of fitting it neatly into any one of these categories, the user will have to spend time consulting every section; such time, however, will be well spent, for one's efforts will turn up a number of useful bibliographical citations. A high percentage of the entries include informative annotations, and there is an excellent index with numerous cross references to ease consultation.

The only guides to literature that could possibly improve on Patterson from an African standpoint are two projected publications in the Gale Information Guide Library.[27] Although both are still in progress, a tentative description of their contents indicates that they will contain useful bibliographical data for the student of South African literature. The work by Lindfors is intended to cover all African literature in English, while Greider will range more widely over all literature in the English language. The researcher will want to watch particularly for the publication by Lindfors, as his scholarship is of a consistently high quality (although often ignoring white South Africa, as in his other forthcoming title with Gale Research[28]).

Of all the bibliographical guides currently available, however, there is not an especially large number to be consulted profitably by the Africanist, and this makes the librarian's selection that much easier when coupled with the fact that most of them are general research guides which the Africana collection may already possess for purposes other than bibliographical inquiry. Thus Duignan is sure to be part of the general reference section in an Africana collection, and Patterson is equally likely to be found in a literary reference section; both are indispensable for their information on bibliographies of bibliographies for Africana and literature. Less worthy of attention are the works by Panofsky and Hartwig and O'Barr. While the former does bring one slightly closer to the present with mention of a few useful literary bibliographies, these few citations may well be found elsewhere without the added cost of Panofsky's book. Therefore, one may place this item and the substitute for Taylor by Hartwig and O'Barr fairly low on a list of priority acquisitions. Certainly Taylor's guide fulfills its *raison d'être* much more adequately than do Hartwig and O'Barr, and in spite of their more recent effort Taylor is still to be preferred. Among the bibliographies of bibliographies *per se* the library will want to have Pearson's revision of *World Bibliography of African Bibliographies,* Bogaert's *Sciences Humaines en Afrique Noire,* Fontvieille's *Bibliographic Guide to the Negro World,* the *Bibliographic Index* from Wilson and *Bibliographische Bericht.* Finally, the most essential guide for South Africa is Musiker's work, but since most of the material in his original publication also appears in Duignan, only the *South African Bibliography Supplement* will be required by the library which already has Duignan.

There are, of course, many more bibliographies of bibliographies that have not been mentioned, but very few of them incorporate data on post-1950 South African literature and so are not included here. More to the point, however, is the fact that there are many other general bibliographies, bibliographical serials and general reference guides to specific types of material which the Africanist will find useful in guiding him to the best bibliographies. However, these materials are not meant to serve primarily as bibliographies of bibliographies and are therefore dealt with in those chapters relevant to their particular functions. Duignan *et al.* have been included in this chapter only because of the general paucity of bibliographies of bibliographies for African studies and the relatively high bibliographical content of these alternative sources of information, which warrants their use as bibliographical guides.

There is, as the preceding pages might indicate, yet again some scope for improving the bibliographical situation *vis à vis* South African literature. In the first place there should be a concerted effort to collect data on *all* general bibliographies of bibliographies with some Africana content and to indicate which of these may be relevant to literature; this would be a single project under the aegis of the proposed center and would be followed by annual or biennial articles pointing out the most recent advances in this specific field in much the same way that Musiker attempts to cover the entire South African scene in his annual surveys. In addition, there is some need for a brief guide along the lines of Taylor but directed primarily at the student of South African literature. Ideally this would be a cooperative effort by scholars and bibliographers and would combine basic comment on the field as a discipline with discussion of the major bibliographical sources. There is no reason to suppose that the center for South African literature would not have all the primary resources necessary for such a project. At present no institution in Britain, and possibly only Yale in the United States, is adequately equipped to provide these resources.

Notes

1. Theodore Besterman, *A World Bibliography of Bibliographies and of Bibliographical Catalogues, Calendars, Abstracts, Digests, Indexes and the Like* (5 vols.; Lausanne: Societas Bibliographica, 1965–1966).

2. Robert L. Collison, *Bibliographical Services throughout the World 1950–59* (Unesco Bibliographical Manuals, no. 9. Paris: Unesco, 1961); Paul Avicenne, *Bibliographical Services throughout the World 1960–1964* (Unesco Bibliographical Handbooks, no. 11. Paris: Unesco, 1969); Paul Avicenne, *Bibliographical Services throughout the World 1965–69* (Documentation, Libraries and Archives: Bibliographies and Reference Works, no. 1. Paris: Unesco, 1972). The series title varies slightly, and with the 1972 volume it changes completely; future volumes should appear under this latest title. Cf. *Bibliography, Documentation, Terminology* (Paris: Unesco, 1961– ; bi-monthly), which contains frequent additions to Avicenne (e.g., vol. 16, pp. 234–53) but without any mention of South Africa.

3. Reuben Musiker, *South African Bibliography: A Survey of Bibliographies and Bibliographical Work* (London: Crosby Lockwood, 1971). Cf. page 73 and note 15 for a fuller discussion of this work and its 1975 supplement.

4. *Bibliographic Index: A Cumulative Bibliography of Bibliographies* (New York: H. W. Wilson, 1938– ; trimestral with annual cumulations).

5. Staatsbibliothek Preussischer Kulturbesitz, ed., *Bibliographische Bericht* (Frankfurt am Main: Verlag Vittorio Klostermann, 1959– ; semi-annual).

6. Richard A. Gray, ed., *Serial Bibliographies in the Humanities and Social Sciences* (Ann Arbor, Michigan: Pierian Press, 1969).

7. In entries 1031–35 Gray mentions the bibliographical sections in the *Journal of Commonwealth Literature* and *Africa* (International African Institute), as well as the *Current Bibliography on African Affairs, Index to Commonwealth Little Magazines* and the International Centre for African Economic and Social Documentation's *Bulletin of Information on Current Research on the Human Sciences Concerning Africa*. These publications will be discussed in later chapters.

8. Robert L. Collison, *Bibliographies Subject and National: A Guide to Their Contents, Arrangement and Use* (Second edition; London: Crosby Lockwood, 1962).

9. Hans E. Panofsky, *A Bibliography of Africana* (Contributions in Librarianship and Information Science, no. 11; gen. ed., Paul Wasserman. Westport, Connecticut: Greenwood Press, 1975). There are brief but informative notes on pp. 29 ff. on the growth of this genre.

10. Percy Freer and Douglas Varley, comps., *A Bibliography of African Bibliographies Covering Territories South of the Sahara* (Fourth edition, rev. by A. M. Lewin Robinson; Grey Bibliographies, no. 7. Cape Town: South African Public Library, 1961). Panofsky, *op. cit.,* p. 29 indicates that a fifth edition is forthcoming, although work on this revision has been suspended for some time.

11. Anthea Garling, comp., *Bibliography of African Bibliographies* (Occasional Papers, no. 1. Cambridge, England: Cambridge University, African Studies Centre, 1968).

12. Jozef Bogaert, *Sciences Humaines en Afrique Noire: Guide Bibliographique (1945–1965)* (Enquêtes Bibliographiques 15. Brussels: Centre de Documentation Economique Sociale Africaine, 1966).

13. Jean-Roger Fontvieille, comp., *Bibliographic Guide to the Negro World: History, Literature, Ethnology* (1 vol. in 2; Yaoundé, Cameroun: Ministry

of Education, Culture and Vocational Training, Direction of Cultural Affairs, 1970).

14. Theordore Besterman, *A World Bibliography of African Bibliographies* (Rev. ed. by J. D. Pearson; Totowa, New Jersey: Rowman and Littlefield, 1975).

15. Reuben Musiker, *South African Bibliography: A Survey of Bibliographies and Bibliographical Work* (London: Crosby Lockwood, 1971); Reuben Musiker, *South African Bibliography: A Survey of Bibliographies and Bibliographical Work. Supplement 1970–1974* (Johannesburg: University of Witwatersrand Library, 1975).

16. Begun in 1958 by D. H. Varley, Musiker continued the series of reports from 1963 to 1971 in *South African Libraries*; since 1971 similar articles by Musiker have also appeared in the *South African Library Association Newsletter* under the title, "Bibliographical Progress." A random sample of these pieces includes the following: 22, no. 8 (1971): 144–47; 23, no. 8 (1972): 250–56; 26, no. 9 (1975): 144–47; 26, no. 11 (1975): 171–72. The *African Studies Bulletin* in 1967 (10, no. 2: 83, 103–106 and 10, no. 3: 117–19) published articles by Musiker with varying titles: "Bibliographical Notes: Southern Africa" and "South African Bibliographical Progress." Later issues of this same journal (11, no. 2: 221–24; 12, no. 3: 305–14) have included reports entitled "Bibliographical Progress in South Africa." Cf. *Africana Library Journal*, 2, no. 1 (1971): 10–11; 3, no. 2 (1972): 21–23 for still other bibliographical reports by Musiker.

17. For example, an article by him entitled "South African Bibliographical Notes and News" has recently appeared in *African Research and Documentation*, 11 (1977): 28–32; this is a new vehicle for Musiker's prolific output.

18. Reuben Musiker, *Guide to South African Reference Books* (Fifth edition; Cape Town: A. A. Balkema, 1971); cf. Reuben Musiker, comp., *Guide to South African Reference Books: Third Cumulative Supplement 1970–1974* (Johannesburg: University of the Witwatersrand, 1975). This most recent supplement exemplifies the up-to-date nature of Musiker's work, mentioning as it does the 1972–73 volume (published in 1974) of the *Bibliography of Overseas Publications about South Africa*.

19. Helen F. Conover, *Africa South of the Sahara* (Washington, D.C.: Library of Congress, 1961); Daniel Matthews, "African Bibliography Today: Selected and Current Bibliographical Tools for African Studies, 1967–68," *A Current Bibliography on African Affairs*, 1, no. 11 (1968): 4–17; Conrad H. Reitz, *South African Bibliography* (Occasional Papers, no. 90. Urbana: University of Illinois, Graduate School of Library Science, 1967); Alan R. Taylor, *African Studies Research; A Brief Guide to Selected Bibliographies and Other Sources for African Studies* (Preliminary edition; Bloomington: Indiana University, African Studies Program, 1964).

20. Panofsky, *op. cit.*, pp. 29–30 and note 2. He cites Taylor's "Bibliographical and Archival Resources for African Studies," which is unpublished but available from the Indiana University Library. Although "probably" prepared in 1972, it may simply be a revision of his 1964 publication, which was intended only as a preliminary edition of a later work. Cf. Alan R. Taylor, "Introduction to the Bibliography of Sub-Saharan Africa at Indiana University," *African Studies Bulletin*, 8, no. 2 (1965): 97–99.

21. Gerald W. Hartwig and William M. O'Barr, *The Student Africanist's Handbook: A Guide to Resources* (Cambridge, Masachusetts: Schenkman, 1974).

22. Gordon D. Gibson, "A Bibliography of Anthropology Bibliographies: Africa," *Current Anthropology,* 10 (1969): 527–66. A revision of this compilation is being prepared by Hans Panofsky.

23. Peter Duignan, ed., *Guide to Research and Reference Works on Sub-Saharan Africa* (Hoover Institution Bibliographical Series, no. 46. Stanford, California: Hoover Institution, 1971); Panofsky, *op. cit.*

24. Peter Duignan, "Review of Panofsky's *A Bibliography of Africana,*" *Africana Journal,* 4 (1975): 316–17.

25. David L. Easterbrook, "Bibliography of Africana Bibliographies 1965–1975," *Africana Journal,* 7 (1976): 101–48; cf. Wendy Simmons, "A Bibliography of Recent Africanist Bibliographies in Journals," *A Current Bibliography on African Affairs,* 9 (1976–77): 317–24.

26. Margaret C. Patterson, *Literary Research Guide* (Detroit: Gale, 1976).

27. Theodore Greider, *Index to American Literature, English Literature and World Literatures in English: A Guide to Information Sources* (American Literature, English Literature and World Literatures in English: An Information Guide Series. Gale Information Guide Library. Detroit: Gale, in progress); Bernth Lindfors, *African Literature in English: A Guide to Information Sources* (American Literature, English Literature and World Literatures in English: An Information Guide Series. Gale Information Guide Library. Detroit: Gale, in progress).

28. Lindfors has indicated that his forthcoming book (tentatively entitled *Criticism on African Literature in English*) to be published by Gale will deal only with criticism by and about black writers. "Letter to G. E. Gorman, 10 September 1976."

Selective Non-Serial Bibliographies

Having waded through the many bibliographies of bibliographies which it is possible to consult in the search for titles relevant to the study and acquisition of South African literature, the following question arises: How does one decide which of the selective bibliographies are most valuable as sources of information about South African fiction in English? Because many of the general bibliographical guides contain few or no annotations, this question is difficult to answer, and consequently one is left with the rather daunting prospect of analyzing for himself the mass of available bibliographies. The field of selective Africana and literary bibliographies certainly has been an area of extensive bibliographical activity, probably because it has been felt necessary to provide different levels of readership and various interest groups with their own subject guides. As a consequence, it is impossible for any single investigation to pretend to cover every available bibliography; in this chapter, therefore, an attempt is made, in the context of South African literature, to evaluate only a small selection of these non-serial bibliographies. In selecting materials an effort has been made to include both the titles of indisputable value in pinpointing South African literary publications and the items most frequently cited in other bibliographies. In this way it is hoped to afford coverage of all listings which are most useful, as well as to indicate which of the other widely known bibliographies may be disregarded in terms of South African fiction.

Selective bibliographies for the sake of convenience may be divided into two broad categories: published library catalogues and guides for specific types of readers. The first category has enjoyed a remarkable vogue in recent years, a phenomenon due in part to the desire of libraries to provide readily available guides to their holdings and also to the growth of G. K. Hall as a publisher of this type of material. Consequently, a number of important institutions now have published catalogues of their holdings, and not a few of these have a place in Africana literary studies. The other main category, as already indicated, has been on the scene for some time, providing various audiences with bibliographical guides of several kinds: general literary

83

bibliographies, general Africana bibliographies, bibliographies for undergraduates and other specific classes of readers, bibliographies with particular subject or area foci. Again, within each of these subdivisions only a handful of titles are discussed, and researchers are encouraged to be on the lookout for other materials which may warrant consultation.

Published Library Catalogues

The one catalogue which fits into neither category noted above is the *National Union Catalog,* which is in fact a guide to the holdings of a large number of American libraries and which appears both in serial and cumulated format.[1] Essentially a cumulative author list, the *NUC* is extremely thorough for those with enough data to make an author approach viable. Appearing in quarterly, annual and quinquennial editions, it caters to the up-to-date requirements of the most avid librarian and researcher and from this standpoint will require frequent consultation. However, for those requiring a subject approach there is little point in spending time with the *NUC,* since it will only result in frustration. Therefore, in general terms the library catalogues which offer a subject arrangement are to be preferred, particularly in terms of retrospective searching.

A number of the most significant library catalogues have been published by G. K. Hall; of those with a strong Africana content four are particularly noteworthy: those of the School of Oriental and African Studies, the New York Public Library, the Royal Commonwealth Society and Northwestern University.[2] The first two were published originally in the early 1960's, with supplements later in the decade and early in the 1970's, and there is every indication that such supplements will continue to appear in an attempt to keep both series fairly up-to-date. On the surface the SOAS catalogue would appear to be preeminent among all published library catalogues for our needs, since this is one of the few institutions devoted entirely to regional studies. The mere size of the catalogue (some 60 volumes to date) suggests that SOAS holds a large number of titles relevant to South African literature, but in this case quantity is far from matched by quality. The original volumes and later supplements are divided into title and subject sections: vols. 1–13 (1963) and two supplements treat title entries, while vols. 14–21 (1963) and two supplements cover the subject arrangement (vol. 15 of the 1963 edition is devoted to Africa). There is also a separate author sequence of eight volumes (1963), and this also has been updated by two supplements (1968, 1973). Of most use are the author and subject volumes, since it is to these that one most often turns in the course of general bibliographical work. However, analysis of both sequences indicates that South African fiction is not a strong point of the SOAS collection. The titles which do appear in the subject catalogue are largely what one would expect in a more general library (e.g., Heinemann's African Writers Series), and some of the more widely read authors (e.g., Gordimer, van der Post) are not represented in their entirety; equally weak are the holdings in literary criticism and history related to African or South African fiction. In short the SOAS *Library Catalogue* may be disregarded by students of South African literature unless future supplements exhibit a marked improvement, but indications from the post-1973 card catalogue suggest that this will not be the case.

The New York Public Library catalogue, on the other hand, is a more comprehensive guide to South African fiction; indeed, with the exception of Northwestern University's compilation (see below) this is probably the best published library catalogue in existence for our subject. As the title indicates, it is a dictionary catalogue, combining author and subject entries in a single sequence; although the original edition is less than half the size of the SOAS effort, the six volumes of supplementary material, again in dictionary format, provide up-to-date coverage equalling that of its sister publication. The holdings of NYPL are not in any sense limited to Negro (i.e., Black American) writings but include South African writers of all colors. Particularly strong is the collection of works by white South Africans, with virtually all of the major "committed" authors represented quite fully (Cope, Gordimer, Jacobson, Lessing, Paton); there are also many books by the more prominent black writers popular in the 1960's (Abrahams, La Guma, Modisane, Mphahlele), as well as a substantial number of bibliographies and general reference materials. An added advantage of this catalogue is that it attempts to include entries for authors whose work appears in anthologies, which can be particularly helpful in view of the general difficulty encountered in tracing such pieces. Therefore, if one is trying to locate the titles of works by South African novelists and has available both the SOAS and NYPL catalogues, chances are that the latter will give more satisfaction.

Only marginally less useful than the NYPL compilation is that of the Royal Commonwealth Society, which is an updating of the 1930–37 *Subject Catalogue of the Royal Empire Society*. The 1971 *Subject Catalogue* includes all new books added to the collection between 1930–37 and 1971; the third and fourth volumes cover Africa under broad subject headings, and the literary coverage of South African materials is quite substantial. Pages 197–200 of Volume One contain a general introduction to Commonwealth literature which the beginning researcher will find helpful. Since the start of this decade financial restrictions imposed on the Society's library have resulted in a decreased acquisitions program, which means that a supplement, were it to appear, would contain rather fewer relevant entries. Nevertheless, the RCS catalogue as it stands provides several citations to items not in the NYPL guide, particularly books published in Britain.

However, the best of these four catalogues is Northwestern's *Catalogue of the Melville J. Herskovits Library*; the compilers state that it includes all

Africana titles catalogued by the University with the addition of libraries cooperating in the *Joint Acquisitions List of Africana*. This means that the compilation is far wider than the title would suggest, since *JALA* involves some two dozen libraries (including the African Studies Centre at Cambridge University). Although modestly claiming to concentrate primarily on the human aspects of tropical Africa, it in fact contains more entries relevant to South African literature in English than any other published library catalogue. There are numerous entries for novels, literary criticism, general literary studies and bibliographies; while the *Catalogue* does not claim to be exhaustive and is strongly American in bias, coverage includes most of the major novels by blacks and whites published up to 1972. The strong point of this compilation, however, lies in the two areas of bibliography and literary criticism, where it lists several titles not found even in subject guides to South African fiction (e.g., works by Nkosi). Unfortunately, arrangement is strictly by author and title, and without any subject index it suffers in comparison with some of the classified catalogues. Either a classified arrangement or a basic subject index would have made the North-western catalogue far more usable, and with their present organization these eight volumes need not be consulted unless a given author or title is being sought.

Of the smaller G. K. Hall library catalogues three may be mentioned in passing: the Musée de l'Homme's *Catalogue Systématique*, Ibadan University Library's *Africana Catalogue* and the International African Institute's *Cumulative Bibliography*.[3] All of these are much less useful than the SOAS or NYPL catalogues, because they are based on relatively small Africana collections and have not yet merited supplements to the original editions. The *Catalogue Systématique* is a classified compilation, which in the Africa section uses only a geographical classification; there are very few entries for African or South African literature and no subject or author indices. It is thus difficult to consult and less useful than the IAI publication in terms of content. The Ibadan catalogue, on the other hand, contains in its two-volume author sequence a surprisingly large number of entries for black African and South African writers. Unfortunately, there is a paucity of material by white South African writers, but this is partly balanced by the catholic collection of literary studies, criticism and anthologies, many with a direct bearing on the South African novel. Obviously a subject index would have added to the usefulness of these volumes, but as it stands one will find the *Africana Catalogue* a useful complement to either the SOAS or NYPL catalogues. The IAI's *Cumulative Bibliography* is divided into a two-volume author sequence and a three-volume classified sequence. In the author section one finds virtually no works by South African novelists, but in the classified sequence under Africa-General (vol. 1, pp. 255–62) there is a fair collection of bibliographies, literary criticism and general literary studies. Although containing marginally more relevant entries than the Musée de l'Homme catalogue, this compilation offers nothing exceptional and so may be disregarded in the search for South African literary titles. Aside from these G. K. Hall publications, a number of libraries have published catalogues through their own institutional presses, and all of them are less useful than those already discussed. Perhaps the most widely available of these house publications are the two Harvard University titles in the Widener Library Shelflist series.[4] Number 34 is a 1971 updating of Shelflist Number 2, which was published in 1965; as the full titles suggest, each volume is divided into four sequences (classification schedule, classified sequence, author sequence, chronological listing). This is a very thorough combination of approaches and so caters to a variety of needs; it is unfortunate that the literary contents do not match the expectations aroused by this thorough arrangement. The 1971 publication with its 20,000 enries represents a 30% increase over the number in the 1965 edition, and one must admit that there is a fair representation of novels published in the mid-1960's. Bibliographically, too, coverage is respectable, including a number of works not found in other of the smaller library catalogues (e.g., Abrash, Davidson, Wilkov). Nevertheless, in terms of overall coverage of both fiction and literary criticism these Harvard catalogues are less complete than the Northwestern compilation and only marginally more representative than some of the African institutional catalogues. This is particularly true ⟩ in terms of works by some of the black South Africans (e.g., Head, Jabavu, Hutchinson) and may well represent a bias toward more easily acquired titles by white South Africans published in America. Furthermore, these two shelflists sometimes err in their classification, placing both Ekwensi and Tutuola under "African Literature Written Originally in English–South Africa —Individual Authors." Therefore, unless one has no other published library catalogue at hand he is best advised to avoid these Harvard shelflists.

Of the less widely available, smaller published catalogues one may regard those of the following institutions as generally representative of the field: Pennsylvania State University, University of Nigeria, Howard University, Missionary Research Library and Disciples of Christ Research Library.[5] The Pennsylvania compilation by Brown and Schwartz is different in that it is not a full catalogue but rather· a bibliography for a single African studies course based on the holdings of the University Library. Although a massive 140-page effort for a particular 1969 undergraduate course, it is clearly biased in favor of political studies and contains precious few references to South African literature in the "substantive" section. Arranged in three sections (countries and bibliography in addition to the subject or "substantive" sequence), emphasis is strongly on periodical literature, which is an interesting innovation for a library-based catalogue. The University of Nigeria publication in the two sections relevant to South African fiction (Literature, pp. 27–30, and Bibliography, pp. 61–64) also contains a sparse selection of useful citations. The Howard University catalogue, which contains some 4,865 entries, need not be consulted because of its dated coverage (mid-1957). All three of these university efforts indicate that the smaller academic libraries have nothing to offer in terms of South African literary studies, and future publications of this sort may be disregarded in good conscience unless, of course, one is aware of a special interest in this subject by the library concerned.

Two slightly different catalogues are those of missionary libraries compiled respectively by Lehman and Dargitz. The first of these, the sixty-five page Missionary Research Library catalogue published in 1969, uses a geographical/subject classification and, as might be expected, contains practically no entries for South African literature with the exception of works by Abrahams and Paton. Finally, the Dargitz compilation focuses in its 431 pages on the collection of another obscure Africana missionary library; using a classified arrangement, it contains some four pages on creative writing (pp. 423–26) but has no indices. Like the Pennsylvania catalogue, this compilation devotes some attention to periodical literature, but in every case reference is to general titles (e.g., *Africa, Africa Report, Africa Today*) with no particular literary interest. As suggested for the university catalogues in the preceding paragraph, one will not need to spend time with either of these highly specialized, rather dated publications.

Indeed, as a general rule one may assume that a particular effort need not be made to consult published library catalogues for bibliographical information about South African literature. This is because these publications are relatively parochial (with the exception of the *NUC*). They are nothing more than catalogues of holdings in particular institutions; just as each library develops a collection to meet the special requirements of those it serves, so its catalogue will merely reflect such specializations. Therefore, since most libraries collect South African fiction only marginally, probably to meet the need for secondary material in non-literary disciplines, one will find in their catalogues only the best known South African novels. In addition library catalogues are dated even before they are compiled, for in even the best acquisitions program it is not unusual for an item to be catalogued at least two years after its publication date. By the time a catalogue itself is published, of course, this date can only have increased. Therefore, unless one is particularly interested in retrospective data there is little hope of finding a given title among the limited entries in these catalogues. Supplements, of course, do make a difference, since they will keep the catalogue more up-to-date, but still they will reflect the eclectic, specialized acquisitions policy of the particular library. Since none of the libraries issuing catalogues has a particular interest in South African literature, even their most up-to-date supplements will be of only marginal use.

The one exception to all of this is the Northwestern University catalogue, since it does embody a comparatively significant interest in this field and also appears in supplement form. The most important fact about this catalogue, however, is its reliance on the *Joint Acquisitions List of Africana* project for bibliographical input. This gives the catalogue its wide coverage, since here the focus is no longer on the collection of a single library. Nevertheless, if one can glean the same information from *JALA* without the additional expense of acquiring this catalogue, it seems to serve very little use other than a cumulative, retrospective one.

Selective Bibliographies

In looking at the remaining types of selective guides which cover South African literature to some degree, one finds a slightly unusual type of compilation in the form of exhibition catalogues. These invariably are prepared for specific exhibitions on African studies and therefore are only as representative as the materials collected for display. By and large such compilations are highly selective and quite dated by the time of publication. Thus one will find little relevant material in such sources as *A Bibliography of African Studies* or *The Commonwealth in Africa.*[6] Marginally more useful are two African entries in the field, Fontvieille's *Bibliographic Guide to the Negro World* and the University of Ife Bookshop's *"Printed and Published in Africa."*[7] Fontvieille, already discussed in the preceding chapter, is a catalogue of the First International Exhibition of African Books (1970). Subject to the limitations mentioned above on page 72, it contains a surprising amount of useful material on literature and literary bibliography (pp. 537–723, 865–67), much of it relevant to South Africa. When compared with the published library catalogues of a similar vintage, it contains a fair proportion of citations not found in those guides (e.g., Taylor's bibliography and novels by La Guma and Mphahlele), which makes it a better guide for its period than any of the more expensive library catalogues. *"Printed and Published in Africa,"* originally published in 1974, was to be updated for the Second World Black and African Festival of Arts and Culture, which was scheduled for November 1975 but did not take place until January-February 1977. To date this revision has failed to appear, although the Festival proceedings have been published as *FESTAC '77* (London: Mohn Gordon, 1977). As it now stands, the 1974 mimeographed document contains a classified listing of African published materials; covering bibliography (p. 3), biography (p. 5), literature and creative writing (p. 23) and periodicals (p. 98), it is generally less representative than Fontvieille and contains few entries relevant to South African literature. Unless a revision appears for a future Festival, one may safely consult Fontvieille in place of the Ife compilation.

Looking to bibliographies geared more directly to the needs of academic research and undergraduate study, one finds the quality of materials to be very mixed. Of the better known guides to Africana, several have already been mentioned in the preceding chapter as bibliographies of bibliographies:

Duignan, Panofsky, Musiker, Hartwig and O'Barr.[8] Most of the comments made in that chapter about these works apply here as well, and one should refer to the relevant pages (73–76) for a fuller discussion of their merits. In the present context it is sufficient to say that Duignan and Musiker are the best general bibliographies, the former being the basic tool for discovering the existence of literary bibliographies published up to 1970. Musiker carries the survey forward a few years and is more helpful for specifically South African material, but neither work is particularly good at listing works of South African fiction. Duignan is too general and now somewhat dated, while Musiker is primarily a national guide and so does not focus on literary titles *per se*. Panofsky resembles Duignan in attempting to cover the whole area of Africana but does so in a less comprehensive, more eclectic fashion, leaving out several titles mentioned by Musiker. Hartwig and O'Barr provide merely a pale imitation of these three guides, listing only a handful of African literary materials on pages 78–80, so their work need not be consulted by any but the most inexperienced student.

There are also a number of general literary bibliographies which treat literature *in toto*; Patterson and Altick and Wright are prime examples of this type of guide.[9] Patterson, also discussed in the preceding chapter (pages 76–77), is like Duignan in attempting to survey the entire field and because of this wide focus has little space to devote to South African literature beyond mention of the basic bibliographical tools. More simply organized and therefore easier to use than Patterson is the work by Altick and Wright; in 586 entries it tries to cover all types of material needed for literary research, including scholarly periodicals, subject catalogues and author bibliographies. Although not particularly useful as a source of information on African literary titles, this is a good introductory guide which may well be a sensible starting point for one about to delve into selective Africana bibliographies.

Less comprehensive than these large general Africana or literary research guides *cum* bibliographies is a massive group of smaller academic bibliographies aimed primarily at undergraduate needs. These bibliographies are much more selective and basic, touching on African literature only incidentally. More often than not such guides are American in origin and emphasis with highly variable contents. In the late 1960's one compilation in particular drew on a number of its predecessors, thereby making them largely obsolete. This is the Ehrman and Morehouse guide, *Preliminary Bibliography on Africa South of the Sahara for Undergraduate Libraries*,[10] which has as its audience librarians wishing to develop undergraduate collections of Africana. Intended originally as a preliminary draft of a final version to be published in 1969, Ehrman and Morehouse relied heavily on a group of similar publications, most of which will be mentioned below: American Universities Field Staff, Conover, Glazier, as well as book reviews in *Choice* and *Africa Report*. Classified by region/country and subject, this work contains an extremely limited number of South African literary titles and mentions virtually none of the more controversial items by radical black writers. Because of its reliance on other published bibliographies, Ehrman was already outdated when it first appeared and since then has become virtually obsolete for anything other than retrospective inquiries.

In 1971 this preliminary guide reappeared as *Africa South of the Sahara* with the added assistance of Peter Duignan.[11] Although shorter by two thirds than the 1967 compilation, it includes a few more of the important literary surveys (e.g., Tucker, Wauthier) but only five entries for specifically South African literature. In place of annotations there are references to reviews and citations in other resources, and these notes can be fairly arduous to trace.

Among the bibliographies on which these two compilations relied were the various American Universities Field Staff publications of the 1960's and early 1970's.[12] Arranged geographically and then by broad subject categories, each edition contains author and title indices with clear annotations for each entry. Every publication is coded A or B to indicate the relative priority which ought to be accorded to it, and although the primary emphasis is on the social sciences and current affairs, there is a reasonable representation of South African fiction. Creative African writing could well benefit from a guide of this sort, for the coding and annotations make one's choice of what to acquire or read relatively effortless. Another work used in compiling this series of guides was Glazier's *Africa South of the Sahara*, which itself went into a revision and updating.[13] Both editions aim to assist students, teachers and librarians in selecting the "best" Africana books by listing a limited choice of titles which have been favorably reviewed in the scholarly press. Each volume contains a mere two hundred English language publications on African studies, literature and the arts arranged alphabetically by author. The basic subject index in neither volume includes more than ten titles relevant to African literature, but a number of these references are to truly seminal works. Thus in the 1969 edition one finds Wauthier's *Literature and Thought of Modern Africa*, Tucker's *Africa in Modern Literature*, Moore's *African Literature and the Universities* and Jahn's *History of Neo-African Literature*. Each of these entries has excellent annotations, including brief review notices, and such information is most useful in guiding one's background reading.

Glazier intended his compilations as supplements to earlier works by Helen Conover, which themselves were also incorporated into the AUFS publications. In 1963 she published *Africa South of the Sahara: A Selected, Annotated List of Writings*, which replaced her two 1950's works of the same name.[14] The 1963 volume is arranged by general subject (items 1761–1859) and includes some nine titles under "Arts and Letters," none of them pertinent to South African fiction. However, the general material is rather more useful (e.g., no. 1761 on *Africana Nova* and no. 1762 on the

University of Cape Town's Bibliographical Series) with its judicious evaluative annotations to help guide one to other relevant sources. Although this work is now sadly dated, it still provides solid background information which with some revision could continue to be of benefit to those requiring basic knowledge of South African literature.

Outside this closely interrelated group of bibliographies are a number of similar guides geared to the requirements of an academic readership. Of these perhaps three will suffice as examples of the field. Gutkind and Webster in 1968 compiled their *Select Bibliography on Traditional and Modern Africa,* which contains some 2,921 entries on books and articles in the humanities and social sciences.[15] Intended as a general introduction to the entire area of African studies, it serves in the field of literature as one of the best guides to various types of publications. Although not dealing specifically with South African literature, Gutkind and Webster on pages 246–52 list nearly all the important general titles, particularly those published between 1962 and 1968. Thus one finds bibliographies by Amosu, Astrinsky, Jahn, Porter and Ramsaran along with such general studies as Moore's *African Literature and the Universities.* Arranged into "Traditional" and "Modern" groupings, the book includes author, subject and keyword indices, all of which make for ease of consultation. Now somewhat dated, one wishes that a revision were in preparation, for along with Conover it is certainly one of the best Africana bibliographies of the 1960's.

A somewhat later and slightly different bibliography was prepared in 1970 by Paden and Soja; intended primarily as a teaching guide and handbook on African studies, it includes two volumes of interest to the literary researcher.[16] Volume IIIA is devoted entirely to an annotated bibliography and is arranged by "Syllabus Modules" (e.g., "society and culture") and "Country Case Studies." Consisting essentially of titles important for undergraduate reading, South African literature figures only marginally. Even in terms of general literary studies coverage is weak and fails to note the major publications (Tucker *et al.*). However, the section devoted to "Country Case Studies" contains a number of novels under South Africa (pp. 616–22), apparently since they (Abrahams, La Guma) are deemed useful in teaching about the Republic. The rather unusual arrangement means that people outside Northwestern University will almost certainly have to rely on the author index, and a basic subject index would have been an added improvement. Volume IIIB is a guide to resources for African studies and contains introductory articles on reference sources, basic journals, audio-visual aids, publishing and the like. This is of little value to the student of South African literature, and one's final judgment must be that Paden and Soja have produced a guide far below the high standards of Africana teaching and library acquisitions which Northwestern University is known to have.

A guide of similar intent but much more limited coverage was prepared in 1969 by Barry Beyer for secondary school students and teachers.[17] It is arranged in two parts, one devoted to the motivation and methodology for teaching African studies and the other to materials for Africana teaching. The latter section consists largely of basic instructional materials and contains some comment on reference sources, publishers and information services. Because of the school audience at which it aims, the volume contains little of value for a university audience; this particular title exemplifies the difficulty in evaluating Africana bibliographies without the benefit of thorough reviews or personal analysis.

Outside the academic sphere there are a number of bibliographical guides either emanating from various research institutes with a particular subject focus or aimed at a general readership. In the former category two works compiled in Britain have enjoyed particular popularity: the International African Institute's *Select Annotated Bibliography* and the Central Asian Research Centre's *Soviet Writing on Africa*.[18] The IAI publication reflects the Institute's concerns in that it is entirely devoted to the social sciences and issues in Third World development. Likewise the Central Asian Research Centre volume, although continuing Holdsworth's earlier work and supplementing the *Mizan Newsletter,* is almost completely functional and does not cover literary studies. One might have expected *Soviet Writing* to include some data on literature in view of the established East European interest in this field (e.g., scholars such as Páricsy and Klima), and there is clearly room for a more comprehensive guide to publications from this bibliographically difficult area. Finally, there is a plethora of material published by government agencies, independent centers and some academic institutions and aimed at civil servants, certain types of students and the general public. Most of these are American undertakings of the 1960's and reflect that country's massive interest in Africa during those years. Particularly active was the African Bibliographic Center with two items in its Special Bibliographic Series, one in 1967 and one in 1968.[19] These were complemented by two government agency undertakings, one by the Library of Congress and the other by the Foreign Service Institute.[20] Finally, in the 1970's these works have been matched by Geoffrion's and Robinson's compilations.[21] In every case the titles are self-explanatory and the contents very basic and general, with a focus on current affairs and background studies. Although not entirely "popular" in nature, most of the items are similar to John Gunther's *Inside Africa* and hold little interest for the student of African literature.

Thus in spite of the massive body of material available in the field of general Africana bibliographies one is left by a process of elimination with only a few publications. Of the library catalogues one may find some assistance in the Northwestern, RCS and NYPL publications, but unless a library already possesses them there is no need to acquire these expensive volumes particularly for South African literary bibliography. Virtually all of the citations in these guides may be located much less expensively in the current bibliographical serials discussed in the following chapter, and unless one is particularly anxious to do retrospective searching for the 1950's, published library catalogues may be completely disregarded. Much the same thing may be said of most of the other selective Africana bibliographies which, because of their date, eclecticism and general readership, contain little of interest to the serious Africanist. In bibliographical terms the 1960's saw a flourishing of Africana scholarship, particularly in America, and one cannot help but feel that the prodigious output was part of a "bandwagon syndrome," with every institution and bibliographer anxious to get into print regardless of the repetition involved. Nevertheless, from a literary standpoint a few of these general guides, although in part out-of-print and therefore difficult to acquire, may be worth consulting if available in a given collection. In this category one may include Fontvieille, Duignan, Musiker, Patterson, Altick and Wright, Glazier, Conover and Gutkind and Webster.

Notes

1. U.S., Library of Congress, *National Union Catalog* (Washington, D.C.: Library of Congress, Resources Committee of the Resources and Technical Services Division, 1956– ; monthly with quarterly, annual and quinquennial cumulations); U.S., Library of Congress, *National Union Catalog: Pre-1956 Imprints* (London: Mansell Information/Publishing, 1968– and New York: Pageant Books, 1968–).

2. University of London, School of Oriental and African Studies, *Library Catalogue* (21 vols.; Boston: G. K. Hall, 1963) and *First Supplement* (13 vols.; 1968), *Second Supplement* (13 vols.; 1973); *Library Catalogue: Author Index* (8 vols.; 1963) and *First Supplement* (3 vols.; 1968), *Second Supplement* (3 vols.; 1973); New York Public Library, *Dictionary Catalog of the Schomburg Collection of Negro Literature and History* (9 vols.; Boston: G. K. Hall, 1962) and *First Supplement* (2 vols.; 1967), *Second Supplement* (4 vols.; 1972), both of which are to be continued in part by G. K. Hall's complementary *Bibliographic Guide to Black Studies* (see Chapter 4, note 23); Royal Commonwealth Society, *Subject Catalogue of the Royal Commonwealth Society* (7 vols.; Boston: G. K. Hall, 1971); Northwestern University Library, *Catalogue of the Melville J. Herskovits Library of African Studies, Northwestern University Library and Africana in Selected Libraries* (8 vols.; Boston: G. K. Hall, 1972).

3. Musée de l'Homme, Bibliothèque, *Catalogue Systématique de la Section Afrique* (2 vols.; Boston: G. K. Hall, 1970); Ibadan University Library, *Africana Catalogue of the Ibadan University Library* (2 vols.; Boston: G. K. Hall, 1973); International African Institute, *Cumulative Bibliography of African Studies* (5 vols.; Boston: G. K. Hall, 1973).

4. Harvard University Library, *Africa: Classification Schedule, Classified Listing by Call Number, Alphabetical Listing by Author or Title, Chronological Listing* (Widener Library Shelflist, number 2. Cambridge, Massachusetts: Harvard University Library, 1965); *African History and Literatures: Classification Schedule, Classified Listing by Call Number, Chronological Listing,*

Author and Title Listing (Widener Library Shelflist, number 34. Cambridge, Massachusetts: Harvard University Library, 1971).

5. J. Cudd Brown and Kraig A. Schwartz, comps., *Africa: A Selective, Working Bibliography* (University Park: Pennsylvania State University Libraries, 1970?); University of Nigeria, *Institute of African Studies Research Library Classified List 1* (Nsukka: University of Nigeria, 1973); Dorothy B. Porter, ed., *A Catalogue of the African Collection in the Moorland Foundation, Howard University Library*. Compiled by Students in the Program of African Studies (Washington, D.C.: Howard University Press, 1958); cf. H. P. Alexander, comp., "Supplement to the Catalogue of the African Collection in the Moorland Foundation of the Howard University Library," unpublished M.L.S. thesis, Catholic University of America, 1963; Robert L. Lehman, comp., and Frank W. Price, ed., *Africa South of the Sahara: A Selected and Annotated Bibliography of Books in the Missionary Research Library on Africa and African Countries South of the Sahara* (New York: Missionary Research Library, 1969?); cf. the slightly earlier *Dictionary Catalog of the Missionary Research Library* (17 vols.; Boston: G. K. Hall, 1967); Robert E. Dargitz, comp., *A Selected Bibliography of Books and Articles in the Disciples of Christ Research Library in Mbandaka, Democratic Republic of the Congo and the Department of Africa and Jamaica of the United Christian Missionary Society in Indianapolis, Indiana* (Indianapolis: The United Christian Missionary Society, Division of World Mission, Department of Africa and Jamaica, n.d.).

6. The Combined Book Exhibit, Inc., *A Bibliography of African Studies* (Scarborough Park, Briarcliff Manor, New York: The Combined Book Exhibit, Inc., 1971?); National Book League and the Commonwealth Institute, *The Commonwealth in Africa: An Annotated List 1969* (London: National Book League, 1969).

7. Jean-Roger Fontvieille, comp., *Bibliographic Guide to the Negro World: History, Literature, Ethnology* (1 vol. in 2; Yaoundé, Cameroun: Ministry of Education, Culture and Vocational Training, Direction of Cultural Affairs, 1970); University of Ife Bookshop, Ltd., *"Printed and Published in Africa:" Catalogue of an Exhibition of Outstanding African Published Materials* (Ile-Ife, Nigeria: University of Ife Bookshop, 1974?). Mimeographed.

8. Peter Duignan, *Guide to Research and Reference Works on Sub-Saharan Africa* (Hoover Institution Bibliographical Series, no. 46. Stanford, California: Hoover Institution Press, 1971); Hans E. Panofsky, *A Bibliography of Africana* (Contributions in Librarianship and Information Science, no. 11; Paul Wasserman, gen. ed. Westport, Connecticut: Greenwood Press, 1975); Reuben Musiker, *South African Bibliography: A Survey of Bibliographies and Bibliographical Work* (London: Crosby Lockwood, 1971) and *Supplement 1970–1974* (Johannesburg: University of Witwatersrand Library, 1975); Gerald W. Hartwig and William M. O'Barr, *The Student Africanist's Handbook: A Guide to Resources* (Cambridge, Massachusetts: Schenkman, 1974).

9. Margaret C. Patterson, *Literary Research Guide* (Detroit: Gale Research, 1976); Richard D. Altick and Andrew Wright, *Selective Bibliography for the Study of English and American Literature* (Fifth edition; London: Collier Macmillan, 1975).

10. Edith Ehrman and Ward Morehouse, eds., *Preliminary Bibliography on Africa South of the Sahara for Undergraduate Libraries* (New York: Uni-

versity of the State of New York, State Education Department, Center for International Programs and Services, Foreign Area Materials Center, 1967).

11. Peter Duignan, Edith Ehrman, Kathleen Hale and Ward Morehouse, eds., *Africa South of the Sahara: A Bibliography for Undergraduate Libraries* (Occasional Publication no. 12, Foreign Area Materials Center, University of the State of New York, State Education Department and National Council of Associations for International Studies. Williamsport, Pennsylvania: Bro-Dart, 1971).

12. American Universities Field Staff, Inc., *A Select Bibliography: Asia, Africa, Eastern Europe, Latin America* (New York: American Universities Field Staff, 1960); there are supplements for 1961, 1963, 1965, 1967, 1969, 1971 and a cumulated supplement for 1961–1971, which was published in 1973.

13. Kenneth M. Glazier, *Africa South of the Sahara: A Select and Annotated Bibliography, 1958–1963* (Hoover Institution Bibliographical Series, no. 16. Stanford, California: Hoover Institution, 1964); *Africa South of the Sahara: A Select and Annotated Bibliography, 1964–1968* (Hoover Institution Bibliographical Series, no. 42. Stanford, California: Hoover Institution, 1969).

14. Helen F. Conover, comp., *Africa South of the Sahara: A Selected, Annotated List of Writings* (Washington, D.C.: Library of Congress, General Reference and Bibliography Division, Reference Department, 1963).

15. Peter C. W. Gutkind and John B. Webster, *A Select Bibliography on Traditional and Modern Africa* (Occasional Bibliography, no. 8. Syracuse, New York: Syracuse University, Program of Eastern African Studies, 1968).

16. John N. Paden and Edward W. Soja, eds., *The African Experience. Vol. IIIA, Bibliography; Vol. IIIB, Guide to Resources* (Evanston, Illinois: Northwestern University Press, 1970).

17. Barry K. Beyer, *Africa South of the Sahara: A Resource and Curriculum Guide* (New York: Thomas Y. Crowell, 1969); cf. McGill University, McLennan Library, Reference Department, *Africa South of the Sahara; A Student's Guide to Selected Reference Sources for African Studies* (Montreal: McGill University, 1973), which is only marginally more scholarly than Beyer in spite of its university origins.

18. Daryll Forde, comp., *Select Annotated Bibliography of Tropical Africa* (New York: The Twentieth Century Fund, 1956; New York: Kraus Reprint, 1969); Central Asian Research Centre, comp., *Soviet Writing on Africa, 1959–61: An Annotated Bibliography* (London: Royal Institute of International Affairs, 1963). The latter is an updated continuation of Mary Holdsworth, *Soviet African Studies, 1918–59: An Annotated Bibliography* (London: Royal Institute of International Affairs, 1961); cf. S. Yu. Abramova, comp., *African Studies in the U.S.S.R.: List of Annotations on Major Works Published in 1952–First Half of 1962* (Moscow: U.S.S.R. Academy of Sciences, Institute of Africa, 1962); "Bibliography of Books and Key Articles on Africa Published in Polish, English and Other Languages in Poland Since 1960, with an Introductory Essay on African Studies in Eastern Europe and the Soviet Union," *Munger Africana Library Notes*, no. 33 (1976).

19. African Bibliographic Center, comp., *African Affairs for the General Reader: A Selected and Introductory Bibliographical Guide 1960–1967*, edited by Daniel G. Matthews (Special Bibliographic Series, vol. 5, no. 4. Washing-

ton, D.C.: African Bibliographic Center, 1967); African Bibliographic Center, comp., *African Affairs for the General Reader, 1968* (Special Bibliographic Series, vol. 6, no. 3. Washington, D.C.: African Bibliographic Center, 1968).

20. U.S., Library of Congress, European Affairs Division, *Introduction to Africa: A Selective Guide to Background Reading* (Washington, D.C.: University Press of Washington, 1952; New York: Negro Universities Press, 1969); U.S., Foreign Service Institute, Center for Area and Country Studies, *Africa, Sub-Sahara: A Selected Functional Bibliography* (Washington, D.C.: U.S. Foreign Service Institute, 1967).

21. Charles A. Geoffrion, *Africa: A Study Guide to Better Understanding* (Bloomington: Indiana University, African Studies Program, 1970); Harland D. Robinson, *Africa, Sub-Sahara: A Selected Functional and Country Bibliography* (Washington, D.C.: U.S. Department of State, 1974).

National Bibliographies and Selected Serial Bibliographies

In the preceding two chapters discussion has concentrated on those materials deemed useful in conducting retrospective bibliographical searches. While it is important to survey such guides in attempting to collect thoroughly and comprehensively in earlier published materials, much of this retrospective searching will have little practical application, since most fiction titles will be unavailable within a few years of publication. To avoid being faced with this dilemma for material currently in print and to insure that one's knowledge is as up-to-date as possible, it is important to have relatively detailed knowledge of the various types of current awareness services and to use them regularly.

This, as any acquisitions specialist well knows, can be an impossible task due to the wide range of current bibliographical publications requiring perusal. As so often happens, South African fiction in English creates special problems in this area both because it straddles the well defined subject areas of literature and Africana and because it is published in so many countries. Therefore, to achieve the fullest possible awareness of presently available titles one must be prepared to scan a wide range of current bibliographical publications. This includes national bibliographies and certain complementary trade publications, serial bibliographies in literature and Africana, some periodicals with a high bibliographical content and even a few acquisitions lists. Each of these in turn is discussed in this chapter, and although it is fair to say that the most revelant items appear in the section on current Africana serials, no publication of this type is complete enough to provide total coverage of the field on its own. For this reason the clearest picture of present output in South African fiction can be obtained only by referring to the more general national and literary bibliographies. To understand the full breadth of materials which one may wish to consult, reference need only be made to *Ulrich's International Periodicals Directory*,[1] which contains literally hundreds of serial bibliographies (general, literary, Africanist and "ethnic") relevant to current awareness needs. As in other chapters, however, only a handful of these are dealt with here, since the criteria for inclusion are either the indisputable value of a given title or its hitherto supposed worth which requires reevaluation in the context of South African fiction. The one type of material not discussed in this chapter is the scholarly journal, either literary or Africanist, which in its review section includes a substantial number of recent publications in the area of South African fiction. Such journals are treated in the appendix to the chapter on periodical literature.

National Bibliographies and Complementary Trade Publications

At first glance it might seem that national bibliographies form a ludicrously expansive category of material to be checked for titles of or on South African fiction, since virtually every Western nation and most African countries have their own national compilations. However, this number can be reduced to three possibilities quite rapidly. First, one need not consult any of the African national bibliographies, since they are either impossibly out-of-date or contain nothing relevant to South African fiction in English. While this may seem a rather sweeping generalization, it nevertheless remains true: with the exception of the Republic, all of the African national compilations published to date contain no titles of South African fiction. For publications about South African creative writing one will find occasional entries in some of the West African compilations, but these are so hopelessly behind that one will have discovered the information a year or two before through other sources. So also one may safely disregard most of the European national bibliographies as containing practically no titles on South African literature. This is particularly true of those two continental undertakings, the French and the German, which one might have thought would list more than a few useful publications. Therefore, the two major French national bibliographies may be safely left aside, along with the two complementary German publications.[2]

By a process of elimination one is thus left with the national bibliographies of three countries: the United States, Great Britain and South Africa, and among them they account for nearly all publications by or about South African novelists. By far the most impressive compilation in this category is the *National Union Catalog*,[3] which has already been discussed in Chapter Three (page 84) under the rubric of library catalogues. Although recording American holdings of titles published throughout the world, the *NUC* concentrates heavily on materials from within the U.S. and so forms a relatively complete guide to American output. Essentially a cumulative author listing, the *NUC* appears monthly with quarterly, annual and quinquennial cumulations, and there are now nearly 500 volumes for pre-1956 imprints. The disadvantage of this publication is that the author listing has no accompanying subject or title index, so one will be able to retrieve data only by an author search. Nevertheless, overall coverage of the more prominent South African novelists is extremely thorough, and with a bit of effort one will find practically every publication by these writers (e.g., Gordimer, Abrahams, La Guma). Another excellent American publication is the *Cumulative Book Index*, which in 1928 began to include material from the entire English-speaking world (but excluding much from South Africa).[4] Arranged in a single alphabetical sequence of authors, titles and subjects, it is both easy to use and extremely up-to-date, covering publications for the immediately preceding year in its frequent issues. Particularly useful are the annual cumulations, which generally contain several titles pertinent to South African literature from a variety of countries, although emphasis naturally falls on American and British publications.

Complementing these supra-national (but essentially American) guides is the *American Book Publishing Record*, which contains information culled from *Publisher's Weekly*.[5] Since 1960, the *Record* has appeared monthly and lists current American publications according to the Dewey classification. Each monthly cumulation includes an author and title index, and there is also an annual cumulative index to make consultation relatively simple. Less international than the *CBI*, the *Record* contains a highly accurate and up-to-date listing of American titles and should not be missed for its frequent references to South African literature published in America.

In addition to these two titles Bowker also produces *The Publishers' Trade List Annual*, which includes two useful annual adjuncts, *Books in Print* and *Subject Guide*.[6] *Books in Print* is essentially a combined index of authors and titles, while the *Subject Guide* is an alphabetical subject listing of titles published in the preceding year. Together these two volumes form an easily used, fairly complete guide to American titles currently on the market. The one advantage of these compilations over the *American Book Publishing Record* is their wide availability, while *ABPR* has the advantage of appearing more frequently for immediate reference. In terms of content there is very little difference between the two publications, for both contain virtually the same South African novels or critical works for a given year.

Turning to the United Kingdom, one again is faced with an admirable series of current bibliographies covering British publications in general. Foremost among these is the *British National Bibliography*, which began in 1950 and in 1973 came under the aegis of the British Library.[7] Issued weekly with semi-annual and annual cumulations, the *BNB* is classified according to the 18th edition of Dewey. The main sequence is supplemented by an alphabetical author and title listing and a subject index, and one will find a wealth of relevant data in each issue due to the fact that several major publishers of South African literature are British (e.g., Heinemann, Evans). The annual cumulations usefully draw together the information contained in the weekly issues, and there are frequent cumulative subject catalogues as well as cumulated indices which serve a useful retrospective function.[8] The *BNB* is clearly the most comprehensive British publication for our needs, so one will have little cause to consult some of the less widely representative guides, whether *British Book News, Whitaker's Cumulative Booklist* or *British Books in Print*.[9] *Book News* is issued by the British Council and contains bibliographical articles with frequent reference to African fiction. However, South African coverage is rather weak in comparison to the other two publications, so one need not consult this compilation. *Whitaker's Cumulative Booklist* is similar to the *American Book Publishing Record* in that it is based on a more frequent trade publication, in this case the *Bookseller*.[10] *Whitaker's* appears quarterly with annual cumulations and lists entries in a classified form; there is an index of authors and titles, but again many publications found in the *BNB* are missing in the *Booklist*. Finally, *British Books in Print*, another Whitaker undertaking, appears annually in two volumes, one for authors and the other for titles. This is the British counterpart of Bowker's *Books in Print* and appears to list most of what is available in a given year. Because it is quite comprehensive and up-to-date, it is the only British guide of value after the *BNB* for tracing current United Kingdom titles on South African fiction.

The remaining national publication which one will need to consult in order to be aware of current material is the *South African National Bibliography*.[11] This began as the mimeographed *Accessions List of Pretoria State Library* in 1933 and in 1959 became a quarterly cumulative publication. Like its British counterpart the *SANB* is compiled on the basis of publications received under the national copyright act; in general such acts in Africa have proved somewhat ineffective, but in South Africa this appears to be less true, since even a small publisher such as Ad. Donker is included in the *SANB*. Arranged by the Dewey Decimal Classification, there are always several entries under literature and fiction, although many of these are translations of foreign works (e.g., Afrikaans versions of Beatrix Potter books). The author and title index plus the annual cumulations ease consultation, and one will want to use the *SANB* regularly for its comprehensive coverage of current South African output.

There are, needless to say, countless other general, current publications with a high bibliographical content, but because of the generally effective coverage afforded by the *SANB, BNB, CBI* and the major American guides, it is unnecessarily time consuming to devote much effort to scanning such periodicals as *Books Abroad, Choice* or *Overseas Books*.[12] This is particularly true in view of the fact that very few academic libraries are without the national guides discussed above, although the *SANB* is not as widely held as it ought to be. All too often librarians tend to treat these national bibliographies and complementary trade publications as purely professional acquisition tools; at best they are left on the shelves and rarely referred to by readers for general reference purposes. In the context of South African literature, researchers should be encouraged to use at least the annual cumulations of the three essential national bibliographical guides, for they frequently contain entries missed in the smaller, more specialized bibliographies. Nevertheless, because these narrow subject guides focus on areas of particular interest to the student of South African literature and so form a more usable source of information, it is to these that he will turn most often.

Serial Bibliographies and Indices: Literature

For general coverage of creative writing in English one will want to consult two major compilations: the *Annual Bibliography of English Language and Literature* and the *International Bibliography of Books and Articles on the Modern Languages and Literatures.*[13] Both of these publications, one British and one American, began in the early 1920's and are surprisingly free from duplication; the British *Annual Bibliography* maintains that there is only a 21% overlap in terms of periodical titles covered, and personal experience has shown this to be the case. In fact both bibliographies are wider in scope than their titles would suggest, for they also index periodical articles in literally hundreds of journals with some literary content. This in itself makes them worth consulting, since periodical literature is notoriously difficult to encompass bibliographically, particularly in an area such as English literature with numerous journals within its range.

The *Annual Bibliography of English Language and Literature* is a highly comprehensive, enumerative, international bibliography of books, pamphlets, reviews and articles from some 700 English language periodicals. For the South Africanist it covers several journals of some importance, among them *English Studies in Africa* and the *Journal of Commonwealth Literature*. At the same time, however, the list of contributors contains not one noted Africanist, and this is partly reflected in the relatively poor coverage afforded to books on South African literature. In the 1972 compilation, for example, one finds only Anna Rutherfoord's edition of the papers from the 1971 Conference on Commonwealth Literature. For periodical literature the entries are rather more comprehensive, since articles relevant to South African fiction occasionally appear in several of the journals regularly scanned. Arrangement is by subject with sections for bibliography, biography and general literature (literary history and literary criticism—fiction), all of which will be of interest to the Africanist. The separate author and subject indices are indispensable for leading one to useful citations, although the author index for any given year suggests that novels by South Africans are not covered with any degree of thoroughness. A final drawback is the slightly dated nature of the *Annual Bibliography*; the 1975 publication was in fact prepared in 1974 for material appearing in 1972, which makes each annual volume a good three years behind in its coverage. In the final analysis this guide is probably most useful as a periodical index and rather less viable as a current bibliography of monograph titles.

In terms of scope of coverage the *MLA International Bibliography* is certainly a more ambitious undertaking, scanning for each annual edition some 2,800 periodical titles and relying on a committee of 150 scholars. Each edition appears in several volumes and is arranged by subject; Volume One includes South Africa within Australian, Canadian and other smaller national English language groupings, while Volume Three covers Africa in general. For each compilation there is only an author index, but the very full table of contents dispenses with the need for a subject index. The *International Bibliography* is slightly more up-to-date than its British counterpart, the 1974 publication having appeared in 1976. In this same volume under the general and African headings there are several critical works relevant to South Africa. Again, this publication serves best as a periodical index and offers relatively poor coverage of monograph titles.

It is clear, therefore, that both the MLA bibliography and the Cambridge compilation are not particularly useful as guides to current South African novels but concentrate instead on literary criticism, especially work of this type appearing in an extremely wide range of literary journals. This in itself makes the two bibliographies worth consulting, but for individual works one will have to rely on the national bibliographies or specifically Africana guides. One may also be tempted to scan some of the less well known bibliographies and indices in the hope of finding current works on South African literature; such publications as *The Year's Work in English Studies, Bulletin of Bibliography and Magazine Notes, Essay and General Literature Index* and the *Fiction Catalog* are frequently regarded as useful items in this category.[14] However, closer scrutiny proves that all of them without fail are not comprehensive enough to include with any degree of thoroughness the area of South African fiction. *Year's Work*, for example, in the 1974 edition included only two paragraphs (pp. 24–25) on African literature as a whole, while the *Fiction Catalog* generally covers about 4,000 titles with a primarily Anglo-American bias. The only other materials worth using are specific periodical indices; since they deal solely with serial articles, they are discussed in the following chapter.

Serial Bibliographies: Africana

In the sphere of current bibliographies devoted to books from or about Africa the field is rather better covered than one might expect; in fact for the student of South African literature the corpus of Africana bibliographies provides an altogether more satisfactory service for recent publications than do the current literary bibliographies. This is due in large part to three factors: 1) the complementary coverage provided by the various serials, which results in relatively thorough information on both creative writing and scholarly studies; 2) the consistent attention paid to literature as part of African studies; 3) the persistent efforts of such individuals as Hans Zell and certain institutions, notably SOAS and the African Bibliographic Center.

However, the situation is not as rosy as these comments suggest, for two of the guides providing national coverage of Africana publications are now virtually defunct, *United States and Canadian Publications and Theses on Africa* and *United Kingdom Publications and Theses on Africa.*[15] However, this is not a great loss, for these compilations have appeared three to four years later than the dates covered and have never expressed more than a marginal interest in creative writing. Thus they have been in effect retrospective guides to recent non-fiction titles published in their respective countries. A still healthy French compilation of this type is CARDAN's "Bibliographie Française sur l'Afrique au Sud du Sahara," which appears annually in the *Bulletin d'Information et de Liaison.*[16] The best that can be said about this effort is its up-to-date appearance; otherwise it has little to offer, since it is no more than an annual two-page listing of selected monographs and periodical articles from the better known French journals (e.g., *Présence Africaine* and *Revue de Littérature Comparée*). Arranged both by subject and country, one will find few references to material relevant to South African fiction, and most of these will have appeared previously in the major English language Africana bibliographies.

Two serial bibliographies still enjoying a healthy existence are *A Current Bibliography on African Affairs* and the *International African Bibliography,* American and British, respectively, but without the national orientation of their defunct series counterparts.[17] *Current Bibliography* is not exhaustive but rather aims to present a representative selection of materials in African studies with emphasis on the most current publications. Coverage includes books and articles, and data is arranged in four sections: 1) original studies and bibliographical essays on specific subjects, 2) short book reviews, 3) listings by general subject and region, 4) author index. For present needs only the last two sections need be consulted, and here one will find both general works such as *Index Africanus* and *African Books in Print* along with a few literary titles, largely those from prominent Western publishers (e.g., Heinemann). Literary criticism has much better coverage than fiction itself within the literature section, and one will not have to look beyond this to the regional section, for there the entries are largely socio-political. Not every issue will contain relevant entries, but by and large this publication requires frequent consultation as the single more comprehensive serial guide to Africana being published in the West.

The *International African Bibliography* is a joint SOAS/International African Institute undertaking under the general direction of J. D. Pearson and also covers books as well as periodical articles. Each issue contains some 750 entries arranged geographically and then by subject and author.

For Africa in general there is a section devoted to language and literature, but the emphasis here is strongly linguistic. Nevertheless, it does contain the occasional reference to otherwise unrecorded pieces (e.g., Panter-Brick's article in the *Journal of Commonwealth and Comparative Politics*) and articles in collected volumes (e.g., R. Smith's *Tradition and Exile*), which is a very useful service. Under South Africa one will find frequent references to periodical articles and essays in *festschriften* with a literary content, but the overall orientation is primarily socio-political. Like the current bibliographies of literature, these two guides are essentially periodical indices and so offer little real assistance in retrieving information about books, either novels or scholarly tomes.

The advantage of these titles is that they are quite up-to-date, certainly more so than the *Africana Journal*, which is another bibliographical guide from America.[18] The somewhat dated nature of the coverage afforded by this publication stems from the fact that it relies primarily on other published bibliographies (e.g., *British National Bibliography, Joint Acquisitions List of Africana, African Book Publishing Record*). Originally edited by Hans Zell, it resembles the *Current Bibliography* in having sections devoted to original bibliographical articles and reviews, but the *Journal* caters more to the literateur with frequent articles on African writers and related topics (e.g., Helene Silver's bio-bibliography of Achebe in vol. 1, 1: 18–22). The bulk of each issue consists of a bibliographical listing classified by subject and country and indexed by author and subject. In both the subject and geographical sections emphasis is entirely on monograph titles, including a fair proportion of novels. Because of this orientation and in spite of its marginally dated entries, it forms an essential supplement to the other serial guides noted above. The journal is genuinely international, listing publications from Europe, North America and Africa and includes frequent reference to titles of South African interest.

Although concentrating to some degree on fiction and including imprints from both the West and Africa, the *Africana Journal* and its sister publications all exhibit a strong Western bias, and this is also true of a more recent series of articles by Eugene de Benko. "A Select Bibliography of Africana" originally appeared in the first issue of the *ASA Review of Books* and is slated to become an ongoing part of this annual serial.[19] Each article begins with a brief but informative summary of major publishing events and trends for the preceding year, and this is followed by a selective listing of items which de Benko considers to warrant acquisition by scholars or libraries interested in African studies. Arrangement is by subject with entries under both bibliography and literature, although to date there have been few entries in either category of interest to collectors of South African fiction. If one assumes that the two articles represent de Benko's view of this genre, then there can be little hope that future compilations will have any greater relevance to creative writing from the Republic.

The Western bias of all of these bibliographies has been remedied of late by two complementary Zell undertakings, the *African Book Publishing Record* and *African Books in Print*.[20] *ABIP* was intended originally to appear in two parts, the second covering French language materials, but it now appears that this idea has been abandoned in favor of a single edition covering both English and French materials.[21] *ABIP* contains some 6,000 titles from 188 African publishers in nineteen countries and includes all types of publications except periodicals and magazines. The volume is carefully arranged by author, title and subject with thorough indices and full form divisions in the subject sequence. Although the 1975 edition does not include exceptionally full coverage of South African titles, one may expect the next edition to do so on the basis of the constantly expanding coverage of the Republic in its sister publication. As the only guide of its kind devoted solely to African imprints, *ABIP* is an indispensable tool for current coverage of South African literature, particularly works by creative writers.

The companion to *ABIP* is the *African Book Publishing Record*, also begun by Zell in 1975. Like its sister publication, *ABPR* is concerned only with African imprints and again deals with all types of material except periodicals. It provides a variety of ancillary services, including notes and news, reports, articles on publishing, information on new periodicals and publisher profiles. By far the largest section of each quarterly issue is devoted to bibliographical coverage of current African output and includes titles from some 200 African publishers. Coverage of South African publishing was originally weak due largely to resistance by the publishers themselves rather than to inefficiency on the part of *ABPR*. While some of the larger firms (e.g., Perskor, Maskew Miller, Timmins) still are quite uncooperative, a number of smaller publishers (e.g., Bateleur, Donker, Ravan) are regularly included in each issue. From the standpoint of creative writing this is an important factor, for it also happens that these same small firms are the very ones which often undertake the publication of "serious" fiction. The larger firms, on the other hand, opt almost entirely for what is commercially viable, and for South Africa this is limited to "popular" fiction; Wilbur Smith is an example of the writers in this category. The entries are classified by subject and region, using the *Sears List of Subject Headings* with slight amendments. The subject headings include the arts, which are further subdivided by place, thereby dispensing with the need to look under the geographical section as well. African literature is subdivided by form (e.g., collections, fiction, bibliography), the headings varying according to the material contained in a given issue. Overall coverage of South Africa under each heading is very good, including both widely known critical texts (e.g., Mphahlele's *Voices in the Whirlwind* and Gordimer's *The Black Interpreters*) and lesser known novels (Stephen Gray's *Local Colour*). At its inception *ABPR* was rather behind in its coverage, but this has improved to the point that titles are often reported some time before publication, as was the case with Beeton's *Pilot Bibliography*. Nevertheless, *ABPR* is indispensable as a guide to current South African creative writing and must be used regularly; *ABIP* for our needs is a useful supplement to *ABPR*, and together these two volumes are the best general guides to current literary output by African publishers.

Complementing the two Zell publications is the *Bibliography of Overseas Publications about South Africa*, compiled by the State Library in Pretoria as a successor to *Africana Nova*, which appeared between 1958 and 1969.[22] As the title suggests, the *Bibliography of Overseas Publications* focuses on overseas material about South Africa and includes publications by South Africans, translations of South African works published abroad, material with substantial but not exclusive reference to the Republic and single issues of foreign periodicals dealing entirely with South Africa. Thus while Zell concentrates on what appears internally, the State Library looks at the other side of the coin and draws together titles from a variety of other countries. At the same time, of course, an undertaking of this sort cannot hope to be exhaustive, and in this case the listing is based on materials acquired by the State Library and listed in the weekly *SANB* card service. Arranged according to Dewey, each biennial edition includes at 823 a wide range of novels and literary criticism (including banned titles). This is a very useful service, considering the high proportion of South African novels which are published abroad. Although the volumes published to date contain frequent references to bibliographically elusive titles (e.g., Klima's *South African Prose Writing in English*) and include an index of authors and titles, their biennial appearance means that some of the items are rather dated. For a service of this sort one would hope for at least an annual volume, as this would make the series much more useful. As it now stands, *Overseas Publications* must be supplemented by the various national bibliographies discussed earlier in the chapter.

The final type of serial bibliography devoted to Africana which the librarian and researcher may want to consult is the acquisitions list. As a rule such lists tend to be rather narrow in scope, since they are the records of materials acquired only by a single library. The few exceptions to this evaluation are the *Joint Acquisitions List of Africana, Africana in Scandinavian Research Libraries* and possibly the *Bibliographic Guide to Black Studies*.[23] *JALA* reports on a bi-monthly basis the acquisitions of some twenty-one major American libraries having strong Africana collections and covers titles published in the current year and the five preceding ones. Arrangement is strictly by author (or title in the case of publications for which an author cannot be ascertained), and the lack of a subject index or cumulative volume can make consultation rather arduous except on a regular basis. Nevertheless, each issue does contain a representative selection of novels by South Africans and related literary criticism published in the Republic and elsewhere.

Another union list is *Africana in Scandinavian Research Libraries*, which reports semi-annually on the acquisitions of more than forty Nordic libraries. Arrangement is by subject (including bibliography, literature and literary history) and lists materials acquired during the preceding six months, although the items listed may have been published up to four years prior to the actual date of acquisition. Rather surprisingly, each issue contains a broad selection of critical titles relevant to the South African novel, recent entries including Wästberg's *The Writer in Modern Africa*, Dale's *The Social and Political World of Alan Paton*, Mphahlele's *African Writing Today* and Cook and Henderson's *The Militant Black Writer in Africa and the United States*. Primary materials, however, are rather poorly represented, and in this respect it resembles *JALA*. At the same time, however, *Africana* usefully complements its sister publication by affording rather better coverage of European publications with an Africana content. As yet unseen is G. K. Hall's *Bibliographic Guide*, which is advertised as an annual accessions list based on the Schomburg Collection of the New York Public Library. However, based on an analysis of this library's *Dictionary Catalog* (see Chapter Three, pages 84–85), one might expect it to contain rather more novels than either *JALA* or the Scandinavian list, since the Schomburg Collection in the past has exhibited a strong interest in this genre. All of these lists will be of most use to the acquisitions librarian with time to scan each issue as it appears, for as a rule most novels and related works will appear in the more conveniently consulted national bibliographies or, in slightly less up-to-date form, in the other serial bibliographies already discussed.

One will see from this survey of the various types of current bibliographies available in the field of South African literature that there are several problems and *lacunae* requiring attention. The national bibliographies as a whole are highly useful guides; the main drawbacks are the number of these tools to be consulted and the ancillary trade publications to be perused for interim publishing data. Taken together, they form too substantial a corpus for any but the most devoted bibliophile. Thus almost inevitably one will have to turn to the more specialized subject services. Here, although bulk may again pose problems, the major sin is that of omission rather than over-indulgence. Bibliographies of literature by and large concentrate on serial articles rather than monographs and are noticeably weak on fiction titles. The current Africana bibliographies, on the other hand, focus very nicely on our area but tend to prefer the social sciences to the humanities, especially literature. Thus on all sides South African fiction loses, as do the humanities in general from within Africa. There is a clear case, therefore, for improving and expanding these services; the most suitable alternative would be expansion of the Africana bibliographies to include fiction, whether creative writing or criticism, within their scope. One must admit, of course, that the *Journal of Commonwealth Literature* provides an annual bibliography on our specific subject, but this compilation suffers from a number of weaknesses to be noted in a later chapter and also is separated quite distinctly from African studies as a whole. One would prefer to see this service provided within the context of African studies or as part of coverage of African literature or, as already suggested in Chapter Four of Part I, as a specific entity in its own right. In any of these alternatives the need for improved coverage is obvious. In the meantime one must be content with the major national guides and current Africana bibliographies.

Notes

1. *Ulrich's International Periodicals Directory: A Classified Guide to Current Periodicals, Foreign and Domestic* (16th edition; New York: R. R. Bowker, 1975–76).

2. Cercle de la Libraire, *Bibliographie de la France; Journal Officiel de l'Imprimerie et de la Libraire* (Paris: Cercle de la Libraire, 1811– ; weekly with monthly/quarterly supplements); *Catalogue Général de la Libraire Française* (Paris: Champion, 1840– ; triennial); Deutsche Bucherei, ed., *Deutsche Nationalbibliographie* (Leipzig: VEB Verlag für Buch- und Bibliothekswesen, 1931– ; in two sections, weekly and bi-weekly); *Deutsche Bibliographie: Wöhentliches Verzeichnis* (Frankfurt am Main: Buchhandler-Vereinigung GmbH., 1947– ; bi-monthly with quadrennial cumulations); cf. Robert L. Collison, *Bibliographies Subject and National: A Guide to Their Contents, Arrangement and Use* (Second edition; London: Crosby Lockwood, 1962), pp. 150 ff. for a brief discussion of these and other national bibliographies.

3. U.S., Library of Congress, *National Union Catalog* (Washington, D.C.: Library of Congress, Resources Committee of the Resources and Technical Services Division, 1956– ; monthly with quarterly, annual and quinquennial cumulations). *Pre-1956 Imprints* has been appearing since 1968 under the Mansell Information/Publishing imprint and now totals nearly 500 volumes.

4. *Cumulative Book Index; A World List of Books in the English Language* (New York: H. W. Wilson, 1898– ; 11 per annum with quarterly, annual and multi-annual cumulations).

5. *American Book Publishing Record* (New York: R. R. Bowker, 1960– ; monthly); cf. *Publishers' Weekly: The Book Industry Journal* (New York: R. R. Bowker, 1877–).

6. *The Publishers' Trade List Annual* (New York: R. R. Bowker, 1873–); cf. *Books in Print* and *Subject Guide* (New York: R. R. Bowker, 1948– and 1957–). Two supplements to *Books in Print* are *Forthcoming Books* (New York: R. R. Bowker, 1966– ; bi-monthly) and *Paperbound Books in Print* (New York: R. R. Bowker, 1955– ; annual with semi-annual supplements).

7. *British National Bibliography* (London: Council of the British National Bibliography for the British Library, 1950– ; weekly with semi-annual and annual cumulations).

8. Cumulative subject catalogues have been issued for 1951–54, 1955–59, 1960–64, 1965–67, 1968–70; cumulated indices exist for 1950–54, 1955–59, 1960–64, 1965–67, 1968–70.

9. *British Book News* (London: British Council, 1940– ; monthly); *Whitaker's Cumulative Booklist* (London: J. Whitaker, 1926– ; quarterly with annual cumulations); *British Books in Print* (2 vols.; London: J. Whitaker, 1874– ; annual).

10. *Bookseller* (London: J. Whitaker, 1858– ; weekly).

11. South Africa, State Library, *South African National Bibliography* (Pretoria: State Library, 1959– ; quarterly with annual cumulations).

12. *Books Abroad; An International Library Quarterly* (Norman: University of Oklahoma Press, 1927– ; quarterly); American Library Association (and others), *Choice* (Middletown, Connecticut: American Library Association, 1964– ; 11 per annum); *Overseas Books* (London: Publishing and Distributing, 1964– ; quarterly).

13. Modern Humanities Research Association, *Annual Bibliography of English Language and Literature* (Cambridge, England: Modern Humanities Research Association, 1920–); Modern Language Association of America, *MLA International Bibliography of Books and Articles on the Modern Languages and Literatures* (New York: Modern Language Association of America, 1921– ; annual, since 1969 issued independently of *PLMA Journal*).

14. English Association, *The Year's Work in English Studies* (London: Murray, 1919– ; annual); *Bulletin of Bibliography and Magazine Notes* (Westwood, Massachusetts: F. W. Faxon, 1897– ; quarterly); *Essay and General Literature Index* (New York: H. W. Wilson, 1900– ; annual with frequent cumulations); *Fiction Catalog* (Eighth edition; New York: H. W. Wilson, 1971; supplements and new editions issued regularly).

15. Hoover Institution on War, Revolution and Peace, *United States and Canadian Publications and Theses on Africa* (Hoover Institution Bibliographical Series. Stanford, California: Stanford University, Hoover Institution, 1962– ; annual for three to four years prior to date of publication). The proposed 1967–1970 cumulation will probably be the last in this series. Cf. Standing Conference on Library Materials on Africa, *United Kingdom Publications and Theses on ˙Africa* (Cambridge: W. Heffer, 1966–1973; publisher varies). The 1973 edition, covering 1967–1968, was published by F. Cass, and the 1969–1970 volume exists only in manuscript form at SOAS.

16. Centre d'Analyse et de Recherche Documentaires pour l'Afrique Noire, "Bibliographie Française sur l'Afrique au Sud du Sahara," *Bulletin d'Information et de Liaison* (Paris: CARDAN, 1969– ; annual for the preceding year).

17. African Bibliographic Center, *A Current Bibliography on African Affairs* (Farmingdale, New York: Baywood, 1962–1967, n.s. 1968– ; quarterly); *International African Bibliography: Current Books, Articles and Papers in African Studies* (London: Mansell Information/Publishing, 1971– ; quarterly).

18. *Africana Journal: A Bibliographic and Review Quarterly* (New York: Africana, 1970– ; previously entitled *Africana Library Journal*).

19. Eugene de Benko, "A Select Bibliography of Africana, 1973–74," *ASA Review of Books*, 1 (1975): 162–84; Eugene de Benko, "A Select Bibliography of Africana, 1974–75," *ASA Review of Books*, 2 (1976): 207–26.

20. *African Book Publishing Record* (Oxford: Hans Zell [Publishers] 1975– ; quarterly); Hans M. Zell, ed., *African Books in Print: An Index by Author, Title and Subject. Part I: English Language and African Languages* (London: Mansell Information/Publishing, 1975).

21. "The second edition of *African Books in Print* is now scheduled for publication early in 1978. We have, however, abandoned our original idea of publishing separate volumes for English and French titles, and the second edition will now also include the output of publishers from francophone Africa, including pre-1973 imprint titles not already listed in *ABPR*. We expect that the second edition will list twice the number of titles than the first edition, i.e., some 13,000 records in all." Hans M. Zell, "Publishing Progress in Africa 1975–76: Problems in Securing Information and the Role of the *African Book Publishing Record*," unpublished paper presented at the SCOLMA Conference on Progress in African Bibliography, Commonwealth Institute, London, March 17–18, 1977, p. 4.

22. South Africa, State Library, *Bibliography of Overseas Publications about South Africa* (Pretoria: State Library, 1973– ; biennial); to date there have been editions covering 1969–1971, 1972–1973 and 1974–1975; cf. South Africa, South African Public Library, *Africana Nova: A Quarterly Bibliography of Books Currently Published in and about The Republic of South Africa, Based on the Accessions to the Africana Department . . . and Including Material Received on Legal Deposit* (Cape Town: South African Public Library, 1958–1969).

23. Northwestern University, Melville J. Herskovits Library of African Studies, comp., *Joint Acquisitions List of Africana* (Evanston, Illinois: Northwestern University Library, 1962– ; bi-monthly); Scandinavian Institute of African Studies, *Africana in Scandinavian Research Libraries* (Uppsala: Scandinavian Institute of African Studies, 1963– ; semi-annual); *Bibliographic Guide to Black Studies* (Boston: G. K. Hall, 1976– ; annual for the preceding year).

Periodical Lists and Periodical Indices

In any academic discipline one of the most difficult areas of bibliographical control for researchers and librarians is periodical literature. The most pressing problem is the discovery of those journals which are relevant to a given field of study, and this is followed closely by the recurrent need to determine the contents of the most useful serial titles once their existence has been ascertained. Part of the difficulty lies in the very nature of the journal publishing industry with its financial uncertainties and esoteric subject specializations, which in turn contributes to the frequent birth, demise, subject reorientation and title changes in the various periodicals. The field of South African literature is not exempt from these general difficulties, and here the problem is compounded by the wide expanse of titles with an interest in Africana, English literature and South African fiction. The range extends from general scholarly publications to specific literary or Africana publications to little magazines devoted to creative writing in the Republic. In an attempt to clarify the confusion and ease the work of those interested in South African fiction this chapter attempts an analysis of relevant periodical literature, including periodical lists and guides and suitable indices to literary and Africana journals; the discussion concludes with an appendix containing notes on those periodical titles felt to be of most use in the field of South African fiction. Because of the wide scope in this area, each section is bound to contain some omissions and to reflect one's personal choice; however, the range of materials discussed should go some way in enlightening others working in the field and perhaps ease the burden of researchers overwhelmed by the wide range of periodical literature of value in the study and collection of South African fiction.

Periodical Lists

For African studies as a whole we are fortunate in having a substantial corpus of guides to serials and periodicals lists; many of these are in effect periodical indices, which serve an additional function as guides to serial titles. Although enjoying a tradition which pre-dates 1961 by several years, it was in that year that the Library of Congress produced the first widely recognized major guide to Africana periodicals.[1] This was Helen Conover's *Serials for African Studies*, which provided bibliographical details on some 2,082 serial titles.[2] Arranged alphabetically by title, this guide is now very dated and contains practically no information on periodicals devoted in any degree to South African fiction (*Contrast* and the defunct *Panafrica* being two exceptions). It is fair to say that the student of modern South African literature need not consult Miss Conover's guide. A similar comment may be made of the Duignan and Glazier 1963 effort, *A Checklist of Serials for African Studies*.[3] While the Conover guide ranges widely over holdings in America, Europe and Africa, its 1963 successor is more narrowly limited to collections at Stanford and the Hoover Institution; its main drawback is the complete lack of indices to facilitate ease of consultation. This along with the relatively early date of the *Checklist* means that its contents need not be scanned for current periodical titles.

By 1969 American university collections had advanced sufficiently to generate a slightly more useful checklist based on library holdings, namely de Benko's *Research Sources for African Studies*.[4] This publication introduces some 2,100 serials available at Michigan State University up to 31 March 1968 and is arranged alphabetically by title with a useful subject/country index. De Benko includes some titles not often found in guides covering material relevant to South African fiction (e.g., *New South African Writing*, the *Bulletin of the Association for African Literature in English* and *Civilisations*), but his work also suffers from certain bibliographical inconsistencies (e.g., listing Heinemann's African Writers Series but not individual titles in this series) and, because of its date, fails to include those new titles of the last ten years which deal substantially with the South African literary scene (*Research in African Literatures* being but one example of what was not available in 1968). Furthermore, *Research Sources* makes no mention of the coverage of literature in general Africanist periodicals; because of these drawbacks, it may be excluded from one's research, although it is the earliest checklist with even marginal usefulness to the student of South African literature.

In the early 1970's the efforts to list Africanist periodicals suddenly blossomed with several useful guides incorporating information on titles with a significant South African content. The first of these was the Panofsky and Koester article in *The African Experience*;[5] this contains some twenty-two pages of entries rather confusingly classified according to the modules developed by Paden and Soja. In spite of this arbitrary arrangement it does mention some of the more general scholarly journals with at least a passing interest in African literature. This attempt was accompanied in the same year by the altogether more substantial Library of Congress publication, *Sub-Saharan Africa: A Guide to Serials*, which in effect updated the earlier *Serials for African Studies* compiled by Helen Conover.[6] Including titles which existed in American libraries at the end of 1968, *Sub-Saharan Africa* records a selection of publications in an alphabetical title listing, and there are also subject and organization indices to assist one in locating relevant journals. Each entry includes the standard bibliographical data (publisher, frequency, dates) which may well have changed in nearly ten years, but there are also scope notes on titles, which continue to be useful. For example, one is told that *English Studies in Africa* includes a select bibliography of books and articles on English literature published in the Republic. The subject index to *Sub-Saharan Africa* covers literary journals arranged by country, and under South Africa one finds some fourteen relevant titles (e.g., *The Classic, Contrast, New Coin, Trek*); here for the first time mention is made of some less well known journals devoted to creative writing in the Republic. Once again, however, there is no mention of general scholarly periodicals with an interest in this field. This along with the relatively dated coverage detracts from the general usefulness of this compilation, yet it remains the best starting point for bibliographical inquiries on periodical literature.

In 1971 the African Bibliographic Center produced *Periodicals for Pan-African Studies,* which on analysis appears to be much more selective than the preceding guide and contains no additional information not already included in the Library of Congress compilation.[7] The recording of Africanist journals then underwent a lull until 1975, when Birkos and Tambs produced *African and Black American Studies.*[8] Aimed primarily at the scholarly writer, this guide provides useful information on titles existing in 1975; data includes the address, frequency, cost, editorial interests and notes for the submission of material. Arrangement is again alphabetical by title, and there are useful chronological and topical indices, the latter including several headings relevant to literature (unrestricted, bibliographical articles, cultural affairs, literature-history and criticism). Entries include for the first time such standard modern undertakings as the *Journal of Commonwealth Literature* and *Research in African Literatures,* and there is also mention of a few of the smaller literary journals (*Ba Shiru, Conch*) but without much emphasis on titles of this type from within South Africa. In spite of this one failing, Birkos and Tambs is the most up-to-date and comprehensive general guide to Africanist periodicals now in existence; therefore, it is a *sine qua non* for both the researcher and librarian, particularly since its closest competitor, *Sub-Saharan Africa,* is no longer generally available. It should be noted, however, that the latter affords rather better coverage of indigenous publications and so should be used wherever possible to supplement Birkos and Tambs.

The only publication which in part supersedes *African and Black African Studies* is the recently completed *Periodicals from Africa: A Bibliography and Union List of Periodicals Published in Africa.*[9] As the title indicates, this guide focuses on indigenous publications and for this reason usefully complements the Western emphasis of Birkos and Tambs. The overall African coverage extends to all titles published in Africa, which must make *Periodicals from Africa* the most comprehensive guide of its kind. For South African output, however, coverage is limited to the holdings of British libraries;[10] this in itself need not be a significant drawback except for the fact that the treatment of South Africa under the SCOLMA scheme is far from adequate. This is seen in the fact that fully 50% of the Republic's literary magazines are not held in Britain and so escape inclusion in *Periodicals from Africa*. For the student of South African literature this becomes particularly debilitating, for such titles as *Bolt, Crux* and *UNISA English Studies* are not cited. Nevertheless, this compilation does manage to list a significant number of indigenous periodicals and for this reason must be consulted. The 17,000 titles are arranged by country (pp. 1–498), and this is supplemented by a full title index (pp. 499–619); for students of literature, of course, this regional approach should also have included a subject index, but with the present arrangement retrieval of literary titles is not particularly difficult. The individual entries are generally clear and relatively complete, including information on dates, publisher and location, frequency and, where applicable, notes on cessations or continuations. One can only hope that future supplements will include a wider range of South African material than is presently the case.[11]

In contrast to these three more or less essential guides there are another three items which for a variety of reasons need never be consulted for data on periodicals with an African Literary content: The *World List of Specialized Periodicals: African Studies,* "Periodicals Published in Africa," *African Periodicals in the Library of the British Museum.*[12] The first of these is devoted solely to the human and social sciences, which excludes literature; the second omits South Africa from its coverage, while the last is based on the holdings of the British Museum (Natural History), a parenthetical addition often omitted in bibliographical citations.

To supplement the important non-serial compilations so far discussed, one will want to make use of a pair of ongoing serial titles for their current information on Africanist periodicals; these are *Periodicals in South African Libraries* and the *African Book Publishing Record.*[13] The former, commonly known as *PISAL,* began in 1961 as a successor to Freer's *Catalogue of Union Periodicals*[14] and is updated with looseleaf additions. Arranged in a single alphabetical sequence, the entries cover a wide range of disciplines represented in titles from a variety of countries. Coverage of indigenous publications is naturally *PISAL*'s forte, although the greatest proportion of these titles deals primarily with the sciences and social sciences and only marginally with creative writing. *ABPR,* on the other hand, is for all practical purposes an excellent guide to African based periodical publishing. Since its origin in 1975, each issue of *ABPR* has included notes on new or defunct magazines and journals, many with a strong South African literary content. Thus one finds in its pages mention of such new titles as *Snarl, Afriscope, New Classic, Ch'indaba* (formerly *Transition*), as well as information on current contents of well established literary journals (e.g., *Black Orpheus*). It is fair to say, therefore, that the *African Book Publishing Record* is probably the best guide to current periodical literature from within Africa and for this reason is not to be overlooked under any circumstance.

Expanding the information found in *PISAL* and *ABPR* is a difficult task, but there is one title which fulfills this function quite admirably, namely *Current South African Periodicals*.[15] Arranged according to Dewey, this compilation and its five supplements cover most titles published in South Africa regardless of their subject or quality, and each edition has a combined author/title/subject index. More inclusive from a literary standpoint than *PISAL*, this compilation includes such valuable titles as *English Studies in Africa, Theoria* and *Contrast*. As the major South African guide to current serials, this State Library publication must be used to complement the more up-to-date information found in *ABPR*, and one will find the forthcoming revision of all six editions an important source of information on literary titles from the Republic.

To complete one's search among general guides to periodical literature there is a strong temptation to return to some of the bibliographies and current awareness publications mentioned in the preceding two chapters. In retrospect, however, it is clear that none of these titles will supply enough additional information on current periodicals to warrant the time spent in consulting them. Instead, one is better advised to turn either to guides to literary periodicals or periodical indices, both of which deal much more directly with serials of use in studying South African fiction.

There were one or two attempts in the 1960's to provide information on African literary periodicals, but by and large these failed to cover the field adequately either because of incomplete data or because their range was not sufficiently limited to be of use to the Africanist.[16] It was not until 1973 that anything approaching a full, general guide to relevant Africana journals was compiled by Hans Zell as part of his guide to African literature. Although not limited to South African fiction, the *Reader's Guide to African Literature* contains in pages 102–11 a selection of literary publications with direct bearing on creative writing in the Republic.[17] In these pages Zell lists a range of both general Africana titles and specific literary magazines with a particular interest in South African fiction. This compilation, however, does not indicate which of the periodicals surveyed has a particular brief to treat Republican fiction, so the researcher must in the end investigate each title for himself.

Although there has not yet been any other attempt to list African literary serials either from the Africanist or literary standpoint, there is in preparation a guide to Commonwealth periodicals which should be a relatively comprehensive listing of both current and defunct titles relevant to South

African literature. This guide is a project of the Working Party on Library Holdings of Commonwealth Literature and so will cover periodicals from the entire Commonwealth which deal with English literature. Begun in the late 1960's, it is intended primarily as a finding list of British library holdings of several serial categories: magazines of general interest with some literary content, scholarly journals concerned at least in part with literature, small press publications and even school and university literary magazines. It will thus be the most comprehensive undertaking of its kind and, because it includes South Africa within the Commonwealth, may well be the most important modern guide yet produced for the student of South African periodical literature.[18] Aside from its function as a finding list, this Working Party compilation will also include as much bibliographical information as possible on more than 3,500 Commonwealth titles issued from colonial times to the present, and this emphasis will be of inestimable value to the librarian attempting to locate data on Africanist literary periodicals.

One problem with this effort is bound to be the worldwide scope encompassed by Commonwealth coverage; because of this, it cannot possibly be expected to appeal specifically to the Africanist unless the indices cater to both the geographical and subject approaches. In a similar fashion Miss Lever's specifically South African guide does not limit itself to creative writing and so includes far more than the literary researcher needs to know.[19] This again exemplifies the problem of overlap which plagues those dealing with a subject/area studies combination. In the following section one will see that the various types of periodical indices for literature and Africana material assist in bridging the gaps in coverage left by these slightly inadequate periodical lists, but even these additional sources of information do not obviate the need for a single comprehensive guide to periodicals dealing with South African literature. Once more, therefore, here is a *lacuna* which merits the attention of the proposed library/bibliographical center for South African literature. What is needed is a complete guide to periodicals (Africanist and literary, Western and African) which deal to some degree with fiction from the Republic; such a guide would provide not only bibliographical details for the librarian but also, following the example of Birkos and Tambs, scope notes for the researcher. In this way much of the frustration inherent in tracing periodical literature would be alleviated. This project could even be divided into two parts, with the Institute for the Study of English in Africa compiling a list of indigenous literary publications (which may already be part of the Institute's forthcoming guide to the South African novel) and the proposed center compiling a list of all Western materials for the study of South African fiction. However the work were divided, one end result must be full coverage of general scholarly literature which deals to any degree with fiction in the Republic, for at present it is quite impossible to know which of these countless titles might include articles relevant to the field except by accident.

Periodical Indices

Turning to serial and monograph indices to periodical literature in the field of South African fiction, one again finds that there are publications of three distinct types: general periodical indices, guides covering literature as a whole and Africana periodical indices. Each of these in turn retrieves data of value to the researcher, so one's time will be well spent in becoming acquainted with the resources in each category. Both within and between these groups there is remarkably little repetition, a fact which requires that one be prepared to scan a number of publications rather than settle on one or two as the most likely sources of information.

Of the general periodical indices three are most widely held by libraries and frequently consulted by researchers: *Readers' Guide to Periodical Literature, Humanities Index* and *British Humanities Index.*[20] The first of these, a Wilson publication, is far too general for our needs and so may be ignored in favor of the much more scholarly *Humanities Index,* also published by H. W. Wilson. This index is certainly the most comprehensive of all the general lists of periodical literature and must be regarded as the starting point in one's search for relevant articles on South African fiction. Each issue consists of a combined author and subject listing of periodical articles, and this format obviates the need for a subject index; there is also a supplementary listing of citations to book reviews and a list of periodicals indexed along with their addresses, subscription costs and frequency of publication. All of this information is of use to librarians who either wish to locate reviews of a given book or wish to subscribe to a journal indexed by this service. For the researcher the index itself is invaluable, listing as it does a widely representative range of scholarly North American periodicals with a strong literary flavor.[21] Thus in any given issue one will find under African or South African literature or literary criticism more than the occasional reference to pieces on African/South African fiction. Although there is fair coverage of some of the African literary periodicals (e.g., *Research in African Literatures* but not the *Journal of Commonwealth Literature*), the *Humanities Index* is most useful as a listing of general literary serials with which the Africanist may be unfamiliar (e.g., *Ariel, Twentieth Century Literature*).

While this guide concentrates heavily on North American titles, the *British Humanities Index* deals with a limited number of more international publications[22] and so usefully complements its sister publication. Each quarterly issue is arranged alphabetically by subject with an author index in each annual cumulation, and under African literature one will generally find one or two relevant entries in each issue. Although *BHI* is much less comprehensive than the *Humanities Index,* it is every bit as up-to-date as the Wilson guide and warrants consultation at least annually. The same cannot be said of the comparable German publication, *Internationale Bibliographie der Zeitschriftenliteratur aus allen Gebeiten des Wissens*;[23] arranged in a classified subject sequence with an alphabetical author index, *IBZ* is very weak on African literature (including neither *Research in African Literatures* nor the *Journal of Commonwealth Literature*) and so may safely be ignored in preference to the more relevant *BHI* and *Humanities Index.*

Of the indices with a specific concentration on literature the two most important publications have already been discussed at some length in the preceding chapter as serial bibliographies.[24] These are, of course, the *Annual Bibliography of English Language and Literature* and the *International Bibliography of Books and Articles on the Modern Languages and Literatures,* both of which are indispensable indices to articles of literary interest. As indicated in Chapter Four, these two undertakings exhibit only a 21% duplication in the periodicals covered, which is important when one realizes that between them these two titles index some 3,500 periodicals. Although the *Annual Bibliography* includes, for the first time among the indexing services so far noted, *English Studies in Africa* and a few other relevant periodicals, it is the MLA index which consistently lists the greater number of articles relevant to South African fiction, so it is to this guide that the researcher will want to turn more frequently.

For coverage of Africana periodicals one has at hand an interesting combination of important monographs, selective serial bibliographies and more limited national undertakings. The two major indices must be *Africa South of the Sahara* and *Index Africanus,* one a Library of Congress compilation and the other an individual effort.[25] The more significant of the two is the LC publication, which is arranged by area and subject within each area/country. Citing some 1,530 periodical titles, *Africa South* concentrates clearly on the major scholarly Africanist periodicals from around the world and also devotes significant attention to some of the less well known African publications; therefore, one will find reference to the contents of journals not normally indexed in the standard services (e.g., *Classic, Phylon, Journal of the New African Literature and the Arts*) along with several standard titles. Although extending back to the beginning of this century, the entries focus primarily on 1960–1970 and so are relatively up-to-date; furthermore, data has been gleaned not only from LC holdings but also from a number of additional sources (e.g., CARDAN, IAI) and so has a genuinely international flavor. An alphabetical listing at the beginning of volume 1 indicates that coverage of African/South African literature occurs under both Africa-General (vol. 1, pp. 204–12, 219–20) and South Africa (vol. 4, pp. 20–22). In both locations one will find a wealth of material relevant to South African fiction, including socio-political analysis and critiques of individual writers. There is in addition an index to literary works by form in volume 4 (pp. 643–744), but the novel naturally figures insignificantly in this section, since one can hardly expect to find entire novels reproduced in periodicals. Nevertheless, for all other purposes the student of South African fiction will have to begin his retrospective search for periodical citations in this compilation, since it is the most comprehensive guide yet available.

Asamani's *Index Africanus* is a much less ambitious project than the Library of Congress publication, although it does cover a wider time span (1885–1965) and contains more than 26,000 numbered entries. The information included, however, is limited to some 230 periodical titles in contrast to the 1,530 journals in the LC index. Furthermore, the citations in Asamani are limited primarily (but not exclusively) to SOAS holdings and so reflect the particular strengths and weaknesses of that library; for the student of South African literature such publications as *Lloyd's Bank Review, English Historical Review* or the *Yorkshire Bulletin of Economic and Social Research* will hold little interest; indeed, coverage of titles with a primary literary interest is rather limited, *Présence Africaine, Transition* and *Black Orpheus* being the major literary periodicals indexed by Asamani. The entries are arranged by subject and by region (subdivided by subject); pages 59–62 (nos. 3267–3482) cover literature, literary criticism and literature in English generally, while pages 418–19 (nos. 22, 812–22, 907) cover South African English literature in particular. In these pages the emphasis is primarily on creative writing in the journals noted above, along with some literary criticism and scholarly analysis. Considering the acclaim which *Index Africanus* received on its publication in 1975, it must be regarded as something of a letdown in terms of South African fiction, for it is neither as full nor as current as the earlier *Africa South of the Sahara.* For the one or two citations on South Africa not found in the LC volumes Asamani is not really worth the effort, and it certainly does not warrant the additional expense of acquisition ($25) by a library able to acquire the LC publication.

The major additions to information provided by *Africa South of the Sahara* are to be culled from serial indices of Africana periodical literature, one of which is the *Index to South African Periodicals.*[26] Published annually by the Johannesburg Public Library, this is a general guide to the contents of approximately 300 South African journals, including the better known scholarly periodicals (e.g., *English Studies in Africa*) but few of the smaller magazines devoted to the dissemination of creative writing by new South African authors. Nevertheless, this is the best indigenous attempt to cover material from the Republic and is relatively up-to-date both in terms of citations included and frequency of issue. Material is arranged in a combined dictionary sequence of authors and subjects (using the LC classification), and each annual issue will require consultation in order to update information from South African sources covered by *Africa South of the Sahara* up to 1970.

The other two important indexing serials, *A Current Bibliography on African Affairs* and the *International African Bibliography,* have been treated in Chapter Three, which should be consulted for general remarks on their format and coverage.[27] As indices of periodical literature with a bearing on South African fiction, these two publications are of unequal value. In *Current Bibliography* one finds reference to articles in selected Africanist journals (e.g., *Journal of Modern African Studies, Journal of African Studies, African Studies Review* and *Issue*) which deal occasionally with literary topics. In addition certain literary journals are also regularly covered (*Transition, Journal of Commonwealth Literature*), thereby providing a balanced but limited insight into serial articles with some bearing on South African literature. Material is retrieved under literature rather than in the regional section, which is entirely socio-political, and there is no list of periodicals indexed in a given issue.

IAB, on the other hand, frequently includes a list of periodicals indexed, and many of these have particular relevance to South African fiction.[28] It appears that the periodicals of some literary interest are better represented in *IAB* than in its sister publication, and for this reason one will want to consult each issue of the *International African Bibliography* as it appears, again concentrating on the general subject section rather than the regional listing, since the latter once more is primarily devoted to the social sciences. This does not mean that *Current Bibliography* may be ignored, for a comparison of this with *IAB* for 1976 shows that both are equally likely to cite articles on South African literature and without a great deal of duplication.

Finally, one will occasionally come across guides to papers or reports sponsored by specific bodies, and some of these also have a bearing on South African literature. The best example of this type of compilation is Dickman's *Abstract/Index to A.S.A. Annual Meeting Papers*, which contains chronologically arranged abstracts of these papers supplemented by subject and author indices.[29] This is a particularly worthwhile index to papers which otherwise would escape one's attention (e.g., John F. Povey, "The Political Theme in South and West African Novels," and Wandile F. Kuse, "The Social Relevance of the South African Novel"). The *IAB*, of course, also indexes papers in collected volumes, which is slightly different from Dickman's concentration, and one will want to watch for future compilations of the latter type.

In spite of the general usefulness of all the periodical indices cited in the preceding pages, Witherell's 1971 observation that ". . . few periodicals on Africa are indexed in the principal serial guides, and information on their contents is elusive"[30] remains true. Because of this, the scholar or librarian pursuing research in South African fiction will have to consult the serial guides with a particular focus on this genre and which are treated in Chapter Seven. As general references, however, several of the preceding indices cannot be overlooked and belong in every library with an interest in the English South African novel: the *Humanities Index, British Humanities Index,* MLA's *International Bibliography, Africa South of the Sahara, Index to South African Periodicals, Current Bibliography* and *International African*

Bibliography. Of the periodical lists discussed in Part A, de Benko's *Research Sources for African Studies,* LC's *Sub-Saharan Africa, Current South African Periodicals,* Birkos and Tambs's *African and Black American Studies* and Zell's *Reader's Guide to African Literature* belong in every library alongside the periodical indices.

Notes

1. For a brief history of the modern recording of African periodicals see Carole Travis, "Recording African Periodicals," unpublished paper presented at the SCOLMA Conference on Progress in African Bibliography, Commonwealth Institute, London, March 17–18, 1977, pp. 1–3.

2. Helen Conover, comp., *Serials for African Studies* (Washington, D.C.: Library of Congress, General Reference and Bibliography Division, Reference Department, 1961).

3. Peter Duignan and Kenneth M. Glazier, *A Checklist of Serials for African Studies Based on the Libraries of the Hoover Institution and Stanford University* (Hoover Institution Bibliographical Series, 13. Stanford, California: Hoover Institution on War, Revolution and Peace, 1963).

4. Eugene de Benko and Patricia L. Butts, *Research Sources for African Studies: A Checklist of Relevant Serial Publications Based on Library Collections at Michigan State University* (East Lansing: Michigan State University, African Studies Center, 1969).

5. Hans E. Panofsky and Robert Koester, "African Newspapers and Periodicals," in *The African Experience. Vol. IIIB: Guide to Resources,* edited by John N. Paden and Edward Soja (Evanston, Illinois: Northwestern University Press, 1970), pp. 33–35.

6. U.S., Library of Congress, African Section, *Sub-Saharan Africa: A Guide to Serials* (Washington, D.C.: Library of Congress, 1970).

7. African Bibliographic Center, *Periodicals for Pan-African Studies: A Selected and Current Guide to Resources* (Current Reading List Series, vol. 8, no. 1. Washington, D.C.: African Bibliographic Center, 1971).

8. Alexander S. Birkos and Lewis A. Tambs, eds., *African and Black American Studies* (Vol. 3 of *Academic Writer's Guide to Periodicals.* Littleton, Colorado: Libraries Unlimited, 1975).

9. Standing Conference on Library Materials on Africa, *Periodicals from Africa: A Bibliography and Union List of Periodicals Published in Africa,* compiled by Carole Travis and Miriam Alman; edited by Carole Travis (Bibliographies and Guides in African Studies, James C. Armstrong, advisory ed. Boston: G. K. Hall, 1977).

10. *Ibid.,* p. ix.

11. For a full critique of this publication see G. E. Gorman and M. H. Rogers, "Review of SCOLMA, *Periodicals from Africa,*" *African Research and Documentation* (forthcoming).

12. Maison des Sciences de l'Homme, Service d'Echange d'Informations Scientifiques, *World List of Specialized Periodicals: African Studies* (Publications

Serie C: Catalogues et Inventaires III. Paris: Mouton, 1969); Standing Conference on Library Materials on Africa, "Periodicals Published in Africa, Parts 1–10," *Library Materials on Africa*, vols. 3–7 (1965–1970), supplements; V. T. H. Parry, *African Periodicals in the Library of the British Museum (Natural History)* (London: SCOLMA, 1974).

13. South Africa, South African Council for Scientific and Industrial Research, *Periodicals in South African Libraries: A Revised Edition of the Catalogue of Union Periodicals* (Pretoria: South African Council for Scientific and Industrial Research, 1961–   ); *African Book Publishing Record* (Oxford: Hans Zell (Publishers), 1975–   ; quarterly).

14. Percy Freer, ed., *Catalogue of Union Periodicals* (Johannesburg: National Research Council and National Research Board, 1943–1952, supplement for 1949–1953).

15. South Africa, State Library, *Current South African Periodicals: A Classified List, July 1965* (Pretoria: State Library, 1966); there have been annual supplements for 1967–1971, and a revision of the entire series is due to appear in 1977.

16. One example of these general guides of the 1960's may be found in R. D. Hamner, comp., "Literary Periodicals in World-English (Commonwealth and Former Commonwealth Countries): A Selective Checklist," *W.L.W.E. Newsletter*, 14 (1968), supplement.

17. Hans M. Zell and Helene Silver, eds., *A Reader's Guide to African Literature* (New York: Africana, 1971; London: Heinemann, 1972).

18. Donald H. Simpson, "Commonwealth Literary Periodicals," unpublished paper presented at the Conference on Library Holdings of Commonwealth Literature, Commonwealth Institute, London, 5 June 1970; cf. Ronald Warwick, "Literary Periodicals of the Commonwealth," *Royal Commonwealth Society Library Notes*, n.s., no. 219: 1–2.

19. Rachelle Lever, *Little Magazines in South Africa Since 1945: A Bibliography* (Johannesburg: University of the Witwatersrand, Department of Bibliography, Librarianship and Typography, 1973).

20. *Readers' Guide to Periodical Literature: An Author Subject Index to Selected General Interest Periodicals of Reference Value in Libraries* (New York: H. W. Wilson, 1900–   ; bi-weekly and monthly with quarterly and annual cumulations); *Humanities Index* (New York: H. W. Wilson, 1967–   ; quarterly with annual cumulations, previously titled *International Index* for 1907–1965 and *Social Sciences and Humanities Index* for 1965–1974); *British Humanities Index* (London: Library Association, 1962–   ; quarterly with annual cumulations, supersedes *Subject Index to Periodicals*, 1915–1961).

21. Among the titles indexed those with a literary/Africanist emphasis include *African Literature Today, Ariel, Books Abroad, Comparative Literature, Comparative Literature Studies, Criticism, Critique, Daedalus, English Literature in Transition, Essays in Criticism, Journal of Modern Literature, Literary Review, Modern Fiction Studies, New Literary History, Novel, Research in African Literatures, Review of English Studies, Southern Literary Journal, Southern Review, Studies in Black Literature, Studies in English Literature, Studies in the Novel, Symposium, Twentieth Century Literature*.

22. The periodicals indexed in *BHI* include *Africa, African Affairs, Essays in*

Criticism, *Journal of Commonwealth Literature, Journal of Modern African Studies, Journal of Southern African Studies, Review of English Studies.*

23. *Internationale Bibliographie der Zeitschriftenliteratur aus allen Gebeiten des Wissens* (Osnabrück, West Germany: Felix Dietrich Verlag, n.s., 1965– ; twelve volumes per annum).

24. See above, pp. 103–04 and note 13, p. 111.

25. U.S., Library of Congress, Reference Department, General Reference and Bibliography Division, African Section, comp., *Africa South of the Sahara: Index to Periodical Literature, 1900–1970* (4 vols.; Boston: G. K. Hall, 1971); there are also two supplements, one published in 1973 for 1971–1972 material and the other due for release in 1978; J. O. Asamani, *Index Africanus* (Hoover Institution Bibliographies, 53. Stanford, California: Stanford University, Hoover Institution, 1975).

26. Johannesburg Public Library, *Index to South African Periodicals* (Johannesburg: Johannesburg Public Library, 1940– ; annual with ten-year cumulations for 1940–1949, 1950–1959).

27. See above, pp. 105–06 and note 17, p. 111.

28. The primary list appears in vol. 3(4): 103–14 with supplements in vol. 4(4): 111–13, vol. 5(4): 111–13, vol. 6(4): 113–15. Periodicals indexed include both the major Africanist publications (e.g., *African Studies Review*) and a significant number of general literary and Africana literary titles (*Ariel, Black Orpheus, Contrast, Critique, Theoria*).

29. Daryl Dickman, comp., *Abstract/Index to A.S.A. Annual Meeting Papers, 1960–1974* (Waltham, Massachusetts: African Studies Association, 1976); cf. O. H. Spohr, "Recent Indexes to Africana Books," *South African Libraries*, 37 (1969): 29–31, which is a supplement to his *Indexes to African Books* (Cape Town: the author, 1967).

30. Julian W. Witherell, foreword to *Africa South of the Sahara, op. cit.*, p. iii. A revisionist view of this situation is provided by Yvette Scheven, "Africana in the Indexes," *History in Africa*, 4 (1977): 207–27.

Appendix

An Annotated List of Selected Africana and Literary Serials

The purpose of this appendix is to list a selection of those journals which devote some coverage to South African creative writing; it includes publications which cater to this field either through scholarly articles, examples of creative work by South African novelists, bibliographies or book reviews. These broad categories have been adopted in order to incorporate both the general scholarly titles as well as those devoted solely to African literature; in this way one hopes to cover the general Africanist periodicals which either should be perused for relevant articles or which, in spite of an avowed interest in the field, appear not to include South African writing within their scope. There is, of course, always the possibility of a reorientation in editorial policy which might suddenly bring this field within the range of a given title. Therefore, the annotations herein must be read with this eventuality in mind.

Due to the limitations of time, space and readily available materials, coverage in this appendix is highly eclectic. In general, titles which, in the course of their existence, have included only one or two relevant articles are excluded (e.g., *Journal of Commonwealth and Comparative Politics*). Furthermore, since the purpose of this listing is to offer some insight into the comparative value of each journal's coverage, many potentially relevant publications not available in Britain and therefore not personally examined are necessarily excluded. This is particularly telling in the case of certain titles from within the Republic (e.g., *Standpunte, Trek, Zonk*); however, there is perhaps some justification for this exclusion on the grounds that unavailability suggests a limited scholarly value, although this is certainly open to disagreement. In addition, since the intention is to list *current* titles, defunct serials are not listed; for coverage of these one will want to turn to the periodical lists discussed in the preceding pages. An important source of information on serials not included in this appendix is Christiane Keane's 1975 F.L.A. thesis, "Commonwealth Literature 1974–1975: A Guide to Sources" (see appendix to Chapter Six). Finally, most newsletters and bulletins of scholarly associations, unless they contain a reasonable percentage of essays or bibliographical material as opposed to information and notes on professional activities, are not treated here but receive some analysis in Chapter Eight, which deals with the various professional/scholarly organizations and their activities.

Each entry includes the date of inception and the most recent publisher or editorial address, but it has not been possible to note the subscription cost, since this varies with alarming frequency. In no case has there been any attempt to provide full bibliographical details, particularly in terms of changes in title, frequency of publication or publisher. Emphasis is entirely on the most current information, as it is this rather than retrospective bibliographical data which most investigators lack. In addition notes on the Africanist literary serials are intended to indicate the type of coverage which they offer (e.g., bibliographies, scholarly essays, reviews, conference proceedings). In this way it is hoped that librarians and researchers will have some indication of the titles most likely to suit their particular needs. An asterisk indicates those titles which provide significant coverage of South African fiction.

Abbia
No. 1–   ; 1963–   , quarterly.
Editions C.L.E., B.P. 4048, Yaoundé, Cameroun

A bilingual journal widely recognized as an important source of scholarly articles on African literature, its contents in fact reveal a primary focus on West African writing. In the past five years there has been only one article of even marginal relevance to South African writing (i.e., Laura Tanna, "African Literature and Its Western Critics" in no. 27/28, pp. 53–63). Therefore, it may be disregarded by the South Africanist.

Africa Current

No. 1–   ; 1975–   , quarterly.
Africa Publishing Trust, 48 Grafton Way, London W1P 5LB, England

The successor to *Africa Digest,* this is largely a socio-political journal with a strong interest in current affairs. It does, however, contain occasional brief news items on literary activities; the February and June issues in 1975, for example, reported on the formation of the Union of Writers of African Peoples. Since this sort of data is often available in more scholarly journals, *Africa Current* is of only marginal interest and need not be consulted unless readily available.

Africa Report

Vol. 1–   ; 1956–   , bi-monthly. Sponsored by the African-American Institute.
833 United Nations Plaza, New York, New York 10017

Like the preceding title, this is an unrestricted, current events journal which in the past has included literature within its frame of reference. Thus in vols. 7(9), 9(7), 11(9) and 13(5) one will find articles on African literature. These are not scholarly in nature and appear with greater infrequency in succeeding volumes. In depth book reviews are sometimes useful from a "popular" standpoint, but in general coverage is no better than that of *Africa Current.*

Africa Today

Vol. 1–   ; 1954–   , quarterly.
Graduate School of International Relations, University of Denver,
University Park Campus, Denver, Colorado 80210

More scholarly than either *Africa Current* or *Africa Report,* this is a general Africanist periodical which includes literary history and criticism in its coverage. There are occasional bibliographical articles and reviews relevant to South African fiction, but since 1968 (i.e., Bernth Lindfors' "Robin Hood Realism in South African English Fiction" in vol. 15, 4: 16–18), there has been little content of a scholarly nature to attract the South Africanist. Should this trend continue, one will prefer to scan other journals of this type noted below.

African Affairs: Journal of the Royal African Society
Vol. 1–   ; 1901–   , quarterly.
Royal African Society, 18 Northumberland Avenue, London WC2N 5BJ, England

Like *Africa Today*, this title has not carried articles of value to literary studies for several years (1972). In its general coverage *African Affairs* includes the occasional literary book review; this information, however, may be gleaned more readily from literary journals, which means that one need not regularly read the review section of *African Affairs*.

African Arts
Vol. 1–   ; 1967–   , quarterly.
African Studies Center, University of California, Los Angeles, California 90024

With this title and an editor (John Povey) whose interest in African literature is well known, one might expect the literary coverage to be substantial. In fact, however, *African Arts* is fast becoming a glossy arts magazine primarily interested in the graphic and performing aspects of artistic creativity. Thus there have been very few articles on literature with the exception of a 1968 piece entitled "Writers in Exile: South Africans in London" (vol. 1, no. 4: 19–25), although the book review section often reports on material from or about South Africa and its literature, and this factor may warrant one's occasional perusal of *African Arts*.

*African Book Publishing Record**
Vol. 1–   ; 1975–   , quarterly.
Hans Zell (Publishers), P.O. Box 56, Oxford OX1 3EL, England

Although primarily a bibliographical journal (see pages 107–08), *ABPR* also includes occasional reports and articles with a bearing on African or South African literature (e.g., Peter Randall's " 'Minority' Publishing in South Africa" in vol. 1: 219–22). For this reason and the increasingly comprehensive bibliographical coverage of indigenous publishing, this journal should be consulted frequently.

*African Literature Today: A Journal of Explanatory Criticism**
No. 1–   ; 1968–   , annual (biennial?).
Heinemann Educational Books, 48 Charles Street, London W.1, England

From 1964 to 1967 this was the *Bulletin of the Association for African Literature in English*; now appearing every two years, each issue focuses on a particular genre (e.g., no. 5 on the novel, no. 7 on criticism). Although primarily West African in orientation, there is the occasional article relevant to South African writing. To date, for example, there have been stimulating contributions by Ernest Emenyonu in no. 5 ("African Literature: What Does It Take To Be Its Critic?," pp. 1–11), D. S. Izevbaye in no. 7 ("The State of Criticism in African Literature," pp. 1–19) and Solomon Ogbede Iyasere in no. 7 ("African Critics on African Literature: A Study in Misplaced Hostility," pp. 20–27). In addition, there are frequent bibliographies of creative writing and literary criticism, those in numbers 1–4 having been compiled by Hans Zell. Because of this and its importance as a vehicle for critical articles by African scholars, one will find it essential to consult future annual issues of *African Literature Today*.

African Research and Documentation
No. 1–   ; 1973–   , trimestral. Jointly sponsored by SCOLMA and the African Studies Association (U.K.).
Centre of West African Studies, University of Birmingham, P.O. Box 363, Birmingham B13 9SA, England

Although concentrating primarily on research in progress and notes on professional activities, *ARD* also includes bibliographical articles (e.g., Reuben Musiker's "South African Bibliographical Notes and News, April 1976: A Checklist of Recent Bibliographies, Articles, Developments and Surveys on Bibliographical Themes, Arranged by Catchword" in no. 11:28–32) and substantial book reviews with some indirect bearing on the South African literary scene. In general, however, this publication has no special value for literary studies. An index to the contents of the first ten issues will appear in 1977.

African Studies: A Quarterly Journal Devoted to the Study of African Anthropology, Government and Languages
Vol. 1–   ; 1941–   , semi-annual.
Witwatersrand University Press, 1 Jan Smuts Avenue, Johannesburg, 2001 South Africa

The successor to *Bantu Studies*, this journal is not often cited with its subtitle, which of course clearly indicates that it focuses primarily on the social sciences. The literary content of *African Studies* deals for the most part with oral literature, and this plus the infrequency of reviews relevant to South African literature means that one need not consult this publication.

African Studies Review
Vol. 1–   ; 1962–   , trimestral. Sponsored by the African Studies Association (U.S.).
African Studies Association, Epstein Service Building, Brandeis University, Waltham, Massachusetts 02154

Formerly the *African Studies Bulletin*, this is a general Africanist periodical which includes literature in its coverage. Rand Bishop has editorial responsibility for this subject, and there is the occasional essay or bibliographical article relevant to South African fiction (e.g., Nancy J. Schmidt's "Something Old, Something New: Recent Studies of African Literature" in vol. 18, no. 2: 129–33). There are also in-depth book reviews catering at times to the literary researcher, and this type of coverage makes the *Review* well worth consulting for material on South African literature.

Africana Journal: A Bibliographic and Review Quarterly*
Vol. 1–   ; 1970–   , quarterly.
Africana Publishing Company, 101 Fifth Avenue, New York, New York 10003

As the subtitle and its earlier name (*Africana Library Journal*) suggest, this is primarily a current bibliography of African studies. It includes excellent bibliographical articles (e.g., Bernth Lindfors' "Reviews of African Literature in Nigerian Periodicals" in vol. 6: 195–231), book reviews and a subject bibliography, all of which frequently direct one to publications with a bearing on South African fiction. Although slightly dated for reasons noted above on page 106, the *Journal* ought to be consulted by anyone interested in keeping abreast of recent literary studies.

Afro-American Studies: An Interdisciplinary Journal
Vol. 1–   ; 1970–   , quarterly. Sponsored by Gordon and Breach Science Publishers, 1127 Carroll Street, Brooklyn, New York 11225

This is one of the many journals devoted primarily to black American studies as opposed to African studies. Although there is an interesting emphasis on teaching in this area, very little of the material is relevant to African or South African literature and so need not claim one's attention. Similar titles dealing primarily with black American culture include *Black Academy Review, Black Creation* and *Black Images*; while their contents are not exclusively North American in orientation, they are so to the extent that it becomes extremely wasteful to spend time scanning them for the very infrequent article relevant to Africa.

Ariel: A Review of International English Literature
Vol. 1–   ; 1960–   , quarterly.
Department of English, University of Calgary, Calgary, Alberta

This is one of several literary journals with an interest in African literature but which tends to be neglected by Africanists. *Ariel* covers literature from throughout the English-speaking world, and although neither the articles nor the reviews deal more than marginally with South Africa's contribution, the presence of Ezekiel Mphahlele on the editorial board suggests that future issues of the journal may well contain fuller African coverage. *Ariel* was formerly known as the *Review of English Literature.*

ASA Review of Books
Vol. 1–   ; 1975–   , annual.
African Studies Association, Epstein Service Building, Brandeis University, Waltham, Massachusetts 02154

   More limited in the volume of its contents than many of the bibliographical/review journals, the *Review* contains enough material on South African literature to make it a marginally worthwhile publication.

Ba Shiru: A Journal of African Languages and Literature*
Vol. 1–   ; 1970–   , semi-annual.
Department of African Languages and Literature, Van Hise Hall, University of Wisconsin, Madison, Wisconsin 53706

   Written partly by and for an undergraduate/postgraduate readership, *Ba Shiru* nevertheless has contained a number of substantial and important articles on all aspects of African culture. Among those which have dealt directly with South African fiction one may cite J. Okpure Obuke's "The Structure of Commitment: A Study of Alex La Guma" in vol. 5, no. 1: 14–20 and Ezekiel Mphahlele's "South African Black Writing 1972–1973" in vol. 5, no. 2: 27–35. Work of this sort makes *Ba Shiru* an important source of material for the student of South African literature.

Black Orpheus: A Journal of African and Afro-American Literature
No. 1–   ; 1957–   , irregular (but promised semi-annually).
Sponsored by the University of Lagos.
University of Lagos Bookshop, Yaba, Lagos, Nigeria

   Although it has enjoyed a stream of highly competent editors (among them Beier, Jahn and Mphahlele) and the critical acclaim of most Africanists, *Black Orpheus* has had a rather checkered career in terms of regular publication and level of contents. It includes creative writing in its coverage, particularly criticism from contributors around the world (among them Mphahlele in vol. 2, no. 3 and Nkosi in no. 19), but by and large emphasis has been on the West African scene. Compared with such efforts as *Transition,* one must say that this is not a title of significance in South African literary studies.

Black Review
1972–   , annual.
Black Community Programmes, 86 Beatrice Street, Durban, South Africa
   Not a scholarly publication by any definition, this is an annual review
of events and trends among the black South African population and
is intended basically to inform this section of the populace of what has
been taking place. It includes a retrospective review of the arts and
entertainment and as such may be somewhat useful for background
information on the literary scene.

Books Abroad: An International Library Quarterly
Vol. 1–   ; 1927–   .
University of Oklahoma Press, Norman, Oklahoma 73069
   Like the Africana Journal, this is primarily a professional journal
which includes critical essays, notes and information and frequent
reviews of South African fiction and literary criticism, as well as more
general essays (e.g., "On African Writing" in vol. 44, no. 3). Each
number carries a review section entitled "World Literature in Review,"
which within the English literature or African sections contains the occasional annotated entry on South African creative writing or criticism.
Scholarly publishing is a particular interest, and from this standpoint
Books Abroad may be of indirect value to South African fiction.

Canadian Journal of African Studies
Vol. 1–   ; 1967–   , trimestral.
Canadian Association of African Studies, Department of Geography,
Carleton University, Ottawa K15 5B6, Ontario
   Comparable to the African Studies Review, CJAS has G. D. Killam
as one of the joint editors and includes critical essays, review articles
and book reviews with some South African literary content. By and
large, however, coverage is devoted to Africa in general, and most of
the articles are therefore only marginally of use to the student of South
African fiction (e.g., Omafume F. Onge's "The Crisis of Consciousness
in Modern African Literature" in vol. 8, no. 2: 385–410). There is
an index to the contents of vols. 1–7 (1967–1973).

Ch'indaba*
No. 1–No. 50, Vol. 1–   ; 1961–1975, 1975–   , quarterly.
Transition, P.O. Box 9063, Accra, Ghana
   Until 1975 Ch'indaba was known as Transition and under that title
developed a reputation as an outspoken politico-cultural review. Important as a radical forum for free discussion of the arts, literature,
society and politics, it is widely regarded as the English language

counterpart of *Présence Africaine.* In the past a special feature has been literary interviews with new and established African writers, and one expects that under the editorial guidance of Wole Soyinka this type of coverage will continue. As a vehicle for general information and commentary on African cultural life, it is an important title for those interested in South African literary activity as it relates to the rest of the continent.

Conch: A Sociological Journal of African Cultures and Literatures
Vol. 1–   ; 1969–   , semi-annual.
Conch Magazine (Publishers), 102 Normal Avenue, Buffalo, New York 14213
For some years *Conch* enjoyed the editorial advice of Gerald Moore and since its founding has devoted much space to African literature. Unfortunately, most of the articles are general literary criticism (e.g., Lloyd W. Brown's "American Image in African Literature" in vol. 4, no. 1: 55–70), which at best provides only background information on South African fiction.

Conch Review of Books: A Literary Supplement on Africa
Vol. 1–   ; 1973–   , quarterly supplement to *Conch.*
Conch Magazine (Publishers), Department of African Studies,
State University of New York, New Paltz, New York 12561
Dealing only with the literary aspect of African studies, this supplement has included some excellent book reviews and general review essays (e.g., Nancy J. Schmidt's "Selective Introductions to African Literature" in vol. 1, no. 1: 6–12) but again is somewhat weak on specifically South African material.

*Contrast: South African Literary Journal**
Vol. 1–   ; 1960–   , quarterly/trimestral.
P.O. Box 3841, Claremont, Cape Town, South Africa
Edited by Jack Cope, this is a South African literary magazine covering the entire range of creative writing: essays, fiction, poetry, book reviews. As one of the few publications of this type emanating from the Republic, it deserves wider circulation in the West, particularly since the reviews and essays frequently deal with indigenous novels.

Critique: Revue Générale des Publications Françaises et Etrangères
Vol. 1–   ; 1946–   , monthly.
Editions de Minuit, 7 Rue Bernard Palissy, 75006 Paris, France
Often cited as an international review of comparative literary studies and therefore thought to be relevant to African literature, *Critique*

in fact concentrates on the Orient and Latin America in terms of its non-European thrust. Therefore, it need not be consulted for articles on South African fiction.

Critique: Studies in Modern Fiction
Vol. 1–   ; 1956–   , trimestral.
Department of English, Georgia Institute of Technology, Atlanta, Georgia 30332

An editorial note informs one that "particular consideration will be given to critical essays on the fiction of writers from any country who are alive and without great reputation," and on the basis of this one might expect to find articles on a number of South African writers. In recent issues, however, only Doris Lessing has been discussed in this category (Barbara F. Lefcowitz's "Dream and Action in Lessing's *Summer Before the Dark*" in vol. 17, no. 2: 107–20). While this belies to some extent the editorial promise, one may still want to consult future issues of *Critique* for possible essays on other South African novelists.

*Current Bibliography on African Affairs**
Vol. 1 (n.s.)–   ; 1968–   , quarterly. Original series published from 1962–1967.
African Bibliographic Center, P.O. Box 13096, Washington, D.C. 20009

Although primarily a bibliographical journal, *Current Bibliography* also includes feature articles and book reviews; while the former do not often deal with literature, these essays can occasionally have in-direct relevance to the study of South African fiction (e.g., Maduka W. Anyakoha's "Publishing in Africa: A Bibliography" in vol. 8, no. 4: 296–319). More valuable is the book review section, which frequently discusses titles of interest to the student of creative writing; for example, Steven Kallish's "African Literary Themes" in vol. 8, no. 4: 383–85 mentions both no. 7 of *African Literature Today* and Dathorne's *The Black Mind*. These reviews plus the occasional mention of South African novels in the bibliographical section make *Current Bibliography* an important source of information.

Drum
1952–   , monthly.
Drum Publications (U.K.), 40–43 Fleet Street, London E.C.4, England

A popular "tabloid" format magazine with separate editions for East, Central and Southern Africa, *Drum* contains occasional reviews and articles on creative writing. However, the limited coverage of South African fiction and the generally superficial quality of most of the pieces give this magazine a limited use.

English in Africa*
Vol. 1–   ; 1974–   , semi-annual.
Institute for the Study of English in Africa, Rhodes University,
Grahamstown, 6140 South Africa

Much less well known than the following title, this is an important publication issued by ISEA, itself one of the more ambitious projects in the area of African literature. Appearing only twice yearly, *English in Africa* carries frequent articles and reports relevant to the study of South African fiction (e.g., Irina Winterbottom's "Towards a Bibliography of South African Literature in English" in vol. 3, no. 1: 49–52). It thus deserves a wider audience among students of this genre and should be consulted frequently by those anxious to keep abreast of developments in the field.

English Studies in Africa
Vol. 1–   ; 1958–   , semi-annual.
Witwatersrand University Press, 1 Jan Smuts Avenue,
Johannesburg, South Africa

Widely regarded as the premier scholarly journal devoted to English literature from within South Africa, *ESA* in fact deals with English *studies* in general. This means that it treats all aspects of English literature from around the world rather than only South African literature in English. Indeed, specifically South African contributions are dealt with rather less than Chaucer, Shakespeare, *et al.* However, there are occasional articles on the Republic's contribution to creative writing and an annual survey entitled "Select Bibliography: Books and Articles on English Language and Literature Published in South Africa." Both the essays and bibliographies may be of passing interest to the student of South African English fiction.

Issue: A Quarterly Journal of Africanist Opinion
Vol. 1–   ; 1972–   , quarterly.
African Studies Association, Epstein Service Building,
Brandeis University, Waltham, Massachusetts 02154

Containing articles of a more controversial nature than those in the ASA's sister publication, *African Studies Review,* one finds that the primary emphasis of material in *Issue* is on matters of political interest. There are, however, occasional articles on African literature, but to date none of these has dealt primarily with South African fiction. A useful recent article in vol. 6, no. 1 ("Proceedings of the Symposium on Contemporary African Literature and the First African Literature Association Conference") is typical of the general coverage afforded to African literature.

*Journal of Commonwealth Literature**
Vol. 1–   ; 1965–   , trimestral. Published by Oxford University Press for ACLALS.
School of English, University of Leeds, Leeds LS2 9JT, England

Together with *Research in African Literatures, JCL* is one of the indispensable serials for the study of South African fiction. As the journal of the Association for Commonwealth Literature and Language Studies, the emphasis on South Africa has fluctuated in relation to that country's tenuous Commonwealth affiliation. Before 1970, for example, South Africa did not feature in the annual bibliographical review but in that year began to appear as an appendix and since then has remained in that position. Nevertheless, this bibliographical survey is the only one of its kind devoted to Republican literature and so is of inestimable value. In addition, scholarly articles on South African fiction are appearing with increasing frequency in the non-bibliographical issues of *JCL*. Volume 11, for instance, carried two contributions with a clear South African focus (N. W. Visser's "South Africa: The Renaissance That Failed," pp. 42–57, and Eric Harber's "South Africa: The White English-Speaking Sensibility," pp. 57–71). For contributions such as these and the annual bibliographical survey it is fair to say that *JCL* is an absolutely essential source of information on the South African novel.

Journal of Modern African Studies: A Quarterly Survey of Politics, Economics and Related Topics in Contemporary Africa
Vol. 1–   ; 1963–   , quarterly.
Cambridge University Press, P.O. Box 92, London NW1 2DB, England

One should not be misled by the subtitle of this journal, for it in fact deals more than occasionally with African literature both in the essay and review sections. South Africa itself receives no special treatment, but the reviews and articles often have an indirect bearing on the Republic (e.g., Solomon O. Iyasere's "Cultural Formalism and the Criticism of Modern African Literature" in vol. 14, no. 2: 322–30 and Alain Ricard's review of Miss Gordimer's *The Black Interpreters* in vol. 14, no. 1: 179). Therefore, *JMAS* is one of the more important general Africanist periodicals in the area of African literature.

Journal of Southern African Affairs: An Interdisciplinary Research Quarterly
Vol. 1–   ; 1976–   .
Southern African Research Association, Room 4133, Art/Sociology Building, University of Maryland, College Park, Maryland 20742

Sponsored jointly by SARA and Afro-American Studies at the University of Maryland, the *Journal* focuses primarily on socio-political affairs but also exhibits a partial interest in the cultural life of Southern Africa. Thus in vol. 2 (pp. 121–29) there appears an article by Bernth Lindfors, "Popular Literature in English in Black South Africa," which suggests that future issues of this periodical may contain material of value for students of literature.

Journal of Southern African Studies
Vol. 1–   ; 1974–   , semi-annual.
Oxford University Press, Press Road, Neasden, London NW10 0DD, England

Like the preceding serial, this is another general Africanist title with a special focus on that part of Africa which includes the Republic. Therefore, one might expect any literary articles to deal more specifically with South Africa, and this is precisely the case, although relevant items do not appear in every issue. Michael Wade's "Myth, Truth and the South African Reality in the Fiction of Sarah Gertrude Millin" (vol. 1, no. 1: 91–108) and Nadine Gordimer's "English-Language Literature and Politics in South Africa" (vol. 2, no. 2: 131–50) are indicative of the type of material which makes *JSAS* one of the more fruitfully consulted general Africanist periodicals. Unfortunately, the review section does not warrant the same consideration, since only rarely does one find mention of a novel or scholarly literary treatise on South Africa.

Journal of the New African Literature and the Arts*
No. 1–   ; 1966–   , quarterly.
The Third Press, 444 Central Park West, New York, New York 10025

As the title suggests, this publication covers the African arts *in toto* but literature in particular; both essays and reviews deal with creative writing, criticism and scholarly analysis. While many of the articles are only indirectly of value for South African fiction, a number of them treat this genre in particular (e.g., J. M. Coetzee's "Alex La Guma and Responsibilities of the South African Writer" in no. 9/10: 5–11, John Povey's "Profile of an African Artist: Dennis Brutus" in no. 3: 95–100 and Bernth Lindfors' "Form and Technique in the Novels of Richard Rive and Alex La Guma" in no. 2: 10–15). For this reason *New African Literature* is an important specialist journal requiring frequent consultation, although recent issues have exhibited a declining coverage of South Africa.

Literary Review
Vol. 1–   ; 1957–   , quarterly.
Fairleigh Dickinson University, Teaneck, New Jersey 07666

Another example of a university literary journal from America, the *Review* is only marginally interested in African literature. In 1969 vol. 11, no. 4 was devoted entirely to African writing, but since then very few essays have dealt with fiction in Africa. Therefore, it is much less important than, for example, the University of Wisconsin's *Ba Shiru*.

Literature East and West
Vol. 1–   ; 1954–   , quarterly.
Box 8107, University Station, Austin, Texas 78912

This is the journal of the MLA's Oriental-Western Literary Relations Group, and each issue tends to be devoted to a specific area. Mainly Eastern in emphasis, only vol. 12, no. 1 in 1968 has dealt specifically with African literature.

Lotus: Afro-Asian Writings
No. 1–   ; 1967–   , quarterly. Previously titled *Afro-Asian Writings*.
Permanent Bureau of Afro-Asian Writers, 104 Kasr el-Aini Street,
Cairo, Egypt

Covering all aspects of Afro-Asian literature, *Lotus* has featured the occasional article on Africa (e.g., "Special Section on South Africa" in no. 12: 144–79). In general, however, this journal is concerned primarily with documenting the various movements encompassing Afro-Asian writers and so has limited scholarly value.

Modern Fiction Studies
Vol. 1–   ; 1955–   , quarterly.
Department of English, Purdue University, Lafayette, Indiana 47907

Devoted solely to European and American fiction, this periodical need not be consulted for articles or reviews on South African literature.

Munger Africana Library Notes
Vol. 1–   ; 1970–   , trimestral.
Munger Africana Library, California Institute of Technology,
Pasadena, California 91125

With each issue devoted to a single essay, the coverage of literature in *Notes* tends to be highly eclectic. Although as yet there has been no special attention to modern South African fiction, past articles indicate that this subject may well be within the journal's frame of reference (e.g., Stephen Gray's "Sources of the First Black South African Novel in English: Solomon Plaatje's Use of Shakespeare and Bunyan in *Mhudi*" in no. 37). There is also some bibliographical coverage, which may indicate future usefulness of *Notes* in this area as well (e.g., no. 33, which contains a bibliography of Polish Africana since 1960).

New Classic*
No. 1–   ; 1975–   , quarterly. Previously titled *The Classic.*
Ravan Press, P.O. Box 31134, Braamfontein, 2017 South Africa

A resuscitation of *The Classic,* which began in the 1960's as a literary magazine geared primarily to assisting black South African writers, *New Classic* should be a useful repository of poetry, short stories and critical essays by and about black writers. On the basis of its predecessor's excellence it is fair to say that *New Classic* may well be the most important indigenous black publication relevant to the South African novel.

New Nation: The South African Review of Opinion and Fact
Vol. 1–   ; 1967–   , monthly.
New Nation Publications, P.O. Box 242, Grahamstown, South Africa

Edited by a group of liberal intellectuals (including Stephen Gray), *New Nation* focuses primarily on current affairs and cultural life but with some attention to creative writing. There have been interviews with prominent writers, Nadine Gordimer included, as well as the occasional brief article on a given author (e.g., Peter Wilhelm's "Remembering William Plomer" in vol. 7, no. 2: 1–2); in general the pieces are journalistic rather than scholarly.

Phylon: The Atlanta University Review of Race and Culture
Vol. 1–   ; 1940–   , quarterly.
Atlanta University, 223 Chestnut Street S.W., Atlanta, Georgia 30314

Phylon includes bibliographical articles as well as critical essays; its scope, however, is widely cultural and primarily American in emphasis rather than essentially literary and African. Consequently, its contents will be of little interest to the South Africanist.

Présence Africaine: Revue Culturelle du Monde Noir
No. 1–No. 16, No. 1 (n.s.)–   ; 1947–1954, 1955–   , quarterly.
18 Rue des Ecoles, 75005 Paris, France

Bilingual since 1965, *Présence Africaine* is undoubtedly a pioneer among the African cultural/literary serials; in general each issue covers all aspects of cultural life as seen from a comparative viewpoint, but occasional special issues deal only with African literature. Entries are generally by well known writers and of a consistently high standard. Essays such as Babatunde Lawal's "The Artist As a Creative Force in Education and Society" in no. 86: 173–77 indicate that *Présence Africaine* is best regarded as a provider of background studies rather than criticism of South African fiction.

Reality: A Journal of Liberal and Radical Opinion*
Vol. 1–   ; 1969–   , bi-monthly.
Reality Publications, P.O. Box 1104, Pietermaritzburg, 3200 South Africa
A general serial published in the Republic, *Reality* frequently includes material on South African writing (e.g., Nadine Gordimer's "Censorship and the Primary Homeland" in vol. 1, no. 6: 12–15, André Brink's "The Position of the Afrikaans Writer" in vol. 2, no. 1: 12–15, Colin Gardner's "Nadine's World of Strangers" in vol. 8, no. 5: 13–15). Liberal to the extent that some articles are banned before publication, it provides an interesting insight into radical literary viewpoints held by South African authors and scholars.

Research in African Literatures*
Vol. 1–   ; 1970–   , semi-annual.
Official journal of the African Literature Committee of the African Studies Association and the African Literatures Seminar of the MLA.
African and Afro-American Studies Research Center, University of Texas, P.O. Box 7457, Austin, Texas 78712

Edited by Bernth Lindfors, *RAL* is a *sine qua non* for the student of South African fiction. Although including articles of particular interest to the researcher in this area (e.g., vol. 6, no. 2), it is most useful for the book reviews, conference reports, data on current research and other professional matters. In this respect it is an important complement to the more scholarly and bibliographical coverage of the *Journal of Commonwealth Literature*.

Review of National Literatures
Vol. 1–   ; 1970–   , semi-annual.
Perboyre Hall, St. John's University, Jamaica, New York 11439
International in scope, the *Review* has occasionally dealt with African literature (e.g., vol. 2, no. 2 on black Africa edited by Albert Gérard) and so should be consulted for the odd essay of significance in South African literary studies.

Revue de Littérature Comparée
Vol. 1–   ; 1927–   , quarterly.
Libraire Marcel Didier, 15 Rue Cujas, 75005 Paris, France
Devoted to the study of comparative literature on an international basis, this periodical from time to time includes a bibliography or essay relevant to South African fiction. In 1974 an entire issue was devoted to African literature and included essays by Gerald Moore (" 'Reintegration with the Lost Self': A Theme in Contemporary Afri-

can Literature," pp. 488–503), Ernest Emenyonu ("African Literature Revisited: A Search for African Critical Standards," pp. 387–97) and others. By and large Africa is not a major concern of *RLC*, but articles of the type noted above mean that it is a journal not to be taken too lightly.

*Snarl: A Critical Review of the Arts**
Vol. 1–   ; 1974–   , quarterly.
Ravan Press, P.O. Box 31134, Braamfontein, 2017 South Africa
    Another Ravan publication, *Snarl* is slightly more scholarly than its sister journal, *New Classic*, and concentrates primarily on controversial literary criticism by both new and established writers. Including substantial book reviews, *Snarl* should be consulted frequently because of its almost exclusively South African content.

Studies in the Novel
Vol. 1–   ; 1969–   , quarterly.
North Texas State University, P.O. Box 13706, Denton, Texas 76203
    Although vol. 4, no. 2 in 1972 was devoted entirely to the Commonwealth novel, this serial focuses primarily on American and European fiction. It is, therefore, not an important title in regard to the South African novel.

Theoria: A Journal of Studies in the Arts, Humanities and Social Sciences
No. 1–   ; 1947–   , semi-annual.
University of Natal Press, P.O. Box 375, Pietermaritzburg, South Africa
    Like *Reality,* this is another general periodical from the Republic, although *Theoria* is more of a scholarly journal than its sister title. There are regular critical essays on literature, but more often than not these deal with Western writers rather than South African authors.

*Twentieth Century Literature: A Scholarly and Critical Journal**
Vol. 1–   ; 1955–   , quarterly.
Hofstra University Press, Hempstead, New York 11550
    While the scholarly essays deal only marginally with African literature, the regular bibliographical section often contains annotated entries on South African fiction. The bibliography is classified by subject and should be scanned regularly to supplement information gleaned from other bibliographical journals.

UNISA English Studies
Vol. 1–   ; 1968–   , trimestral.
Department of English, University of South Africa, Pretoria, South Africa

This university publication is concerned primarily with grammar and linguistics rather than creative writing; more directly related to literature is *UNISA*, which is the annual journal of the same university. Reputed to contain regular critical articles on South African literature, *UNISA* is not widely available in the West.

*World Literature Written in English**
Vol. 1–   ; 1962–   , semi-annual. Successor to *CBCL Newsletter,* published by English Group 12—World Literature Written in English of the MLA. Department of English, University of Texas at Arlington, Arlington, Texas 76019

Like *Research in African Literatures, WLWE* has an MLA sponsorship and includes Bernth Lindfors on its Texas-based editorial board. This particular publication, however, performs less of an information function than *RAL* and has exhibited a particularly strong interest in South African fiction. Recent articles with a South African orientation have included the following: Lloyd W. Brown's "The Shape of Things: Sexual Images and the Sense of Form in Doris Lessing's Fiction" in vol. 14: 176–86, Roberta Rubenstein's "Outer Space, Inner Space: Doris Lessing's Metaphor of Science Fiction" in vol. 14: 187–97, Michael Wade's "Apollo, Dionysius and Other Performers in Dan Jacobson's South African Circus" in vol. 13: 39–82, Valerie Carnes' " 'Chaos, That's the Point': Art as Metaphor in Doris Lessing's *The Golden Notebook*" in vol. 15: 17–28, Charles R. Larson's "Protest—the South African Way" in vol. 15: 42–45. Clearly, therefore, *WLWE* is an important source of provocative essays on South African literature, although appearing mildly obsessed with Doris Lessing, who in vol. 12: 148–206 has an entire section devoted to her work in addition to those essays cited above.

Dissertations, Theses and Research in Progress

The individual undertaking research in South African fiction, like his colleagues in other disciplines, generally expresses an interest in dissertations and theses merely to insure that someone else has not already laid claim to his own esoteric field of investigation. This limited interest reflects in part the highly variable quality to be found in such writing both in terms of content and style, as well as the fact that most theses investigate an extremely limited topic of little interest to other researchers. At the same time the scholar with more than a perfunctory interest in graduate research will quickly find his enthusiasm dampened by the dearth of readily available, suitable bibliographical guides to theses on South African literature. As a result, one will expend much time and effort in scanning a wide variety of marginally relevant material for citations of useful research. For example, the appendix to this section, which lists only seventy-one Ph.D. dissertations and M.A. theses relevant to the South African novel in English, is based on information gleaned from more than three dozen guides, many of them very difficult to locate and ultimately not worth consulting. In some ways this appendix obviates the need for others interested in the South African novel to consult these sources, yet a review of the materials may usefully indicate the breadth of coverage and also point out pitfalls to be avoided.

Theses

Bibliographies of theses (a term including both doctoral dissertations and M.A. theses) take several forms, beginning with international, multidisciplinary compilations and finishing with guides to African studies research at individual universities. In between one finds compilations covering all disciplines in two or three countries, resources limited to African studies in selected countries, national guides to academic research generally or Africana in particular and finally regional or single country bibliographies of theses on African literature. Furthermore, these compilations appear in a variety of published forms: ongoing or cumulative serial publications, serial articles, monographs, sections of larger bibliographies. In the following pages only those titles in each category which deal *specifically* with theses either in whole or in part are discussed, so the reader will also want to consult the chapter on serial publications, as some journals in their bibliographical sections indicate recently completed theses on the South African novel.

The basic bibliographical introduction to this aspect of scholarship is *A Guide to Theses and Dissertations: An Annotated, International Bibliography of Bibliographies*; published in 1975, it includes entries up to the end of 1973 and is a model of clarity, sound judgment and reasonably comprehensive coverage.[1] Reynolds has arranged this compilation by subjects, including useful sections on national/regional bibliographies, area studies and literature; for African literature, however, there is but one entry, so one will have to consult the more general sections for this subject. With its concise annotations, and subject, author/title and institutional indices, Reynolds must be regarded as an essential starting point for the student of African literature.

Whether or not one chooses to consult this guide, one will certainly not want to bypass the most ambitious of all thesis bibliographies, *Dissertation Abstracts International,* which was originally known as *Microfilm Abstracts* (1938–1951) and then as *Dissertation Abstracts*.[2] Having adopted its present name in 1969, the publication appears in two monthly fascicles, of which Part A is devoted to the humanities and social sciences. It consists of abstracts of dissertations submitted to the publisher by more than 375 universities and which are available either on microfilm or as Xerographic reproductions. Coverage is very wide, covering both North American and some European universities, but limits itself to those institutions which have agreed to cooperate with University Microfilms by making their dissertations available for reproduction and purchase; in this sense it is a very extensive catalogue arranged by subject and disciplinary subdivisions; thus under III A (Language–Literature–Linguistics) one finds the following categories of interest to the Africanist: general literature, comparative literature, modern literature, English literature. With this careful breakdown of the field, one cannot help but wish for an additional section on African literature, but there is some compensation in the thorough keyword-in-title and author indices for each monthly fascicle. The abstracts are of a consistently high quality and in most cases indicate whether a given dissertation is worth reading in full. Each volume has an annual cumulative index which saves much time, since its keyword-in-title section provides the full title after the keyword, which can often indicate whether the abstract itself is worth consulting. There is also a retrospective subject and author index to vols. 1–29, which makes consultation of these volumes relatively efficient and rapid.[3] Because of its wide coverage and commendable promptness of publication, *Dissertation Abstracts International* is an essential tool, a particularly significant and important part of which is the annual index.

Of a similar but much less commendable nature is AUPELF's *Répertoire des Thèses de Doctorat: Soutenues devant les Universités de Langue Française.*[4] Issued biennially since 1970, the publication aims to cover all universities throughout the world which conduct their teaching at least partly in French, and it is therefore particularly strong in West African coverage. The listing is rather poorly organized by university and then researcher; this is partly overcome by the subject index, which includes African literature. But since most of the universities listed are, as one might expect, not known as centers of research for African literature in English, one is best advised not to spend time consulting this guide; this judgment is reinforced by the fact that the *Répertoire* has been in existence only since 1970, which makes it irrelevant for theses prior to that date.

Pollak and Pollak have made a significant attempt to list all Sub-Saharan Africana theses on an international basis in their 1976 compilation;[5] published by G. K. Hall, it contains more than 2,400 dissertations accepted at some 200 institutions in 30 countries between 1884 and 1974. Arrangement is by subject and country with which the research deals; within each subject/country subdivision the entries are listed chronologically and then alphabetically by author. For South African linguistics, literature and communications (pp. 159–66) there are some eighty dissertations listed, while the same subjects for Central and Southern Africa (pp. 168–71) include an additional forty-seven theses. Combining these two geographical listings, one finds that nearly every recent North American dissertation on South African fiction has been listed. However, the same cannot be said for theses from the Republic, for a number of those noted in the appendix to this chapter are not included in Pollak and Pollak. While this strong Western bias detracts from the usefulness of *Theses and Dissertations on Southern Africa,* there is a full author index and a very informative chapter on the bibliography of Africana theses which is particularly worth reading.

On the national side there are several worthy compilations; once again the most thorough coverage is for the United States. The best of the American efforts is produced by University Microfilms as *American Doctoral Dissertations,* which has existed under a variety of titles since 1934 (covering 1933/34).[6] Originally somewhat limited in coverage, it now encompasses doctoral research at more than 200 universities in America and Canada. Arranged by subject and institution, each annual volume has an author index. Like *Dissertation Abstracts International, American Doctoral Dissertations* consists primarily of abstracts of theses submitted to the publisher by the sponsoring universities; because this compilation appears quite regularly, researchers seeking information on current Africana dissertations in North America will find it an indispensable bibliographical tool. At the same time, however, one must realize that much of this information will also appear in *Dissertation*

Abstracts International, albeit somewhat later. In addition the thirty-four volumes of University Microfilms' *Comprehensive Dissertation Index 1861–1972* should be regarded as a useful summary of *American Doctoral Dissertations* up to 1972. This compilation (volumes 29 and 30 are devoted to languages and literature) attempts to list all traceable dissertations, including those not available from the publisher.[7] Canada also has its own national compilation, *Canadian Theses,*[8] but the inclusion of this country in *American Doctoral Dissertations* makes the former superfluous for all theses except those submitted to smaller universities not participating in the University Microfilms scheme. Britain is rather poorly served by ASLIB's generally out-of-date *Index to Theses Submitted for Higher Degrees,* which appears annually but is at least two years behind in its coverage.[9] At present, however, an attempt is being made to bring this publication more up-to-date by making it semi-annual. Using a classified arrangement subdivided alphabetically by institution, it contains the occasional reference to African literature, as well as author and subject indices.

Several other countries have compilations of this sort, many of them listed in the *Guide to Theses and Dissertations;* however, since very few of the guides listed include data relevant to South African English literature, one is well advised to concentrate primarily on North America, Britain, possibly France and Germany, and certainly South Africa. For France there are two relevant publications, *Catalogue des Thèses de Doctorat Soutenues devant les Universités Française* and *Bibliographie de la France.*[10] The former publication, which originally ran from 1885 to 1959 and began a new series in the latter year, is regarded as the official compilation of French dissertations. Each fascicle is arranged by faculty and subdivided by university and type of doctorate; this arrangement along with a simple author index means that consultation can be time consuming. However, one will come across some dissertations on West African literature, and these may occasionally have an indirect bearing on South African fiction. The *Bibliographie de la France* since 1932 has contained a section entitled "Thèses," which lists all dissertations received in the Bibliothèque National under the French legal deposit scheme. Less comprehensive than its sister publication, it is arranged by broad subject headings and subdivided by institution and type of doctorate. The annual author and institutional indices do little to compensate for this typically Gallic organization, which makes "Thèses" a difficult and generally unrewarding section to consult.

The two German efforts, *Jahresverzeichnis der Deutschen Hochschulschriften* and *Reihe C* of the *Deutsche Nationalbibliographie*[11] tend not to fare so badly due largely to the inclusion of subject indices for each issue. The *Jahresverzeichnis,* however, dropped its subject index in 1965 and now has only an author index; each annual volume is arranged by place and university with a substantial subdivision for dissertations in each case. The entries, like the South African compilation discussed below, try to indicate publication information where applicable, which may save trouble in trying to acquire a given dissertation from its covetous depository. However, until quite recently there has been very little German interest in South African literature and a correspondingly inconsequential amount of graduate research in this area. *Reihe C: Dissertationen und Habilitationsschrift* of the German national bibliography is more usefully arranged by topic and has both author and subject indices; again there is some attempt to provide publication data, but the entries for South African literature are very sparse indeed.

The one compilation worth consulting regularly along with *American Doctoral Dissertations* is the *Union Catalogue of Theses and Dissertations of the South African Universities.*[12] Although the original volume is now rather dated, the annual supplements attempt to keep abreast of current output. Each edition is arranged by major subject areas and is further subdivided by institution; there is also mention of the location of copies within South Africa and notes on publication data where applicable. The lack of a detailed subject or keyword index in addition to the regular author index is not really critical in view of the small size of each volume. Each supplement will warrant consultation as it appears, since one may expect South Africans to take a strong interest in their own literature.

The growth in popularity of area studies has generated a number of publications devoted to theses on Africa, and once again the United States has both the most and best titles of this type. In 1962 the Library of Congress opened the way with *A List of American Doctoral Dissertations on Africa,* which was followed in 1967 by Miss Cruger's supplement, *A List of American Doctoral Dissertations on Africa, Covering 1961/62 through 1964/65.*[13] Both of these were updated by Peter Duignan's compilation, *United States and Canadian Doctoral Dissertations on Africa,* and all three were consolidated by Bratton and Schneller in *American Doctoral Dissertations on Africa, 1886–1972.*[14] To further expand their coverage Bratton and Schneller also drew upon entries in *American Doctoral Dissertations* (Library of Congress, 1912–1938), *Doctoral Dissertations Accepted by American Universities* (Association of Research Libraries, 1933–1955), *American Doctoral Dissertations* (University Microfilms, 1955–1971) and *Dissertation Abstracts International* (University Microfilms, 1951–1972). Their work thus represents a comprehensive survey of all American dissertations on Africa up to 1972 and in its 2,540 entries contains several items on South African literature. However, this is not the end of the story, for in 1976 Sims and Kagan brought out *American and Canadian Doctoral Dissertations and Master's Theses on Africa, 1886–1974.*[15] This to date represents the culmination of the American effort to record Africana theses, for it not only updates Bratton and Schneller but also includes M.A. work and Canadian material through 1974. The 6,070 entries are sensibly arranged by area/country and then by subject and author with both subject and author indices. If one is able to begin his search with this publication, there is no need to consult any of the preceding American compilations or the National Library of Canada's *Canadian Theses*. Furthermore, the work of Sims and Kagan will be supplemented by "Dissertations on Africa" in the *African Studies Newsletter*; this section appears very frequently and includes Ph.D., M.A. and some other types of theses post-1974.[16] This is essentially an alphabetical author listing of recently completed work and indicates the country focus of the research. The ongoing nature of this project also obviates the need to consult such compilations as Sackett's "Master's Theses in Literature" and Schmidt's two bibliographies of theses on African literature,[17] since this type of material presumably will be included in the *Newsletter*. Sackett is an alphabetical author listing of 895 theses with subject and author/title indices, while Schmidt includes only about thirty-five dissertations written between 1923 and 1969; neither adds to the Sims and Kagan volume. The only additional publication which may still warrant consultation is the Hoover Institution's *United States and Canadian Publications on Africa*, which with the 1965 volume began to include dissertations under the form division for books and pamphlets within the major area divisions for Sub-Saharan Africa and specific regions/countries.[18] This may be a useful annual survey of theses reported piecemeal in the *African Studies Newsletter*; however, it must be noted that it covers research of up to four years prior to the date of compilation and with the 1967–1970 cumulation will probably cease publication.

In Britain the tools for tracing theses on South African literature are altogether less praiseworthy. The first attempt to record Africana dissertations for our period was by Colman in an appendix to an article in the *African Studies Bulletin*.[19] This is a five-page topical listing with no items for African literature, and after this 1959 effort nothing appeared for five years. In 1964 SCOLMA entered the field with *Theses on Africa Accepted by Universities in the United Kingdom and Ireland*, which is a geographical and subject listing of some 1,142 theses prepared between 1920 and 1962 at twenty-two universities.[20] A supplement covering 1963–1975 is currently being compiled by John McIlwaine of the School of Library, Archive and Information Studies at University College London for publication in 1978; additions to this supplement may be listed annually in *African Research and Documentation*. The 1964 SCOLMA publication has been supplemented regularly by *United Kingdom Publications and Theses on Africa*,[21] which is very similar to the Hoover Institution's annual compilation, even in being three years or more behind in its coverage. Each volume contains a section entitled "Supplement to *Theses on Africa*" in which the theses are arranged geographically and with an author/subject index.

Because the coverage provided by the SCOLMA compilation is so very out-of-date and generally uneven, one will have to rely more on "Research in Progress" in *African Research and Documentation*,[22] if it is able to expand its currently weak coverage. At present this section relies on the cooperation of readers in informing the editor of their work, which sometimes includes postgraduate degree research. In the past two years there have been no entries for South African literature, and one hopes that with the gradual decline of *U.K. Publications and Theses* some attempt will be made to establish "Research in Progress" on a more solid foundation. The other publication to consult in an attempt to fill the gaps in British coverage is the Institute of Commonwealth Studies compilation, *Theses in Progress in Commonwealth Studies*, which includes South Africa within its scope.[23] The present volume supersedes the 1975 issue and is arranged by region/country, then alphabetically by author. Although there is at present only one reference to African literature, one will want to watch for future issues, since the cooperation of more than twenty British centers is bound to uncover further relevant research. However, it must be remembered that this guide is limited to research in progress, and once a thesis is completed it is no longer listed.

Since 1969 the French have made a fairly thorough attempt to keep abreast of Africana theses in the CARDAN publication, *Bulletin d'Information et de Liaison: Études Africaines*, which is published in four annual parts; "Inventaire de Thèses et Mémoires Africanistes de Langue Française: Soutenances" is the collection devoted to recently completed theses.[24] After an initially slow start, each volume now covers material from the preceding year and includes items both from within France and from French-speaking institutions elsewhere. Arrangement is geographical with broad subject subdivisions, and there are both author and subject indices. As is the case with most French Africana work, little appears in thesis form of importance to South African literature. Another French language publication, Rial's guide to Swiss Africana theses, is equally limited in its relevance to South Africa.[25]

In effect, therefore, one finds that the only useful compilations of theses dealing with South African literature to any degree are *Dissertation Abstracts International, American Doctoral Dissertations, Union Catalogue of Theses and Dissertations of the South African Universities*, Sims and Kagan, *U.S. and Canadian Publications on Africa, U.K. Publications and Theses on Africa* and *Theses in Progress in Commonwealth Studies* (all of them subject to the limitations noted above). Certainly this handful of resources will provide one with enough information without requiring him to turn to the plethora of guides to theses undertaken at individual institutions, which only rarely mention work on South African literature.[26]

Research in Progress

Having determined what has already been written in thesis form, one may also want to know about theses or postgraduate research currently under way, and there are again several resources from which to choose. With the demise of the MLA's "Research in Progress in the Modern Languages and Literatures"[27] in 1960 there ceased to be a useful guide to literary research, but there are some tools yet extant specifically for the Africanist. One of the best of these has been *Current Africanist Research: International Bulletin*,[28] which draws information not only from CARDAN and the African Studies Association (both U.S. and U.K.) but also from questionnaires designed specifically for this publication. The volumes, which together form a cumulative survey of current research, are arranged by region and subject with a number of relevant entries under language and literature both for Africa in general and Southern Africa. These include researchers as well as degree candidates, and there are useful indices of countries, organizations, names and subjects. To complement this publication, the IAI has recently published its *International Guide to African Studies Research*, which completely updates the earlier *International Register of Organisations Undertaking Africanist Research.*[29] It also includes *Current Africanist Research* no. 4, and it is extremely useful to have these two publications together. The *Guide* itself is arranged geographically and provides details on institutions undertaking Africanist research in all countries (African, Western and Eastern). Although missing a major South African center, the Institute for the Study of English in Africa, as well as that country's National English Documentation Centre and the National Documentation Centre for Afrikaans Language and Literature, it does cover a wide range of institutions with an interest in African literature. This may usefully provide one with some general contacts in the field, while the section on research may give more specific names of individual researchers. Unfortunately, however, the current listing contains no data on South African literary projects.

The other major guide to current research is the African Studies Association's *Research in Progress*, which is based on questionnaires sent to members of the Association and includes theses, dissertations and postdoctoral projects.[30] This has now been updated by Miss Frey's compilation,[31] which in its thirty-nine page subject arrangement provides a very good indication of current literary research; it is again based on questionnaires sent to Association members and includes contact addresses as well as author and geographical indices. This in turn will be kept up-to-date by further notices in the *African Studies Newsletter*, and with this ongoing project at hand the researcher will have little trouble in keeping abreast of American activities.

For Britain the African Studies Association (U.K.) has made a beginning effort to inform researchers of current activities, but as yet the coverage afforded by *African Research and Documentation* is still very haphazard.[32] Much better, and with far greater potential, is the Institute of Commonwealth Studies publication, *Theses in Progress*, which is limited to graduate research but nevertheless systematically covers many more universities than the ASA undertaking.[33] What one would like to see is a concerted annual effort by the editors of *African Research and Documentation* to collect and publish data on current Africanist research throughout Britain. Personal experience has shown that even a fairly substantial research guide of this sort is neither difficult nor expensive to compile,[34] and the need clearly exists for the collection of data on African studies research. Certainly CARDAN has made a valiant effort to serve French needs with its "Inventaire de Thèses et Mémoires Africanistes de Langue Française en Cours" in the *Bulletin d'Information et de Liaison: Études Africaines*, which is an annual listing of theses in progress in France and French-speaking institutions elsewhere.[35] It is arranged geographically with subject subdivisions and has author, subject and supervisor indices. Once again, however, one will find little of value concerning South African literature in this compilation and may well be advised to ignore future issues.

Somewhat more useful are two South African undertakings, *Register of Current Research in the Humanities at the Universities* and *Register of Research*.[36] The former, which has been appearing annually since 1949, covers the humanities in general and occasionally refers to literary research related to the South African novel. The *Register of Research*, on the other hand, deals only with projects in African studies being undertaken in the Republic. Although not personally examined, users have said that it includes research on English literature and is scheduled to appear in supplementary form from time to time.

Finally, there have been a few attempts to disseminate information on research dealing specifically with African/South African literature. Although sporadic and variable in their usefulness, these brief reports can be very enlightening when located. It so happens that *Research in African Literatures* has carried several of the more informative reports and so may be expected to continue this coverage in future issues. Miss Sullivan in "Work in Progress in African Literatures" presents a list of research by geographical base; it includes researchers' names but does not mention any addresses or the planned output.[37] A slightly different approach from this and related reports in *RAL* has been taken by André de Villiers, who deals with South African literary research based in the Republic.[38] His is a most informative article, including as it does notes on projects at the Institute for the Study of English in Africa along with a checklist of recently completed or ongoing research in South African universities. One hopes that articles of this type will continue to present an annual review of similar proportions.

Aside from this indigenous effort, most of the reports on research in progress deal to a disappointing degree with South African literature. At present the best sources of information are the guides prepared by the African Studies Association (U.S.), the International African Institute and Institute of Commonwealth Studies. For work in progress within the Republic, however, all of these efforts are rather sketchy, and there is as yet no suitable vehicle for keeping abreast of indigenous literary research on a regular basis.

Notes

1. Michael M. Reynolds, *A Guide to Theses and Dissertations: An Annotated, International Bibliography of Bibliographies* (Detroit, Michigan: Gale Research, 1975); cf. Oliver B. Pollak and Karen Pollak, *Theses and Dissertations on Southern Africa: An International Bibliography* (Boston: G. K. Hall, 1976), pp. ix–xiii for a discussion of thesis guides relevant to Southern Africa.

2. *Dissertation Abstracts International; A: The Humanities and Social Sciences* (Ann Arbor, Michigan, and High Wycombe, Bucks.: University Microfilms International, 1969– ; monthly); cf. *Dissertation Abstracts: Abstracts of Dissertations and Monographs Available in Microfilm* (Ann Arbor, Michigan: University Microfilms, 1938–1966; monthly); *Dissertation Abstracts; A: The Humanities and Social Sciences* (Ann Arbor, Michigan: University Microfilms, 1966–1969; 3 vols., monthly).

3. *Dissertation Abstracts International; Retrospective Index, Volumes 1–29* (Ann Arbor, Michigan: Xerox University Microfilms, 1970; 9 vols. in 11). Vol. 8 includes literature, and vol. 9 contains the author index.

4. Association des Universités Partiellement ou Entièrement de Langue Française, *Répertoire des Thèses de Doctorat Soutenues devant les Universités de Langue Française* (Quebec: Université Laval, Centre de Documentation de la Bibliothèque, 1970– ; semi-annual).

5. Oliver B. Pollak and Karen Pollak, *Theses and Dissertations on Southern Africa: An International Bibliography* (Boston: G. K. Hall, 1976).

6. *American Doctoral Dissertations* (Ann Arbor, Michigan: University Microfilms, 1965– ; annual); cf. *Doctoral Dissertations Accepted by American Universities* (New York: H. W. Wilson, 1934–1956; 22 nos. in 18 vols., annual); *Index to American Doctoral Dissertations* (Ann Arbor, Michigan: University Microfilms, 1957–1964; 8 vols., annual).

7. University Microfilms, *Comprehensive Dissertation Index 1861–1972* (34 vols.; Ann Arbor, Michigan: University Microfilms, 1973).

8. National Library of Canada, *Canadian Theses/Thèses Canadiennes* (Ottawa: National Library of Canada, 1962– ; annual); cf. National Library of Canada, *Canadian Theses/Thèses Canadiennes, 1947–1960* (2 vols.; Ottawa: National Library of Canada, 1973).

9. ASLIB, *Index to Theses Accepted for Higher Degrees by the Universities of Great Britain and Ireland and the Council for National Academic Awards* (London: ASLIB, 1953– ; annual and semi-annual, for academic year two years prior to date of publication).

10. France, Direction des Bibliothèques de France, *Catalogue des Thèses de Doctorat Soutenues devant les Universités Françaises* (Paris: Direction des Bibliothèques de France, 1885–1959; annual) and *Catalogue des Thèses de Doctorat Soutenues devant les Universités Françaises; Nouvelle Série* (Paris: Cercle de la Librairie, 1960– ; annual); "Thèses . . . ," *Bibliographie de la France* (Paris: Cercle de la Librairie, 1932– ; annual, issued in fascicles). There is no need to consult Marion Dinstel, *List of French Doctoral Dissertations on Africa* (Boston: G. K. Hall, 1966), since it affords no coverage of literature.

11. Deutsche Bucherei, comp., *Jahresverzeichnis der Deutschen Hochschulschriften* (Leipzig: Verlag für Buch- und Bibliothekswesen, 1887– ; an-

nual); *Deutsche Nationalbibliographie; Reihe C: Dissertationen und Habili-tationsschrift* (Leipzig: VEB Verlag für Buch- und Bibliothekswesen, 1968– ; monthly). This supersedes *Reihe B,* which from 1931–1967 contained a substantial number of dissertations.

12. S. I. Malan, comp., *Union Catalogue of Theses and Dissertations of the South African Universities, 1942–1958* (Potchefstroom: Potchefstroom University, Department of Librarianship, 1959); Potchefstroom University, F. Potsma Library, *Union Catalogue of Theses and Dissertations of the South African Universities: Supplement* (Potchefstroom: Potchefstroom University, 1959– ; annual).

13. U.S., Library of Congress, African Section, comp., *A List of American Doctoral Dissertations on Africa* (Washington, D.C.: U.S. Government Printing Office for the Library of Congress, General Reference and Bibliography Division, Reference Department, 1962); Doris M. Cruger, *A List of American Doctoral Dissertations on Africa, Covering 1961/62 through 1964/65; France, Covering 1933/34 through 1964/65; Italy, Covering 1933/34 through 1964/65* (Ann Arbor, Michigan: University Microfilms Library Services, 1967).

14. Peter Duignan, comp., *United States and Canadian Doctoral Dissertations on Africa* (Ann Arbor, Michigan: University Microfilms, 1973); Michael Bratton and Anne Schneller, comps., *American Doctoral Dissertations on Africa, 1886–1972* (Waltham, Massachusetts: African Studies Association, Research Liaison Committee, 1973).

15. Michael Sims and Alfred Kagan, comps., *American and Canadian Doctoral Dissertations and Master's Theses on Africa, 1886–1974* (Waltham, Massachusetts: African Studies Association, 1976).

16. "Dissertations on Africa," *African Studies Newsletter* (Waltham, Massachusetts: African Studies Association). In vol. 7 (1974) this section appeared three times: no. 3 (p. 14), no. 4 (p. 2) and no. 6 (p. 18); cf. "Master's Theses on Africa," *African Studies Newsletter,* which since 1973 has been an annual alphabetical listing by author of recently completed and currently in progress American M.A. theses.

17. S. J. Sackett, "Master's Theses in Literature Presented at American Colleges and Universities, July 1, 1964–June 30, 1965," *Fort Hays Kansas State College Language and Literature Series,* no. 7 (1966): 89–165; Nancy J. Schmidt, "Bibliography of American Doctoral Dissertations on African Literature," *Research in African Literatures,* 1 (1970): 62–65; Nancy J. Schmidt, "A Bibliography of American Dissertations and Theses on African Literature," *Research in African Literatures,* 5 (1974): 89–92.

18. Hoover Institution on War, Revolution and Peace, *United States and Canadian Publications on Africa* (Hoover Institution Bibliographical Series. Stanford, California: Stanford University, Hoover Institution, 1962– ; annual).

19. James S. Colman, "Research on Africa in European Centers: Appendix B; Ph.D. Dissertations on African Subjects Completed at British Universities, 1950–1956," *African Studies Bulletin,* 2, no. 3 (1959): 18–22.

20. Standing Conference on Library Materials on Africa, *Theses on Africa Accepted by Universities in the United Kingdom and Ireland* (Cambridge: W. Heffer, 1964).

21. Standing Conference on Library Materials on Africa, *United Kingdom Publications and Theses on Africa* (Cambridge: W. Heffer, 1966– ; an-

nual). The volume for 1967–1968 was edited by Miriam Alman and published in London by F. Cass in 1973. The series has now ceased publication; the typescript of the 1969–1970 edition is available for consultation in the library of the School of Oriental and African Studies.

22. "Research in Progress," *African Research and Documentation* (Birmingham: African Studies Association [U.K.] and the Standing Conference on Library Materials on Africa, 1973– ; trimestral).

23. University of London, Institute of Commonwealth Studies, *Theses in Progress in Commonwealth Studies: A Cumulative List* (London: University of London, Institute of Commonwealth Studies, 1976). Each entry lists author, subject/title, supervisor's name, university and date commenced.

24. Centre d'Analyse et de Recherche Documentaires pour l'Afrique Noire, "Inventaire de Thèses et Mémoires Africanistes de Langue Française: Soutenances," *Bulletin d'Information et de Liaison: Etudes Africaines* (Paris: CARDAN, 1969– ; annual).

25. Jacques Rial, *Inventaire des Thèses Suisses Consacrées à l'Afrique au Sud du Sahara, à l'Ethiopie et à Madagascar, 1897–1970* (Berne: Commission Nationale Suisse pour l'Unesco, 1972).

26. Examples of this type of compilation include: Peter C. Garlick, "Theses on Africa Accepted by Howard University, Washington, D.C.," *African Studies Bulletin*, 11 (1968): 259–68; R. Philip Hoehn and Jean Judson, "Theses on Sub-Saharan Africa Accepted by the University of California at Berkeley," *African Studies Bulletin*, 12 (1969): 157–66; Indiana University, African Studies Program, *Dissertations on Africa: A List of Titles of Dissertations on Africa That Were Completed at Indiana University from 1938 to the Present* (Bloomington: Indiana University, African Studies Program, 1976?); Makerere College Library, *Annotated List of Theses Submitted to University of East Africa and Held by Makerere College Library* (Kampala: Makerere College Library, 1970); Yvette Scheven, comp., *Africa-Related Theses and Dissertations at the University of Illinois at Urbana-Champaign, 1921–1974* (Urbana-Champaign: University of Illinois, African Studies Program, 1976); University of Wisconsin-Madison, African Studies Program, *Africa-Related Doctoral Dissertations and Masters Theses Completed at University of Wisconsin-Madison Through 1973* (Madison: University of Wisconsin-Madison, African Studies Program, 1974).

27. Modern Language Association, "Research in Progress in the Modern Languages and Literatures," *Modern Language Association Publications* (New York: MLA, 1948–1960; annual and biennial).

28. International African Institute, Research Information Liaison Unit, *Current Africanist Research: International Bulletin* (London: International African Institute, 1971– ; annual). Due to lack of funds the *Bulletin* has ceased publication. No. 4 of this series was issued as part of the *International Guide to African Studies Research*; see note 29 below.

29. International African Institute, *International Guide to African Studies Research; An Enlarged and Revised Edition (1974) of the "International Register of Organisations Undertaking Africanist Research in the Social Sciences and Humanities," Together with "Current Africanist Research" Number 4* (London: International African Institute, 1975); cf. International African Institute, Research Information Liaison Unit, *International Register of Organisations Undertaking Africanist Research in the Social Sciences and*

Humanities (London: International African Institute, Research Information Liaison Unit, 1971).

30. African Studies Association, *Research in Progress 1972–1974: A Selected Listing of Current Research on Africa* (Waltham, Massachusetts: African Studies Association, 1974). This publication updates the volume for 1970–71 prepared by the ASA's Research Liaison Committee.

31. Mitsue Miyata Frey, comp., "Research in Progress, 1975–76," *African Studies Newsletter*, 9, no. 2 (1976): special insert.

32. See note 22 above.

33. See note 23 above.

34. The compilation of *Development Studies: Register of Research in the United Kingdom 1975/76* (Brighton, England: Institute of Development Studies, 1976), which covers some 450 projects at 46 centers, required only eight weeks of work following the distribution and return of questionnaires. For a smaller project the time involved should be significantly less.

35. Centre d'Analyse et de Recherche Documentaires pour l'Afrique Noire, "Inventaire de Thèses et Mémoires Africanistes de Langue Française en Cours," *Bulletin d'Information et de Liaison: Études Africaines* (Paris: CARDAN, 1969– ; annual).

36. South Africa, Human Sciences Research Council, *Register of Current Research in the Humanities at the Universities* (Pretoria: Human Sciences Research Council, 1949– ; annual); cf. the Council's *Research Bulletin*, which is issued ten times annually and contains a listing of research projects in South African universities along with reports from researchers funded by the Council; African Studies Research Committee, *Register of Research* (Pietermaritzburg, Natal: African Studies Research Committee, 1974).

37. Sally L. Sullivan, "Work in Progress in African Literatures," *Research in African Literatures*, 5 (1974): 213–14; reports with the same title have been presented by Ian Munro in vol. 2 (1971): 28–38, Reinhold Sander in vol. 3 (1972): 54–59, Barney C. and Rae G. McCartney in vol. 4 (1973): 209–15.

38. André de Villiers, "South African Research Since 1969 in the Literatures of the Republic: Some Notes and a Checklist," *Research in African Literatures*, 6 (1975): 237–46.

Appendix

Dissertations and Theses on the
South African Novel in English Since 1950

This listing of theses has been gleaned from all the resources cited in the preceding pages and therefore is only as complete as these materials themselves. An attempt has been made to indicate which items have been published, as this may obviate the need to borrow items through an interlibrary loan system. Also, where theses have been cited in more than one form or with varying dates, a note or query appears to this effect, since it has not been possible to verify the citations with individual universities. A few items dealing only indirectly with the novel have been included for their useful background coverage of the field.

Alcorn, Noeline Elizabeth. "Vision and Nightmare: A Study of Doris Lessing's Novels." Ph.D. dissertation, University of California (Irvine), 1970/71.

Arab, Si Abderrahmane. "The Individual and the Urban Situation in the Negro African Novel from 1934 to 1966." Ph.D. dissertation, University of Algeria, 1973.

Awoonor, Kofi. "A Study of the Influences of Oral Literature on the Contemporary Literature of Africa." Ph.D. dissertation, State University of New York (Stony Brook), 1972.

Baraitser, M. D. "Pauline Smith and Arnold Bennett—a Study in Affinities." M.A. thesis, University of Cape Town, 1971.

Barnett, Ursula Annemarie. "African Writing in English in Southern Africa." Ph.D. dissertation, University of Cape Town, 1971?

Baxter, C. "Pessimism and Protest in Modern American and South African Fiction—A Comparative Study." Ph.D. dissertation, University of Cape Town, 1974?

Bishop, David Rand. "African Critics and African Literature: A Study of Critical Standards, 1947–1966." Ph.D. dissertation, Michigan State University, 1970/71.

Brown, V. M. "The Study of South African Life through Its Novels." M.A. thesis, Pennsylvania State College, 1929.

Buelow, George David. "The Ethnographic Novel in Africa." Ph.D. dissertation, University of Oregon, 1973.

Burkom, Selma Ruth. "A Reconciliation of Opposites: A Study of the Works of Doris Lessing." Ph.D. dissertation, University of Minnesota, 1970/71.

Carey, Alfred A. (John Leonard). "Doris Lessing: The Search for Reality—a Study of the Major Themes in Her Novels." Ph.D. dissertation, University of Wisconsin (Madison), 1964/65. This is also cited as Cary, Alfred Augustine. "Doris Lessing: The Search for Reality: A Study of Six Major Themes in Her Novels."

Chavis, Helen D. "The New Decorum: Moral Perspectives of Black Literature." Ph.D. dissertation, University of Wisconsin (Madison), 1971.

Christie, S. H. "The African Writing of William Plomer and Dan Jacobson." M.A. thesis, University of the Witwatersrand, 1972.

Couzens, T. J. "The Role of the Writer in African Literature." Ph.D. dissertation, University of the Witwatersrand, 1974?

David, R. "South African Prose Fiction of the Past Two Decades (with Special Reference to Nadine Gordimer, Dan Jacobson and Alan Paton)." M.A. thesis, University of Liverpool, 1966/67.

Davis, Gail Marie. "The Effect of Islam and Christianity on Modern African Literature." M.A. thesis, Midwestern University, 1974.

Davis, Reginald Victor. "Roy Campbell: A Critical Survey." M.A. thesis, Potchefstroom University, 1957.

Dabo, S. K. "A Comparative Study of the Treatment of Human Relationships in Fiction by Modern African Writers in French and in English." B.Litt. thesis, University of Oxford, 1966/67.

De Koker, Benjamin. "The Short Stories and Novels of Nadine Gordimer: A Critical Study." M.A. thesis, Potchefstroom University, 1962.

Ebert, R. "A Study of South African Imaginative Writing in English." M.A. thesis, University of Cape Town, 1971.

Essa, Ahmed. "Four Stories about South Africa." M.A. thesis, University of Southern California, 1962.

————. "Postwar South African Fiction in English: Abrahams, Paton and Gordimer." Ph.D. dissertation, University of Southern California, 1968/69.

Gakwandi, A. "The African Novel in English and the Politics of Independence." M.Litt. thesis, University of Edinburgh, 1971/72.

Gleason, Judith Sargent Illsley. "African Novels." Ph.D. dissertation, Columbia University, 1964.

Gray, S. "The Making of Fiction—a Critical Study of the Works of Herman Charles Bosman." D.Litt. dissertation, Rand Afrikaans University, 1974?

Hall, S. J. "The Role of Education in African Literature." M.A. thesis, Teachers College, Columbia University, 1966/67.

Hammond, Dorothy B. "The Image of Africa in British Literature of the Twentieth Century." Ph.D. dissertation, Columbia University, 1962/63.

Haresnape, Geoffrey. "A Study of the Works of Pauline Smith." M.A. thesis, University of Cape Town, 1960. Published as *Pauline Smith* (Twayne's World Authors Series. New York: Twayne Publishers, 1969).

Hart, M. Jerome. "The Imagery of Alan Paton." M.A. thesis, Immaculate Heart College (California), 1957/58.

Heinrich, F. "Stuart Cloete's 'Turning Wheels': Als Brücke zwischen Afrikaans und Englisch." Ph.D. dissertation, University of Vienna, 1951.

Herring, Maben Dixon. "The Defined Self in Black Autobiography." Ph.D. dissertation, University of Notre Dame, 1974.

Iyasere, Solomon Ogbede. "The Rhetoric of African Fiction." Ph.D. dissertation, State University of New York (Binghamton), 1972.

Keane, Christiane. "Commonwealth Literature 1945–1975: A Guide to Sources." F.L.A. thesis, Library Association (U.K.), 1975.

Krooth, Ann Baxandall. "Aesthetics of the Novel of Social Protest in South Africa and the United States." M.A. thesis, University of Wisconsin, 1967.

Larson, Charles Raymond. "Patterns of African Fiction." Ph.D. dissertation, Indiana University, 1969/70. Incorporated in *The Emergence of African Fiction* (Bloomington: Indiana University Press, 1972).

Lobel, R. F. "Twentieth Century South African Literature with Special Reference to the Novel." M.A. thesis, University of Leicester, 1974?

Luck, James William. "Identity and Image Development of Students through Black Literature." Ph.D. dissertation, University of South Carolina, 1971/72.

McDowell, Robert Eugene. "The African-English Novel." Ph.D. dissertation, University of Denver, 1965/66.

Makward, Idris. "Negro-African Novelists: A Comparative Study of Themes and Influences in Novels by Africans in French and English." Ph.D. dissertation, University of Ibadan, 1968.

Milette, M. "Le Personage Noir Africain dans Queleques Romans de Langue Anglaise." M.A. thesis, University of Montreal, 1964.

Millar, Clive John. "The Contemporary South African Short Story in English (with Special Reference to the Work of Nadine Gordimer, Doris Lessing, Alan Paton, Jack Cope, Uys Krige and Dan Jacobson)." M.A. thesis, University of Cape Town, 1962.

Mostert, Cornelius Wickaum. "The Native in the South African Novel in English." M.A. thesis, University of the Orange Free State, 1955.

Mphahlele, Ezekiel. "The Non-European Character in South African English Fiction." M.A. thesis, University of South Africa, 1957.

————. "The Wanderers: A Novel of Africa." Ph.D. dissertation, University of Denver, 1968/69. Published as *The Wanderers* (New York: Macmillan, 1971).

Musisi, Charles J. "African Background in Recent Fiction." M.A. thesis, University of Montreal, 1961.

Mutiso, Gideon-Cyrus Makau. "Socio-Political Ideas in African Literature in English, 1945–1967." Ph.D. dissertation, Syracuse University, 1969. Incorporated in *Socio-Political Thought in African Literature: Weusi?* (New York: Barnes and Noble, 1974).

Petrukhina, M. A. "The Modern English Colonial Novel." In Russian; Kandid. Diss., Moscow State University, 1971.

Prinsloo, Willem Jacobus de Villers. "The Regional Novels of Arnold Bennett and Mary Webb: A Study in Contrasts." M.A. thesis, Potchefstroom University, 1960.

Rabkin, D. "The Development of the English Novel in South Africa, with Particular Regard to the Works of Olive Schreiner, Pauline Smith, Sarah

Gertrude Millin and William Plomer, and with Regard to the Moral and Aesthetic Problems of Prose Fiction in a Culturally and Racially Diverse Society." M.A. thesis, University of Cape Town, 1973.

Roloff, Barbra Jean. "Gordimer: South African Novelist and Short Story Writer." M.A. thesis, University of Texas (Austin), 1962.

Rossouw, Daniël Gerhardus. "The Poetic Image in South African English Literature: A Critical and Comparative Study of Its Functions, Varieties and Values Considered as Criteria of Literary Merit." D.Litt. thesis, University of the Orange Free State, 1962.

Saratovskaya, L. B. "Modern Realist Prose in the Republic of South Africa (1945–1964)." In Russian; Kandid. Diss., Moscow State University, 1964.

Schlueter, Paul George. "A Study of the Major Novels of Doris Lessing." Ph.D. dissertation, Southern Illinois University, 1968/69.

Smith, Diane E. Sherwood. "A Thematic Study of Doris Lessing's *Children of Violence.*" Ph.D. dissertation, Loyola University, 1970/71.

Smith, Rowland James. "Lyric and Polemic: The Literary Personality of Roy Campbell." Ph.D. dissertation, University of Natal, 1967.

Spann, Patricia Ann. "Descriptive Survey of Creative African Literature and the Social Forces Influencing It." Ph.D. (M.A.?) dissertation, University of Chicago, 1964/65.

Stanislaus, Joseph. "The Growth of African Literature: A Survey of the Works Published by African Writers in English and French." Ph.D. dissertation, University of Montreal, 1952.

Stopforth, Lourens Daniel Marthinus. "Some Exponents of the South African Short Story in English." M.A. thesis, Potchefstroom University, 1954.

Tejani, Bahadur. "Local Significance and the Importance of the Local Audience in Modern African Writing: Studies in Ngugi, La Guma, Mphahlele, Okara and Peters." Ph.D. dissertation, University of Nairobi, 1975?

Thomas, A. L. "An Interpretive Analysis of Symbols in the Black South African Short Story; a Critical Analysis of Literature and Life." M.A. thesis, Howard University, 1969.

Tucker, Martin. "A Survey of the Representative Modern Novel in English about Africa." Ph.D. dissertation, New York University, 1965/66 (1963?). Incorporated in *Africa in Modern Literature: A Survey of Contemporary Writing in English* (New York: Frederick Ungar, 1967).

Van Zyl, John Andrew Fullard. "The Afrikaner Way of Life As Depicted in South African English Fiction." M.A. thesis, University of the Orange Free State, 1959.

Venter, Susanna Sophia. "The Contemporary Novel in English." M.A. thesis, University of the Orange Free State, 1958.

Wade, Michael. "The Liberal Tradition in South African Fiction in English." D.Phil. dissertation, University of Sussex, 1973.

Waiyaki, D. Nyoike. "Alienation and Betrayal in Caribbean and African Writing, with Particular Reference to the Work of George Lamming and Peter Abrahams." M.A. dissertation, University of Nairobi, 1974?

Ward, M. R. "An Analysis of the Ways in Which Colonialism, Tribalism and Associated Political Themes are Handled in Novels by the African Authors Peter Abrahams, Chinua Achebe and James Ngugi." M.Phil. thesis, University of Leeds, 1968/69.

Washington, L. E. "Treatment of the South African Native in Fiction of the South African Union." M.A. thesis, Howard University, 1936.

Weinstock, Donald Jay. "The Boer War in the Novel in English, 1884–1966: A Descriptive and Critical Bibliography." Ph.D. dissertation, University of California at Los Angeles, 1967/68.

Wessels, J. H. "From Olive Schreiner to Nadine Gordimer: A Study of the Development of the South African Short Story in English." M.A. thesis, University of the Orange Free State, 1974.

Wroblenski, Nancy F. "The Autobiography: Its Theory and South African Forms." M.A. thesis, Kent State University, 1969.

Wulf, H. "Die Natur in der südafrikanischen Literatur: Ihre Darstellung und Ihre Funktion." Ph.D. dissertation, University of Kiel, 1966.

Bibliographies of African and
South African Literature

The final source of bibliographical information in the field of South African English fiction is, of course, the bibliography devoted solely to this subject. Although investigators such as Gérard and Musiker would have us believe that the *lacunae* in Africana literary bibliography are almost insurmountable,[1] the fact is that in recent years there has been significant activity aimed at closing the gap between the published literary output and its bibliographical recording. As a result, in 1973 Lindfors could devote a single review article to as many as five major literary bibliographies;[2] since then, titles have continued to flow steadily from both Western and African presses. As has been the case in all other areas investigated in the preceding six chapters, these materials cover the field with a varying degree of success and from several standpoints. Some of the results are excellent, while others hardly seem to deserve a place in even the most basic collection.

The purpose of this chapter is to provide a relatively complete guide to those bibliographies which merit a place in any library hoping to serve the requirements of users interested in the South African novel. An attempt has been made to analyze every available monograph bibliography in this field published since 1950, as well as a wide selection of bibliographical articles appearing in a broad range of serials. It would be impossible for a single individual to cover the latter category entirely, but every effort has been made to touch upon the serial articles cited most frequently for their literary content. The keen researcher will, of course, want to seek additional bibliographical articles in the various publications discussed in Chapter Six and its appendix.

The titles in the present discussion have been divided into two categories, general Africana literary bibliographies and bibliographies of South African fiction. Within each category coverage includes both the widely heralded, substantial guides and the less well known but still useful publications. Because some attempt has been made to offer a reasonably comprehensive

161

selection of titles, one cannot avoid a certain number of rather dubious compilations, yet it is felt that only by this method can the researcher realize both what to consult and what to avoid.

General Africana Literary Bibliographies

Most scholars active in the field of Africana bibliography regard three works as important precursors of the major literary bibliographies; without fail they cite Amosu, Abrash and Ramsaran as the key early guides to African literature. The first of these was Margaret Amosu's *Creative African Writing*, which appeared as a supplement to *African Notes*, the bulletin of the Institute of African Studies at Ibadan University.[3] In only thirty-five pages this compilation covers all writing from the nineteenth century up to 1963, and in view of its brevity and the more substantial later works one will find no information here which cannot be had more fully in the newer guides. Pages 20–24 cover South Africa with forty-three entries on poetry, short stories, autobiography and the novel; with the exception of works by Paton and one or two other important novelists, there are few fiction titles to be gleaned from the listing. Therefore, while many have praised Amosu for its wide coverage, in the present context one must suggest that breadth and brevity here combine to present far too incomplete a picture of South African writing.

In 1967 Barbara Abrash produced *Black African Literature in English*,[4] which is an altogether more satisfactory compilation; indeed up to this date it must be regarded as the best general Africana bibliography containing notes on South African fiction. It includes bibliographies, critical monographs and articles, and an alphabetical author listing of novels, stories and anthologies. Each entry is thoughtfully and fairly annotated. The early sections dealing with the scholarly apparatus of literary research include both general bibliographies and a few South African contributions in much greater detail than is often found in purely indigenous guides (e.g., Davidson). For the novels themselves, one finds a judicious (but incomplete) selection of South African works by Abrahams, Mphahlele *et al.*; the annotations include variant publishers as well as complete subtitles, and there is also a very useful author index. A serious drawback is the limitation to black writing, an exclusiveness which we have seen appearing throughout the bibliographical spectrum. Nevertheless, even with this color barrier Abrash is the best starting point for general bibliographical inquiries up to 1967.

Three years later Ramsaran issued *New Approaches to African Literature*, which was in fact the second edition of a 1965 work by the same title; this in turn had superseded a joint effort with Jahn entitled *Approaches to African Literature*.[5] Like Abrash, Ramsaran saw fit to exclude works by whites but in this case expanded the geographical coverage to include the Caribbean and America. As a result, the focus is less clearly African and therefore loses value; in addition Ramsaran includes languages other than English, which again detracts from the focus required by the student of South African fiction. *New Approaches* is much more than a bibliography, for it includes extensive data on the background of the literature for those requiring a general orientation to the field. Chapter Two covers modern African literature, and fiction is dealt with on pages 28–45; here one finds what is essentially a list of works classified by genre and language, and there is limited coverage of the South African novel. Compared with Abrash, this section is neither as complete (omitting some works by La Guma and Mphahlele) nor as bibliographically accurate. Therefore, of these three important early bibliographies which include South Africa in their coverage, one will want to consult only Abrash as both the most comprehensive and accurate compilation.

Surrounding these frequently cited but marginally useful bibliographies is a plethora of ancillary compilations produced between 1960 and 1970. Many of these are worth consulting as supplements to the Abrash undertaking, while far more ought to be avoided by any but the most ambitious retrospective searcher. Some have appeared as monographs, while many others have found their way into various serials; all of them are widely available and frequently cited and because of this must be mentioned at least in passing.

An early bibliographer of Africana was Dorothy Porter, who in five years produced three articles in addition to her Howard University catalogue (see pages 87–88 and note 5 above). "Notes on Some African Writers," "Fiction by African Authors" and "African and Caribbean Writings" all have two things in common:[6] based largely on collections at Howard University and the Library of Congress, they exhibit both a strong black orientation and neglect of South African writing, which factors suggest that all three articles be bypassed for more relevant essays by such scholars as Douglas Killam. Since 1965, he has produced a number of bibliographical articles,[7] the most recent having appeared in the *Canadian Journal of African Studies* as an updated version of an earlier essay in *Twentieth Century Literature*. Including bibliographies, criticism and creative works arranged by country, the *CJAS* article once again excludes white South Africans, thereby denying access to rather more than half of the South African output. In the bibliographies listed there are only twenty for all of black Africa, but it does mention some American efforts not encountered in other lists (e.g., Middleton, Priebe).

Similar to Killam's effort is the 1973 coverage by Bishop of African literary criticism, which itself has been supplemented by Bernth Lindfors.[8] In the Bishop bibliography one has a fairly comprehensive guide to literary criticism by African commentators. Most of the citations refer to periodical articles, and from the South Africanist's viewpoint the bulk of the criticism shows a disproportionate emphasis on West African fiction. Lindfors, on the other hand, has been able to include a substantial number of South African works in his single country supplement to Bishop. Many entries in Lindfors carry annotations, which are essentially quotations from book reviews. These two efforts clearly exemplify the variations in coverage which one is likely to find in literary bibliographies.

At about the same time that Killam compiled his first bibliography Martin Tucker wrote *Africa in Modern Literature,* an important scholarly work which on pages 265–309 includes a section entitled "Selected Reading List of Modern African Literature through 1966."[9] For the period covered and considering the limitations inherent in a list of this type, it affords generous coverage of South African literature; arranged by region and type of publication, there are listed several novels (Abrahams, Mphahlele, La Guma) and a few critical essays, although in the mid-1960's not much criticism of merit had been produced. Very similar in style to Tucker is Wilson's *Working Index,* which includes a selective listing of South African novels but unfortunately mentions little that cannot be found in more readily available titles.[10]

Wilson directed his compilation primarily at university teachers working in African studies, and there have been a number of similar attempts to provide information for academic audiences at different levels. One of the more widely quoted of these has been Mutiso's *Messages,* which was prepared in 1970 as a working guide to African English literature available in America and suitable for use at a pre-university level.[11] It may well be an ideal guide of its kind, but like Beyer's work mentioned earlier (see pages 92–93 and note 17 above) it has no place in the more advanced study of South African fiction. Much the same is true of lists bearing the National Book League imprint; these are not geared for schools but instead aim at the general reading public and so are neither particularly comprehensive nor notably scholarly in their contents.[12]

Like Crooke's *British and Commonwealth Fiction* prepared for the NBL, two recent works have dealt with African writing in the context of Commonwealth literature.[13] Brady's *Selective Bibliography* is a very brief (55 pages) and highly unrepresentative selection of titles from the English-speaking world. Although partly annotated and primarily post-1945, it is only an introductory bibliography with no value for serious research in South African fiction. New's bibliography is reported to be a very substantial undertaking (432 pages) with some space devoted to South Africa and Rhodesia (pp. 208–29). Finally, two works in progress also may be adopting exclusive policies which mitigate against full coverage of South African fiction.[14] The MLA's Commonwealth bibliography may well regard South Africa as outside its parameters, while Bernth Lindfors has clearly indicated that his bibliography will deal only with black writings. Therefore, it is clear that with the exception of Abrash, all of these smaller Africana literary bibliographies may be passed over in favor of the major guides to the field.

It is not until one turns to these major bibliographies that the full range of South African imaginative writing even begins to become apparent. The most ambitious of these post-1970 undertakings certainly must be Jahn and Dressler's *Bibliography of Creative African Writing*,[15] which has been reviewed in glowing terms on several occasions. The reviewers may well be right in applauding this work as an "impressive bibliographical achievement"; however, for South African literature one is immediately disappointed by Jahn's black bias. Because of this limitation, not one of the 2,180 titles listed is by a white South African, which must give this bibliography a relatively limited value. Otherwise the Jahn and Dressler compilation is quite catholic in including all types of creative writing from both before and after 1900, although the latter era covers only fiction itself and not criticism. South Africa is included within "Austral Africa" (pp. 268–373), and this section is arranged by author and title in three subdivisions: secondary literature, anthologies, individual works. This is a less than satisfactory arrangement, as the instructions for use (some 30 rules) might suggest.

To give Jahn and Dressler its due, one must say that the coverage is quite full for black South African authors, including as it does nearly all of their works published up to 1970. Each entry lists the various editions and translations of a given work along with numerous book reviews, which means that for those authors included one has a remarkably complete bibliographical picture. In addition there is an index of authors and editors plus three author lists classified by (1) language in which they write, (2) language of translations, (3) nationality. The last category is particularly useful, since the bibliography itself is not arranged by country. Overall, therefore, Jahn and Dressler must be regarded as the standard reference guide to black South African fiction.

Unfortunately, this work is now becoming rather dated and seems not to have generated supplementary bibliographies, as did Jahn's 1965 compilation.[16] For example, an important but often neglected supplement to Jahn (1965) was prepared by Páricsy in 1969.[17] Arranged in two parts, it includes additions to Jahn and a preliminary bibliography of African writing (1965–1968). Although listing some 360 items overlooked by Jahn, Páricsy's *New Bibliography* itself was superseded by Jahn and Dressler. However, Lindfors has said that his present work, *Criticism on African Literature in English*, will go some way in updating Jahn and Dressler's 1971 effort (see page 81, note 28).

In 1971 Hans Zell and Irene Silver also entered the bibliographical ranks with their *Reader's Guide,* which Zell himself has updated on at least one occasion.[18] Like Jahn and Dressler, Zell and Silver also exclude white authors from their coverage; pages 54–59 therefore list only works by black writers from the Republic. Although frequently cited in the same breath as the preceding and following bibliographies, *Reader's Guide* is much less comprehensive, intending primarily to provide an introductory guide to the field. Therefore, as a bibliography one will want to bypass this work in favor of Jahn and Dressler.

On the heels of these two 1971 publications came a rather different bibliography, Herdeck's *African Authors*, which is both a bibliography and a biographical guide.[19] The entries, arranged in an alphabetical author sequence, provide brief biographies to which bibliographies are appended. There are useful appendices of authors, countries, languages, bibliographies, critical studies and the like. Although not as comprehensive as Jahn and Dressler in the sense that it ignores literary criticism, Herdeck is far more generous in its coverage of South African authors (see page 63 above). Unfortunately, here too black is the only acceptable color, but in spite of this Herdeck remains an essential supplement to Jahn and Dressler in terms of its date and additional authors listed. Taken together, Herdeck, Jahn and Dressler, Zell and Silver clearly leave much to be desired from a South African viewpoint, so it is to materials compiled specifically to meet the bibliographical requirements of South African literature (black *and* white) that one must turn in the end.

South African Literary Bibliographies

Without a doubt the vast bulk of bibliographical work on South African fiction has been undertaken by students of librarianship at the University of Cape Town and the University of the Witwatersrand. While this work is subject to the limitations common to all student compilations (i.e., lack of time and available resource materials), it nevertheless forms a substantial corpus of some significance in filling the many *lacunae* in South African literary bibliography. Of the two centers, Witwatersrand's Department of Bibliography, Librarianship and Typography has shown a more consistent interest in this field, resulting in at least a dozen bibliographies on literary figures or topics.[20] While many of them are very brief, occasionally no more than eight pages, and now somewhat dated, they are still in many cases the only extant bibliographies in their field and for this reason deserve wider circulation. Furthermore, several of them are better than one might expect; Elizabeth Davidson's bibliography of black writing is a good example of the excellence which can be achieved in this area.[21] This work contains some 550 entries for 188 authors and includes autobiography, poetry and drama along with fiction; arranged in an alphabetical author sequence, it has useful indices of authors and titles by genre. Having scanned a variety of sources for relevant data, Davidson is one of the most complete guides to black writing, especially for the period 1960–1970, and deserves recognition as a useful South African supplement to Jahn and Dressler.

In most respects Davidson is a rather better effort than a comparable

Cape Town undertaking by Aviva Astrinsky.[22] Similar in length to the former, Astrinsky has a decided advantage in dealing with both black and white writers. Unfortunately, in the 290 entries for 140 authors there is a considerable amount of "pulp" fiction, particularly romances and mysteries, which makes the effort less valuable than Davidson's concentration on "serious" writing. Astrinsky is arranged alphabetically by author, and there are occasional notations which appear to be little more than dust jacket review notices. Title and chronological indices complement the main author listing. Although this guide wisely, in our view, disregards color, it also disregards literary merit and so retrieves several items not worth mentioning. Overall, therefore, it must be seen as a less useful compilation than Davidson. However, one must not judge the entire Cape Town effort by this one example, as there are bound to be some guides of merit on authors or topics not discussed elsewhere.[23] In fact titles in the Cape Town series suggest that its orientation is primarily topical, and for this reason alone it serves as a useful complement to the author focus of the Witwatersrand series. Libraries with a collection of South African fiction would be well advised to make some effort to collect these titles, particularly those which, taken together, form a relatively comprehensive sequence (e.g., Wilkov for 1944–1960, Davidson for 1928–1971, Holson for 1870–1950). Many of the compilations devoted to individual authors are now too dated to be of much value, and several of these writers have received more current treatment in a variety of sources.

There have, of course, been several attempts outside the two universities to record fiction titles with varying degrees of thoroughness. One of the better compilers has been Ursula Laredo, who in 1970 and 1971 prepared two bibliographies on South African creative writing as a whole.[24] The first compilation is fairly extensive, covering only four years in twenty-one pages; the late 1960's saw a great deal of activity by South African novelists, and a number of their works are included in the main Laredo article and its 1971 supplement. A slightly earlier piece by Bernth Lindfors deals with "short fiction" and so has limited value in terms of the novel, but it does show which anthologies and serials have devoted some space to fiction (e.g., *Drum*).[25]

These individual efforts to record published fiction have been attended by more substantial, ongoing bibliographies; a particularly useful one is that in the *South African P.E.N. Yearbook*. In a series of bibliographies the *Yearbook* managed to cover much indigenous output from the 1950's; this provides data on a period often neglected in other bibliographies, and for this reason one would be well advised to acquire copies of the four issues from the mid-1950's.[26] Unfortunately, the *Yearbook* appears to have ceased publication in 1960, so one must turn elsewhere for more current surveys. These exist in two serials, *English Studies in Africa* and the *Journal of Commonwealth Literature*. As stated in Chapter Five,[27] *ESA* covers

English literature in general from a South African standpoint and so lacks a clear focus on indigenous creative writing. *JCL*, on the other hand, carries an annual appendix on South African writing within its bibliographical survey of Commonwealth literature. Now appearing regularly in the December issue, each list provides extensive coverage of all creative writing from South Africa, novels as well as criticism; this is the most complete and up-to-date guide to the field and as such must not be overlooked under any circumstance.[28]

Each compilation is prepared by a single individual, currently Tim Couzens of Witwatersrand University, and one wonders to what degree gaps in coverage may be due to the inability of a single bibliographer to collect data thoroughly from around the world for an entire year. The most obvious deficiencies occur in the generally inadequate information on new publishers (e.g., Donker in vol. 9, no. 2: 141) and in the coverage of critical essays and bibliographical articles appearing in non-South African serials. On the other hand, Couzens does try to include material regardless of its place of origin, having most success in the area of individual novels and essays published within South Africa. Each bibliography covers all imaginative writing and is arranged by genre, including bibliography, novels and criticism (both on individuals and more general studies). With each compilation coming to some 8–10 pages and including a brief but informative survey of the year's publishing activity, this is clearly an energetic attempt to cover as much as possible. One wonders to what degree some sort of collaboration with a compiler in the West would widen the present coverage of the *JCL* bibliography.

In addition to these general surveys there have been a number of attempts to record in full the works of individual authors, among them Doris Lessing, Peter Abrahams and Alan Paton.[29] While each of these compilations, particularly those on Lessing and Paton, is remarkably full, they are no substitute for a single bibliographical guide to South African English literature. There was hope that Beeton's recently published *Pilot Bibliography* might go some way toward providing just such a tool, but this has proved not to be the case.[30] Beeton's work covers all aspects of creative writing to 1971, and in only 102 pages he cannot be expected to present a complete picture of the novel, let alone all other forms of South African literature. To be fair to Beeton, he does say that the compilation aims to provide only ". . . a representative listing of the most significant South African writing in English" and that it ". . . does not pretend to be complete, comprehensive or definitive in any way."[31] Even so, there can be little rationale for ignoring Zell and Silver or Jahn and Dressler among the general bibliographies, not to mention such important authors as Hutchinson, Jabavu, Matshikiza and Mphahlele.

Coverage is divided into three main parts; Part I includes sections on general bibliographies, general criticism, collections, criticism by genre and journals and magazines; Part II contains an alphabetical listing of South African writers and their works (i.e., first editions and major criticism only), while Part III contains chronological and genre indices and an appendix of further names to be consulted. The core of the work is Part II, which includes only creative writers with at least one volume to their credit; "in the case of those regarded as indisputably major writers . . . as full a compilation as possible was attempted."[32] With this intention, how could the compilers have missed Doris Lessing's important 1957 work, *Going Home,* or two titles on Paton, Edward Callan's *Alan Paton* and Lea Bentel's *Alan Paton; A Bibliography*? These are only a few of the gaps discovered in a rapid perusal of this UNISA compilation, and it is on the basis of such omissions that we find little to recommend in this bibliography. Perhaps for a library with extremely limited holdings this book will have some value; however, one hopes that it will not be much consulted by students of South African literature, for it is apt to be misleading to any but the most knowledgeable researcher interested primarily in first editions of works by a limited number of writers. The one useful section is the listing of journals and magazines (pp. 29–33), which includes some fourteen extant literary magazines devoted to fiction in South Africa among the numerous defunct titles. Otherwise, the most that can be said in favor of *A Pilot Bibliography* is that it displays in one place a selection of novels and critical works.

There is, however, some hope on the horizon in the form of the *Bibliography of South African English Literature,* a project of the Institute for the Study of English in Africa under the general direction of André de Villiers and Reuben Musiker.[33] Begun in 1974, it is intended to cover all of South African literature from its beginning up to that date and will include all forms of creative writing, both primary and secondary works. The major limitation is the focus on monograph material only, but there is to be a companion volume covering individual poems and stories in serials and newspapers as well. To present an adequate picture of South African writing, the editors have decided to include all works which have an obvious connection with the Republic, as well as works by native South Africans regardless of the South African-ness of these novels. In this way the bibliography should make a significant contribution to the recording of imaginative writing from and about South Africa. In format the work will consist of ten parts with sections devoted to general bibliography, general criticism, South African journals and each type of literary genre; prose fiction will be divided into general bibliographies, general criticism and an alphabetical author listing, the latter again being subdivided into bibliographies, individual works and criticism. There will be at least 8,000 separate items in the completed work, and one hopes that its publication in 1978 will provide us with a guide matching the impressive description of this important undertaking.

Assuming that ISEA will be providing *the* definitive bibliography of South

African fiction down to 1974, one will want to use this for all bibliographical inquiries to that date. Ongoing coverage will continue to be supplied by the annual bibliography in the *Journal of Commonwealth Literature*. However, in view of the *JCL*'s slightly erratic efforts one might hope that ISEA will undertake an annual supplement to its own bibliography; if this were to cover all material published within the Republic, the proposed international or U.K. bibliographical center could compile a complementary list of titles produced elsewhere. Should an ideal of this type come to fruition, the student of South African fiction would have an excellent series of guides to satisfy his bibliographical inquiries.

Notes

1. Albert Gérard, "Bibliographical Problems in Creative African Literature," *Journal of General Education*, 19, no. 1 (1965): 25–34; Reuben Musiker, "South African English Literature: Bibliographic and Biographical Resources and Problems," *English Studies in Africa*, 13 (1970): 265–73.

2. Bernth Lindfors, "Africana Bibliomania," *Africana Journal*, 4, no. 1 (1973): 21–24.

3. Margaret Amosu, comp., *Creative African Writing in the European Languages: A Preliminary Bibiliography* (Ibadan: University of Ibadan, Institute of African Studies, 1964); cf. Margaret Amosu, "Selected Bibliography of Critical Writing," in *Introduction to African Literature: An Anthology of Critical Writing from "Black Orpheus,"* edited by Ulli Beier (London: Longman, 1967), pp. 265–70. This is a much more limited effort with no particular attention to South African fiction, but it does show Miss Amosu in a rather more flattering light in terms of accuracy and thoroughness.

4. Barbara Abrash, comp., *Black African Literature in English Since 1952: Works and Criticism* (New York: Johnson Reprint, 1967).

5. John A. Ramsaran, *New Approaches to African Literature: A Guide to Negro-African Writing and Related Studies* (Second edition; Ibadan: University of Ibadan Press, 1970); cf. Janheinz Jahn and John A. Ramsaran, *Approaches to African Literature* (Ibadan: University of Ibadan Press, 1959).

6. Dorothy B. Porter, "Notes on Some African Writers," *Africa and the United States: Images and Realities* (African Series 26, Department of State Publication 7332. Washington, D.C.: Department of State, 1961), pp. 165–73; Dorothy B. Porter, "Fiction by African Authors: A Preliminary Checklist," *African Studies Bulletin*, 5, no. 2 (1966): 54–66; Dorothy B. Porter, "African and Caribbean Writings: A Bibliographic Survey," *African Forum*, 1, no. 4 (1966): 107–11.

7. G. D. Killam, "Recent African Fiction," *Bulletin of the Association for African Literature in English*, 2 (1965): 1–10; cf. G. D. Killam, "Modern Black African Writing in English: Selected Bibliography," *Twentieth Century Literature*, 17 (1971): 37–47; G. D. Killam, "Modern Black African Writing in English: A Selected Bibliography," *Canadian Journal of African Studies*, 9 (1975): 537–66.

8. Rand Bishop, "A Bibliography of African Literary Criticism, 1947–1966," *Africana Library Journal*, 4, no. 2 (1973): 2–31; Bernth Lindfors, "Reviews of African Literature in Nigerian Periodicals," *Africana Journal*, 6 (1975): 195–231.

9. Martin Tucker, "Selected Reading List of Modern African Literature through 1966," in *Africa in Modern Literature: A Survey of Contemporary Writing in English* (New York: Frederick Ungar, 1967), pp. 265–309.

10. Richard Middlewood Wilson, *A Working Index to African Literature, with Selective Bibliographies in the Novel and Theater in Africa* (Evanston, Illinois: EPDA, Institute for College Teachers, Program of African Studies, 1970).

11. Gideon-Cyrus M. Mutiso, *Messages: An Annotated Bibliography of African Literature for Schools* (Upper Montclair, New Jersey: Montclair State College Press, 1970); cf. Vincent P. Bol and Jean Allary, *Littératures et Poètes Noirs* (Léopoldville, Congo: Bibliothèque de l'Etoile, 1964), which is another example of a guidebook prepared primarily for teachers of literature.

12. Arthur Crooke, ed., *British and Commonwealth Fiction Since 1950* (London: National Book League, 1966); National Book League, *Creative Writing from Black Africa, Sub-Sahara; a Checklist* (London: National Book League, 1971).

13. Sister Mary William Brady, comp., *A Selective Bibliography of Literature Written in English in Africa, Australia, Canada, New Zealand, West Indies* (St. Paul, Minnesota: The College of St. Catherine, 1975); William H. New, *Critical Writings on Commonwealth Literatures: A Selective Bibliography to 1970, with a List of Theses and Dissertations* (University Park: Pennsylvania State University Press, 1975).

14. Modern Language Association, *Bibliography of Commonwealth Literature* (provisional title, in progress); Bernth Lindfors, *Criticism on African Literature in English* (see page 81, note 28).

15. Janheinz Jahn and Claus Peter Dressler, *Bibliography of Creative African Writing* (Nedeln, Liechtenstein: Kraus-Thomson, 1971); cf. Janheinz Jahn, *A Bibliography of Neo-African Literature from Africa, America and the Caribbean* (London: André Deutsch, 1965).

16. Pál Páricsy, "A Supplementary Bibliography to J. Jahn's *Bibliography of Neo-African Literature from Africa, America and the Caribbean,*" *Journal of the New African Literature and the Arts*, 4 (1967): 70–82; Bernth Lindfors, "Additions and Corrections to Janheinz Jahn's *Bibliography of Neo-African Literature* (1965)," *African Studies Bulletin*, 11 (1968): 129–48.

17. Pál Páricsy, *A New Bibliography of African Literature* (Studies on Developing Countries, no. 24. Budapest: Center for Afro-Asian Research of the Hungarian Academy of Sciences, 1969); cf. Pál Páricsy, comp., "The History of Black African Literature (A Select Bibliography of Criticism)," *Studies on Modern Black African Literature*, edited by Pál Páricsy (Studies on Developing Countries, no. 43. Budapest: Center for Afro-Asian Research of the Hungarian Academy of Sciences, 1971), pp. 99–121. The latter compilation inadvertently competes with Jahn and Dressler by having been published in the same year; of the 217 entries on literary criticism, only 17 deal specifically with the Republic.

18. Hans M. Zell and Helene Silver, eds., *A Reader's Guide to African Literature* (New York: Africana, 1971; London: Heinemann, 1972); cf. page 62 and note 32 on page 68 above; cf. Hans M. Zell, "African Literature 1971–1972: A Checklist," *Africana Library Journal*, 4, no. 4 (1973): 7–16.

19. Donald E. Herdeck, *African Authors: A Companion to Black African Writing. Vol. 1: 1300–1973* (Washington, D.C.: Black Orpheus Press, 1973); cf. page 63 and note 34, page 68 above.

20. Bibliographies from the Department of Bibliography, Librarianship and Typography at the University of the Witwatersrand include the following compilations: Judith Beinash, *Books and Pamphlets by South African Jewish Writers* (1965); Lea Bentel, *Alan Paton: A Bibliography* (1969); Helen Camberg, *Daphne Rooke; Her Works and Selected Literary Criticism: A Bibliography* (1969); Shora Gertrude de Saxe, *Herman Charles Bosman: A Bibliography* (1971); Catherina Ipp, *Doris Lessing: A Bibliography* (1967); Fanelle Levy, *The Works of Sarah Gertrude Millin, 1952–1968: A Bibliography* (1969); Racilia Jilian Nell, *Nadine Gordimer, Novelist and Short Story Writer: A Bibliography of Her Works and Selected Literary Criticism* (1964); A. Wilkov, *Some English Writings by Non-Europeans in South Africa, 1944–1960* (1962); Myra Yudelman, *Dan Jacobson: A Bibliography* (1967).

21. Elizabeth Davidson, comp., *Some Writings by Non-European South Africans (1928–1971): A Bibliography* (Johannesburg: University of the Witwatersrand, Department of Bibliography, Librarianship and Typography, 1972).

22. Aviva Astrinsky, comp., *A Bibliography of South African English Novels, 1930–1960* (Cape Town: University of Cape Town: School of Librarianship, 1965).

23. Bibliographies from the School of Librarianship at the University of Cape Town include: Valerie Margaret Davis, *Bibliography of the Works of Ignatius Roy Dunnachie Campbell* (1954); M. B. Holson, *A Select Bibliography of South African Novels in English, 1870–1950* (1952); S. Kiersen, *English and Afrikaans Novels on South African History: A Bibliography* (1958); Maureen J. Stern, *South African Jewish Biography, 1900–1966: A Bibliography* (1972); Rowse Ushpol, *A Select Bibliography of South African Autobiographies* (1958); D. J. Weinstock, *The Boer War in the Novel in English, 1884–1966: A Descriptive and Critical Bibliography* (1968); Morag Whyte, *The Works of Sarah Gertrude Millin: Bibliography* (1952).

24. Ursula Laredo, "Bibliography of South African Literature in English, 1964–1968," *Journal of Commonwealth Literature*, no. 9 (1970): 1–27; Ursula Laredo, "Supplement to Bibliography of South African Literature in English," *Journal of Commonwealth Literature*, 6 (1971): 1–5; cf. O. F. Raum, "Some Recent African Novels in English," *New South African Writing*, n.s., no. 5 (n.d.): 30–49.

25. Bernth Lindfors, "A Preliminary Checklist of English Short Fiction by Non-Europeans in South Africa, 1940–1964," *African Studies Bulletin*, 12 (1969): 272–91.

26. South African Centre of the International P.E.N. Club, "Selected Bibliography (of Works by South African Writers) 1945–1954," in *South African P.E.N. Yearbook* (Johannesburg: Central News Agency, 1954), pp. 81–92; cf. articles of the same title covering 1954–55 in the 1955 issue, pp. 124–27;

1955–57 in the 1957 issue, pp. 116–20; and a longer survey, "Fifty Years of the South African Novel," in the 1960 edition covering 1959.

27. See page 135 above.

28. South Africa appears in the following issues: no. 9 (1969): 1–27 (Laredo's bibliography cited above, note 24), no. 10 (1970): 123–31, vol. 6, no. 2 (1971): 110–19, vol. 7, no. 2 (1972): 136–47, vol. 8, no. 2 (1973): 147–57, vol. 9, no. 2 (1974): 140–48.

29. Selma P. Burkom, *Doris Lessing; a Checklist of Primary and Secondary Sources* (Troy, New York: Whitston, 1973); "Peter Abrahams: A Selected Bibliography," *World Literature Written in English,* 13, no. 2 (1974): 184–90; Edward Callan, *Alan Paton,* trans. Rolf Italiaander (Hamburger Bibliographien Band II. Hamburg: Hans Christian Verlag, 1970), pp. 35–80.

30. D. R. Beeton, ed., *A Pilot Bibliography of South African English Literature (from the Beginnings to 1971)* (Documenta 14. Pretoria: University of South Africa, 1976); cf. G. E. Gorman, "Review of *A Pilot Bibliography of South African English Literature,*" *African Book Publishing Record,* 3 (1977): 91; Stephen Gray, "Review of *A Pilot Bibliography of South African English Literature,*" *South African Libraries,* 44 (1977): 170–71.

31. Beeton, *op. cit.,* p. vii.

32. *Ibid.,* p. viii.

33. Irina Winterbottom, "Towards a Bibliography of South African Literature in English," *English in Africa,* 3, no. 1 (1976): 49–52.

Selected Publishers
and Scholarly Societies

Publishers

In addition to the international directories of publishers commonly used by most librarians, the individual charged with acquiring South African fiction is fortunate in having at hand a number of directories devoted partly or entirely to African publishers.[1] In recent months, however, these somewhat dated guides have been completely superseded by Hans Zell's *African Book World and Press*.[2] It is possible that Taubert's forthcoming volume may supplement Zell, but in view of the latter's excellence any substantial improvement will be extremely difficult to achieve. The bulk of *African Book World* consists of some 2,347 entries arranged in an alphabetical country sequence. Within each country the listing is divided into several sections: university, college and public libraries; special libraries; booksellers, publishers, institutional publishers; periodicals and magazines; newspapers; book industry associations and literary societies. Thus on pages 136–90 one has a complete picture of South African publishing, libraries and related interests. In terms of actual publishing houses, entries 1526–83 (publishers) and 1584–1604 (institutional publishers) present very full coverage of the field, listing both major South African publishing houses and the very small institutional presses. Without a great deal of effort one can discover the name, address, senior staff and· special interèsts of virtually every South African publisher likely to include fiction in its list.

More than this, and slightly outside the scope of this chapter, *African Book World* provides many other benefits to the user. The appendices (pp. 241–96) include a subject index to special libraries, subject index to periodical titles, list of African book clubs and literary prizes, a calendar of trade events, directories of government printers and overseas Africana book dealers and an updated bibliography of publishing and book development, the original version of which first appeared in *ABPR*.[3] Here, then, one will find a representative sampling of almost anything having to do with African publishing.

175

For the librarian seeking publishers of South African fiction, which are the important indigenous houses in this area? The major houses specializing in creative writing (Human and Rousseau, Perskor, Tafelberg and Timmins) in fact concentrate very heavily on "popular" fiction and writing in Afrikaans and other African languages; therefore, their lists will be of little value in collecting English language titles. One is left with a mere handful of very small South African publishers, none with a list of more than a few dozen titles, who exhibit an interest in creative English writing. One of the largest of these is David Randall's Ravan Press (Pty.) Ltd. (P.O. Box 31134, Braamfontein, 2017 South Africa). Committed more or less to the radical voice in imaginative writing, Ravan concentrates on short fiction, poetry and criticism (e.g., Nadine Gordimer's *The Black Interpreters*). Ravan also acts as agent for a slightly newer imprint, Bateleur Press, which was founded in 1975 by Lionel Abrahams and Patrick Cullinan. The policy of Bateleur is to publish works by writers who cannot readily find an outlet under present South African conditions (e.g., Bessie Head, *Serowe, Village of the Rain Wind*). Although the accent in the current list of eight titles lies clearly on short stories and poetry, Bateleur's co-publishing links with Davis-Poynter and Heinemann suggest that future expansion may well include novels. A Ravan-size firm is Ad. Donker (Pty.) Ltd. (P.O. Box 41021, Johannesburg, 2000 South Africa), which was established in 1973 and has some three dozen titles in its current list. A recent innovation by Donker is New Writing from South Africa, a series obviously devoted to creative writing; the degree to which book-length fiction will figure in this series must await future developments. Two other houses important for their interest in imaginative writing are BLAC Publishing House (P.O. Box 17, Athlone, Cape Town, South Africa) and David Philip Publisher (Pty.) Ltd. (3 Scott Road, Claremont, Cape Town, 7700 South Africa).

Aside from these three smaller companies (Bateleur, Donker and Ravan), one will not find much of interest being published within the Republic and so must turn to the multinationals which have exhibited a willingness to publish African writing. Without a doubt the earliest and most important international publisher in the field has been Heinemann with its African Writers Series, begun in 1962 and issued entirely in paperback. Although covering writing from Africa as a whole, there has been a sustained interest in works by both new and established novelists from the Republic (Modikwe Dikobe's *The Marabi Dance* and D. M. Zwelonke's *Robben Island*, Bessie Head's *A Question of Power* and Doris Lessing's *The Grass Is Singing*). In addition Heinemann also specializes in literary criticism with its Studies in African Literature series, which has included several titles relevant to South Africa (e.g., Pieterse and Munro's *Protest and Conflict in African Literature*, Palmer's *Introduction to the African Novel*, Killam's *African Writers on African Writing*); some of these have been issued in America under the Africana Publishing Company imprint (101 Fifth Avenue, New

York, New York 10003). Clearly, Heinemann is a publisher whose lists on African literature (48 Charles Street, London W1X 8AH) will require frequent scrutiny.

Somewhat behind Heinemann both in terms of its appearance on the Africana scene and relevance to South African fiction is the Longman Group (Longman House, Burnt Mill, Harlow, Essex GM20 2JE), which now incorporates Lane and Penguin in its lists. Longman's catalogue invariably includes a section on African writing in English, but this contains relevant titles only under the Penguin imprint (e.g., works by Paton, Cary, Schreiner). Recently, however, Longman has launched the African Creative Writing Series, which is to include drama, poetry and fiction in its coverage; under the editorship of Michael Echeruo the focus has been primarily on West African writers, but there is no reason why the series may not in time extend to South Africa. Slightly more relevant is the Modern African Writers series published by Evans Brothers (Montague House, Russell Square, London WC1B 5BX). Edited by Gerald Moore, it is devoted to critical studies of individual authors and already has included one work on a South African novelist (i.e., *Peter Abrahams* by Michael Wade). Another series by a different publisher, Fontana Modern African Novels (William Collins Sons, 14 St. James's Place, London SW1A 1PS), concentrates on fiction in paperback, and has recently issued one of Mphahlele's novels under this imprint.

Although most of these series, either those devoted to creative writing or to criticism, have not yet managed to bring South Africa clearly within their purview, they have potential importance in view of their general focus on African imaginative writing. Much less specific in their interests are Oxford University Press (Press Road, Neasden, London NW10 0DD) and Twayne Publishers. OUP has an inexpensive paperback imprint, Three Crown Books, which is designed to provide an outlet for new creative writing in English produced anywhere in the world. While Three Crowns makes no pretense of focusing on South Africa, one might have expected Oxford University Press Southern Africa, Ltd. (P.O. Box 1141, Cape Town, 8000 South Africa) to provide one or two titles by Republican novelists; however, this is not the case, for to date its prose offerings have not included a single South African work. Much the same is true of Macmillan South Africa (Pty.), Ltd. (Total Centre, P.O. Box 31487, Braamfontein, 2077 South Africa), which to date has published only one modern South African novel (i.e., Sheila Fugard's *The Castaways*). Slightly surprising, therefore, is the appearance of several studies of South African novelists in Twayne's World Authors Series (e.g., *Alan Paton* by Edward Callan and *Pauline Smith* by Geoffrey Haresnape); this series is issued by Twayne Publishers (c/o G. K. Hall and Company, 70 Lincoln Street, Boston, Massachusetts 02111), an American firm not generally recognized as a publisher of Africana.

Aside from these few South African and Western commercial publishers, one is likely to come across imaginative writing from South Africa under almost any imprint, for South African novelists, like other writers, do not limit their manuscripts to certain publishers. The same may be said of critical studies on the South African novel, which may appear in the lists of almost any scholarly or university press. Such works, either creative or critical, one will learn of through normal trade channels, but it will save much time if one is able to be directly in touch with those publishers noted above, since they are more or less specialists in South African fiction. In addition there are a few bibliography and reprint houses whose lists frequently cite titles of importance in the study of this genre. Among the publishers of bibliographies an important name to be aware of is Gale Research with its interest in literary bibliography. Its American Literature, English Literature and World Literatures in English: An Information Guide Series is scheduled to include relevant guides by both Theodore Greider and Bernth Lindfors in the near future. So too one will want to peruse the lists of R. R. Bowker and G. K. Hall, both of which have included a number of bibliographies cited frequently in the preceding chapters; these two publishers concentrate on Africana in general and so should not be expected to produce guides specifically on literature/African literature. Likewise one should be aware of the dissertation publishing undertaken by University Microfilms, since it occasionally produces theses relevant to African or South African literature.[4] Finally, the Kraus-Thomson Organization (Nedeln, Liechtenstein and Millwood, New York) frequently issues reprints of journals and monographs important in this field.[5]

Scholarly and Professional Organizations

If one intends to keep up with the various scholarly activities which have some bearing on South African literature, then it is important to maintain contact with the professional bodies devoted to this field. In looking at these societies one finds a wide range of interests encompassed in relatively few established groups. Although no more than twelve in number, they represent everything from general Africanist groups to literature societies to professional librarianship organizations, and each individual must decide which of these offer activities or services most akin to his particular interests.

The two bodies which encompass African studies as a whole and which include South African literature within their scope are the African Studies Association (U.S.) and the African Studies Association (U.K.). The former is by far the more active of the two and is well worth considering for membership even by scholars resident outside North America. The American ASA not only holds frequent meetings and conferences but also reports on African studies through a wide range of publications which should be of particular interest to librarians: *African Studies Review, African Studies Newsletter, Issue* and *ASA Review of Books*. These titles cover every aspect of African studies from scholarship to meetings and from controversy to book reviews.

Librarians in particular will find the *Newsletter* and *Review of Books* worth reading, since they keep one abreast of current Africanist activities, research and recent publications; the scholar, on the other hand, will find the *African Studies Review, Issue* and the *Newsletter* useful for both scholarship and professional information. Membership in ASA is open to all Africanists and may be obtained from the Association at Epstein Service Building, Brandeis University, Waltham, Massachusetts 02154; receipt of the *Newsletter, Review* and *Issue* are included with membership.

There are also several regional American associations devoted to African studies, among them the Rocky Mountain Southwest African Studies Association (Department of Political Science, North Texas State University, Denton, Texas), the Western Association of Africanists (Office of International Affairs, University of Houston, Houston, Texas 77004) and the Southern Association of Africanists (Center for African Studies, University of Florida, 470 Grinter Hall, Gainesville, Florida 32611). Most of these groups publish newsletters, but their contents deal primarily with professional activities in a limited geographical area. Because of this, one will probably wish to look to the larger associations for information of a more generally useful nature.

Another American group worth knowing about is the Southern African Research Association (Room 4133, Art/Sociology Building, University of Maryland, College Park, Maryland 20742). SARA has a special interest in research on Southern Africa and sponsors symposia and conferences on various topics relating to this region. It also publishes the *Journal of Southern African Affairs* (see above, pp. 136–37), which is well on the way to becoming an important organ in its field. Both the *Journal* and SARA's general activities exhibit wide ranging interest in all aspects of Southern African affairs, including literature. Therefore, although the Association is of recent vintage, one may well want to consider membership in it, if for no other reason than to receive the *Journal.*

Much less active than its American counterpart is the British African Studies Association, which holds fewer meetings and has fewer divisions, activities and publications. With SCOLMA it publishes *African Research and Documentation.* While membership for British Africanists is important in order to keep up with relevant activities in the U.K., it is probably more useful on an international level to belong to the American ASA. Nevertheless, membership in the British Association is inexpensive and brings with it a subscription to *African Research and Documentation;* this publication is useful as a means of learning about current research in Britain and other matters of interest to librarians in particular. The Association may be contacted at the Centre of West African Studies, University of Birmingham, P.O. Box 363, Birmingham B15 2SD, England.

Among the many general literature associations catering to scholarly interests the premier body is the Modern Language Association of America

(62 Fifth Avenue, New York, New York 10011). Begun in 1883, the MLA now includes several divisions specializing in various aspects of literary studies. Most important for the Africanist are the Division on English Literature Other Than British and American (ELOTBAA) and English Group 12. ELOTBAA (Department of English, Simon Fraser University, Burnaby 2, British Columbia) appears to be an interest group of recent vintage and has not yet undertaken any activities which merit the attention of Africanists. English Group 12, on the other hand, has existed for some time, having started as the Conference on British Commonwealth Literature (CBCL). Under that name it produced the *CBCL Newsletter,* which now appears as *World Literature Written in English*; this is an excellent newsletter with notes on professional activities, bibliographies and semi-scholarly essays. Membership and subscription information may be obtained from the Department of English, University of Texas at Arlington, Arlington, Texas 76010. Because English Group 12–World Literature Written in English has exhibited a strong interest in South African fiction (see page 142 above), it is a group well worth joining. In addition, the African Literatures Seminar of the MLA jointly sponsors with the African Literature Committee of the African Studies Association one of the best periodicals in this field, *Research in African Literatures* (see page 140 above), and this too is a title/group with which one should be constantly in touch (African and Afro-American Studies Research Center, University of Texas, P.O. Box 7457, Austin, Texas 78712).

The one society devoted specifically and wholly to African literature is yet another American body, the recently formed African Literature Association.[6] While it does not concentrate only on literature in English, the ALA through its *Newsletter* and conferences has exhibited a clear interest in African literature in this language. Because it is American, the Association naturally reflects the interests of scholars on that side of the Atlantic, but its meetings and news to date have been of direct value to the South Africanist. Therefore, one should consider membership in the ALA as a *sine qua non,* and details may be obtained from the French Department, Pennsylvania State University, University Park, Pennsylvania 16802.

Somewhat less well known among students of South African fiction is an association with a Commonwealth focus, the Association for Commonwealth Literature and Language Studies (ACLALS) and its various branches (see page 26 above). Begun in 1965, ACLALS has gradually built up a significant South African content in the pages of its important serial, the *Journal of Commonwealth Literature.* In addition to this title, ACLALS also publishes the *Commonwealth Newsletter* and *ACLALS Bulletin.* Taken together, these three serials provide an important source of information on South African fiction, whether this be scholarship or notes on professional activities. ACLALS also sponsors conferences which frequently include discussions on creative writing in the Republic; for all of these reasons the

Association is a significant but still underrated organization in African literary studies. Therefore, the benefits of membership are well worth the cost, since ACLALS publications alone will do much to keep one aware of current scholarship; details may be obtained from Dr. H. Maes-Jelinek, 4 Avenue des Ormes, 4.200 Cointe-Sclessin, Belgium. For some time the Canadian branch of ACLALS, which is known as CACLALS (Canadian Association for Commonwealth Language and Literary Studies) has expressed an interest in enrolling more members with an interest in African literature, and this has been reflected in the growing Africanist content of *Moko*, the CACLALS regional newsletter. This, however, is not part of the general ACLALS membership and may be obtained from R. R. Robertson, Department of English, University of Saskatchewan, Saskatoon, Saskatchewan, Canada S7N OWO.

In Africa itself there are virtually no societies or associations devoted to the study of African literature in English. For some years there was the Association for African Literature in English, which was based in Sierra Leone and published a bulletin; the Association is now defunct, and its newsletter has been incorporated in *African Literature Today*. As yet no other indigenous society of this type has been formed, but South Africa itself has become the location for an institutional response to the interest in English literature from Africa. This refers, of course, to the Institute for the Study of English in Africa at Rhodes University (Grahamstown, 6140 South Africa). This was established in 1964 and has enjoyed a remarkably low profile since then. The Institute concentrates very broadly on the study of English in Africa and sponsors research, collects information and provides liaison with local and overseas scholars in the field. ISEA publishes *English in Africa* and an annual report of research activities, not to mention the forthcoming bibliography (see pp. 169–70 above). For the last item alone ISEA deserves wider recognition, but the Institute is also important as the one indigenous undertaking of primary importance in this field. Scholars and librarians alike must be encouraged to obtain all of the Institute's publications, since they will keep them in touch with both academic and professional activities of some significance in the study of South African English fiction.

To summarize, the best sources of information on African literature, as opposed to African studies generally, must be the African Literature Association, the Association for Commonwealth Literature and Language Studies and the Institute for the Study of English in Africa. Among them they publish the most relevant newsletters or bulletins carrying information on professional activities related to South African fiction. In addition they provide, through the pages of *English in Africa* and the *Journal of Commonwealth Literature*, important scholarly essays on this branch of creative writing. Less important as professional bodies are the associations related to the MLA and African Studies Association (U.S.), but the two serials,

Research in African Literatures and *World Literature Written in English*, should be part of every collection devoted to South African fiction. It is only by using such tools as these that one can hope to be well informed of those activities in which English literature from South Africa plays an important part.

Notes

1. Sigfred Taubert, ed., *African Book Trade Directory 1971* (Munich: Verlag Dokumentation; New York: R. R. Bowker; London: André Deutsch, 1971). Under the same editor this is scheduled to reappear late in 1977 as *The Book Trade of the World. Vol. III: Africa and Asia* (Munich: Verlag für Buchmarkt-Forschung; New York: R. R. Bowker; London: André Deutsch). Cf. *Publishers' International Directory* (Fifth edition, 2 vols.; Munich: Verlag Dokumentation; New York: R. R. Bowker, 1972), of which volume 2 deals with Africa.

2. Hans M. Zell, ed., *The African Book World and Press—a Directory*, compiled by *African Book Publishing Record* (Oxford: Hans Zell [Publishers], 1977).

3. Hans M. Zell, "Publishing and Book Development in Africa: A Bibliography," *African Book Publishing Record*, 2 (1976): 95–103.

4. University Microfilms International, *Doctoral Dissertations on Africa* (London and Ann Arbor, Michigan: University Microfilms International, 1976?).

5. *Kraus Bibliographical Bulletin*, 16 (1977) is a special issue on "black Africa" and includes notes on Jahn and Dressler's *Bibliography of Creative African Writing* as well as such periodicals as *African Affairs, Africa South* and *Africa South in Exile*. Cf. Janheinz Jahn, ed., *The Black Experience I: 400 Years of Black Literature from Africa and the Americas* (Nedeln, Liechtenstein: Kraus Reprint, 1970?), which is in effect a listing of reprints available from Kraus.

6. Thomas Hale, "Establishment of African Literature Association," *Research in African Literatures*, 6 (1975): 60–63.

Conclusion

The South African novel in English already enjoys a certain degree of popularity in a variety of academic programs, and there is no reason why its acceptance as a legitimate field of study should not continue to expand. This present popularity, however, is not matched by knowledge of the appropriate bibliographical apparatus on the part of either librarians or researchers; indeed, the bibliographical framework itself is rather incomplete and uninspiring in many ways. It is because of both factors—the lack of knowledge and the bibliographical *lacunae*—that the present study has been undertaken. To provide some analysis of the literature and its bibliographical requirements, attention has focused on the various types of material required by both the librarian and the scholarly investigator. The main purpose of this discussion has been to create a basic reference tool which will go at least some way in meeting the requirements of those interested in the South African novel.

However, a bibliographical guide of this type can be nothing more than a beginning, for the basic need is for a variety of specific bibliographies in the categories discussed in Part II. Throughout the preceding pages a constant refrain has been the lament over the bibliographical *lacunae* which exist in every field; there is no adequate biographical dictionary of South African authors, no guide to relevant serials or theses and, most important of all, no complete bibliography of the novel since 1950 or, even if there were such a compilation, no project aimed at providing an ongoing bibliography of the field. At best, therefore, the preceding pages can only outline the variety of resources which are to be used in place of these non-existent bibliographies. There are, as we have seen in Part II, many categories of material which together go some way in meeting the requirements of those seeking bibliographical data on South African novels: biographical directories, bibliographies of bibliographies, national bibliographies, selective guides to literature and Africana, periodical indices, lists of theses and even the occasional bibliography of South African literature. In an attempt to reduce this mass of titles to reasonable proportions, each chapter in Part II has tried to indicate the best (and worst) publications in each category. In this way it is hoped that interested users will have at least some guidelines in finding their way through the bibliographical maze.

Ultimately, of course, the only real solution can be in the provision of two indispensable resources: (1) a comprehensive and complete bibliography of the South African novel and literary criticism in English, (2) an ongoing guide to current output, whether this be creative writing or its attendant criticism. The first of these essential tools is, as we have seen, currently being prepared by the Institute for the Study of English in Africa, but the latter guide has not yet been attempted on any notable scale. It is in this context that a tentative solution has been suggested in the form of a bibliographical committee/center devoted to collecting and disseminating information on the South African novel. Some institutions, particularly the above mentioned ISEA in South Africa and the African collection at Yale University, already attempt to collect comprehensively in the field of South African literature; what we have suggested in Chapter Four of Part I is an expansion of this work to provide adequate bibliographical coverage of South African imaginative writing. Whether this expansion takes the form of an international center, a national bibliographical collection or a committee for the bibliography of South African literature is for others to decide. Whatever option is chosen, some attempt must be made to close the gaps in present bibliographical coverage. It is only in this way that those of us with an interest in South African fiction can hope to have an adequate system for satisfying bibliographical inquiries in this increasingly important field.

Bibliography

The materials listed in this bibliography include only those items cited in the preceding pages or used for general background information. Therefore, this must not be taken as an exhaustive compilation but rather as a partial guide to resources relevant to the study of South African fiction. The bibliography does not list works in progress or personal correspondence; reference to these items may be found in the notes at the end of each chapter. Titles in the following compilation are classified according to their function in the preceding chapters, and because several items serve more than one purpose, they are cited more than once. The section on general background materials covers all citations found in Part I; the remaining sections correspond to Chapters 1–8 in Part II.

General Background Literature

Achebe, Chinua. "English and the African Writer," *Transition*, 18 (1965): 27–30.

Altbach, Philip G. "Publishing in Developing Countries: A Select Bibliography," *Scholarly Publishing*, 6 (1975): 267–79.

————. " 'Third World' Publishing: Problems and Prospects," *Scholarly Publishing*, 5 (1973): 247–53.

Anyakoha, Maduka W. "Publishing in Africa: A Bibliography," *A Current Bibliography on African Affairs*, 8 (1975): 269–319.

Apartheid: Its Effects on Education, Science, Culture and Information. Paris: Unesco, 1967. Pp. 149–60.

Armstrong, James C. "Africana Acquisitions Trip Report—1975," *Africana Libraries Newsletter*, no. 2 (1975): 13–23.

Armstrong, Robert P. "The Arts in Human Culture," in *Expanding Horizons in African Studies: Proceedings of the Twentieth Anniversary Conference, 1968, Program of African Studies, Northwestern University.* Edited by

Gwendolen M. Carter and Ann Paden. Evanston, Illinois: Northwestern University Press, 1969. Pp. 119–27.

―――. "The University Press in a Developing Country," *Scholarly Publishing*, 5 (1973): 35–40.

Astrinsky, Aviva, comp. *A Bibliography of South African English Novels 1930–1960*. Cape Town: University of Cape Town, School of Librarianship, 1965.

Bantock, G. H. "Literature and the Social Sciences," *Critical Quarterly*, 17 (1975): 99–127.

Beeton, D. R. "South African English Literature from the Perspective of the Seventies," *South African Libraries*, 40 (1972): 148–57.

Blair, Dorothy. "African Literature in University Education," in *African Literature and the Universities*. Edited by Gerald Moore. Ibadan: Ibadan University Press, 1965.

Blotner, Joseph. *The Modern American Political Novel, 1900–1960*. Austin: University of Texas Press, 1966.

―――. *The Political Novel*. Garden City, New Jersey: Doubleday, 1955.

Brutus, Dennis. "South Africa: The Tortoise Literature," in *Studies on Modern Black African Literature*. Edited by Pál Páricsy. Studies on Developing Countries, no. 43. Budapest: Center for Afro-Asian Research of the Hungarian Academy of Sciences, 1971. Pp. 85–88.

Carter, Gwendolen M. "African Studies in the United States," in *Proceedings of a Conference on African Languages and Literatures Held at Northwestern University, April 28–30, 1966*. Edited by Jack Berry, Robert P. Armstrong and John Povey. Evanston, Illinois: Northwestern University, 1966. Pp. 2–8.

―――. "African Studies in the United States: 1955–1975," *Issue*, 6, nos. 2/3 (1976): 2–4.

Cartey, Wilfred. "Contemporary African Literature," in *The African Experience*. Edited by John N. Paden and Edward W. Soja. Evanston, Illinois: Northwestern University Press, 1970. Vol. I. Pp. 502–91.

―――. *Whispers from a Black Continent: The Literature of Contemporary Black Africa*. London: Heinemann, 1971 [1969].

Clark, Alden H. "Publishing in Sub-Saharan Africa," *Scholarly Publishing*, 2 (1970): 67–74.

Clarke, D. A., ed. *Acquisitions from the Third World: Papers of the LIBER Seminar, 17–19 September 1973*. London: Mansell Publishing, 1975.

―――. "South Africa: Politics and Economics," in *Conference on the Acquisition of Material from Africa, University of Birmingham, 25th April 1969*. Edited by Valerie Bloomfield. Zug, Switzerland: Interdocumentation, 1969. Pp. 116–17.

Collison, Robert, comp. *The SCOLMA Directory of Libraries and Special Collections on Africa.* Third edition revised by John Roe. London: Crosby Lockwood Staples, 1973.

"Commonwealth Literature: Its Study and Sources," *Royal Commonwealth Society Library Notes,* n.s., no. 204 (1974).

"Company Profiles," *African Book Publishing Record,* 2 (1976): 15, 21–23.

Cook, David. *Literature: The Great Teaching Power of the World.* Nairobi: East African Literature Bureau, 1971.

Cook, Mercer, and Stephen E. Henderson. *The Militant Black Writer in Africa and the United States.* Madison: University of Wisconsin Press, 1969.

Cotezee, J. M. "Alex La Guma and the Responsibilities of the South African Writer," *Journal of the New African Literature and the Arts,* 9/10 (1971): 5–11.

Crossey, J. M. D. "Building a Working Collection on Africa: Notes on Bibliographic Aids and Dealers," *Africana Library Journal,* 1, no. 2 (1970): 18–22.

Dathorne, O. R. *African Literature in the Twentieth Century.* London: Heinemann, 1975.

————. *The Black Mind: A History of African Literature.* Minneapolis: University of Minnesota Press, 1974.

de Benko, Eugene. "Books and Publishing in Selected African Countries: Excerpts from a Report on a Library Acquisitions and Publications Survey Tour in Africa, November 1970–May 1971," *Africana Library Journal,* 3, no. 2 (1972): 3–14.

"Declaration of African Writers," *Issue,* 4, no. 4 (1974): 8.

Dodson, Don. "The Four Modes of *Drum*: Popular Fiction and Social Control in South Africa," *African Studies Review,* 17 (1974): 317–43.

Downey, J. A. "A Blanket Order Supplier: A Resumé of the Work of the African Imprint Library Services," *Africana Libraries Newsletter,* no. 5 (1976): 1–8.

Duerden, Dennis, and Cosmo Pieterse, eds. *African Writers Talking.* London: Heinemann, 1972.

Eleazu, U. O. "African Studies and the Study of the Future," *Issue,* 4, no. 4 (1974): 3–7.

Emenyonu, Ernest. "African Literature Revisited: A Search for African Critical Standards," *Revue de Littérature Comparée,* 48 (1974): 387–97.

Erb, Karen Simmons. "Books on Africa in the Local Library: A Critique," *Bulletin of the Southern Association of Africanists,* 5, no. 2 (1977): 5–30.

Frey, Mitsue Miyata, and Michael Sims, comps. *Directory of African and*

Afro-American Studies in the United States. Fifth edition. Waltham, Massachusetts: African Studies Association, 1976.

Gérard, Albert. "Bibliographical Problems in Creative African Literature," *Journal of General Education,* 19, no. 1 (1965): 25–34.

Goodwin, K. L., ed. *National Identity: Papers Delivered at the Commonwealth Literature Conference, University of Queensland, Brisbane, 9–15 August, 1968.* London: Heinemann, 1970.

Gordimer, Nadine. *The Black Interpreters: Notes on African Writing.* Braamfontein, South Africa: Ravan Press, 1973.

―――. "English-Language Literature and Politics in South Africa," *Journal of Southern African Studies,* 2, no. 2 (1975): 131–50.

―――. "Literature and Politics in South Africa," *Southern Review,* 7, no. 3 (1975): 205–27.

―――. "The Novel and the Nation in South Africa," in *African Writers on African Writing.* Edited by G. D. Killam. London: Heinemann, 1973. Pp. 33–52.

Hammond, Dorothy, and Alta Jablow. *The Africa That Never Was: Four Centuries of British Writing about Africa.* New York: Twayne Publishers, 1970.

Harris, Chauncey D. "Area Studies and Library Resources," *Library Quarterly,* 35 (1965): 205–22.

Harvard University, Faculty of Arts and Sciences. *Report of the Faculty Committee on African and Afro-American Studies.* Cambridge, Massachusetts: Harvard University Press, 1969.

Herbstein, Denis. "The Man with the Golden Typewriter," *The Sunday Times Magazine,* 11 April 1976, pp. 55–60.

Heywood, Christopher, ed. *Perspectives on African Literature: Selections from the Proceedings of the Conference on African Literature Held at the University of Ife, 1968.* London: Heinemann, 1971.

Horne, A. J. "An Outline of U.K. Library Holdings of Commonwealth Imaginative Literature: Statistics." Paper read at the Conference on Library Holdings of Commonwealth Literature, Commonwealth Institute, London, 5 June 1970 (Mimeographed).

International African Institute. *International Guide to African Studies Research.* London: International African Institute, 1975.

Izevbaye, D. S. "African Literature Defined: The Record of a Controversy," *Ibadan Studies in English,* 1 (1970): 56–69.

Jahn, Janheinz. *A History of Neo-African Literature: Writing in Two Continents.* Translated by Oliver Coburn and Ursula Lehrburger. London: Faber and Faber, 1968.

————. "Modern African Literature: Bibliographical Spectrum," *Review of National Literatures*, 2, no. 2 (1971): 224–42.

————. *Muntu: An Outline of Neo-African Culture*. Translated by Marjorie Greene. London: Faber and Faber, 1961.

————, and Claus Peter Dressler. *Bibliography of Creative African Writing*. Nedeln, Liechtenstein: Kraus-Thomson, 1971.

Jeanpierre, W. "Negritude and Its Enemies," in *African Literature and the Universities*. Edited by Gerald Moore. Ibadan: Ibadan University Press, 1965.

Jeffares, A. Norman. "The Study of Commonwealth Literature," *Journal of the Royal Society of Arts*, no. 5149 (1968): 16–33.

Joyaux, Georges J. "On African Literature," *African Studies Review*, 15 (1972): 307–18.

Kettle, M. R., and R. P. Moss, eds. *Southern African Studies: Report of a Symposium Held at the School of Oriental and African Studies in the University of London on 24th September 1969 by the African Studies Association of the U.K.* Birmingham, England: University of Birmingham, Centre of West African Studies, 1970.

Killam, G. D. "Modern Black African Writing in English: A Selected Bibliography," *Canadian Journal of African Studies*, 9 (1975): 537–66.

Klima, Vladimir. *South African Prose Writing in English*. London: C. Hurst, 1971.

Knoke, Susan. "Report on a Library Acquisitions Trip to Africa, December 1969–March 1970," *Africana Library Journal*, 1, no. 4 (1970): 14–23.

Kotei, S. I. A. *Persistent Issues in African Bibliography*. Department of Library and Archival Studies, University of Ghana, Occasional Paper No. 7. Legon: University of Ghana, 1972.

Laredo, Ursula. "African Mosaic: The Novels of Nadine Gordimer," *Journal of Commonwealth Literature*, 8, no. 1 (1973): 42–53.

Larson, Charles R. "Alan Paton's *Cry the Beloved Country* after Twenty-Five Years," *Africa Today*, 20, no. 4 (1973): 53–57.

————. *The Emerence of African Fiction*. Revised edition. Bloomington: Indiana University Press, 1972.

————. *The Novel in the Third World*. Washington, D.C.: Inscape, 1976.

Legum, Colin, ed. *Africa: A Handbook*. Second edition. London: Anthony Blond, 1965.

Lessing, Doris. *Going Home*. St. Albans, Herts.: Panther Books, 1968 [1957].

Lindfors, Bernth. "American University and Research Library Holdings in African Literature," *African Studies Bulletin*, 11 (1968): 286–311.

————. "Introduction: Proceedings of the First Symposium on Contemporary

African Literature and First African Literature Association Conference," *Issue,* 6, no. 1 (1976): 3.

―――. "Robin Hood Realism in South African English Fiction," *Africa Today,* 15, no. 4 (1968): 16–18.

MacRae, Donald. "A World of Riches," *The Sunday Times,* 13 April 1975, p. 40.

Madubuike, Ihechukwa. "The African Novel in the 1970's: Basic Identity and Categorization," *Issue,* 4, no. 4 (1974): 15–18.

Maes-Jelinek, Hena, ed. *Commonwealth Literature and the Modern World.* Brussels: Editions Marcel Didier, 1975.

Makouta-Mboukou, J. P. *Black African Literature: An Introduction.* Washington, D.C.: Black Orpheus Press, 1972.

Masters, Brian. *Sartre: A Study.* London: Heinemann, 1974.

May, Rollo. *Power and Innocence: A Search for the Sources of Violence.* London: Fontana, 1976.

Moore, Gerald. *The Chosen Tongue: English Writing in the Tropical World.* London: Longman, 1969.

―――. " 'Reintegration with the Lost Self': A Theme in Contemporary African Literature," *Revue de Littérature Comparée,* 48 (1974): 488–503.

Morehouse, Ward, ed. *The Comparative Approach in Area Studies and the Disciplines; Problems of Teaching and Research on Asia: Selected Papers Presented at the Conference on Asian Studies and Comparative Approaches Sponsored by the Comparative Studies Center, Dartmouth College, September 13–17, 1965.* Occasional Publication no. 4. New York: Foreign Area Materials Center, University of the State of New York, State Education Department, 1966.

Mphahlele, Ezekiel. "South African Black Writing 1972–1973," *Ba Shiru,* 5, no. 2 (1974): 27–35.

―――. *Voices in the Whirlwind and Other Essays.* New York: Hill and Wang, 1972 [1967].

Musiker, Reuben. "South African English Literature: Bibliographic and Biographical Resources and Problems," *English Studies in Africa,* 13 (1970): 265–73.

Mutiso, Gideon-Cyrus Makau. "African Socio-Political Process: A Model from Literature," in *Black Aesthetics: Papers from a Colloquium Held at the University of Nairobi, June 1971.* Edited by Andrew Gurr and Pio Zirimu. Nairobi: East African Literature Bureau, 1973. Pp. 104–74.

―――. *Socio-Political Thought in African Literature: Weusi?* New York: Barnes and Noble, 1974.

"Nadine Gordimer: The Solitude of a White Writer," *The Listener,* 96, no. 2480 (1976): 514.

Nathan, Manfred. *South African Literature: A General Survey.* Cape Town: Juta, 1925.

Nazareth, Peter. *Literature and Society in Modern Africa.* Nairobi: East African Literature Bureau, 1972.

Nitecki, André, ed. *African Studies in the Seventies: Selected Papers Presented at a Conference on Problems of Classification for Africana Held at the University of Ghana, 22–24 November 1973.* Department of Library and Archival Studies, University of Ghana, Occasional Paper no. 8. Legon: University of Ghana, 1974.

Niven, Alastair. "Commonwealth Literature Studies in British Universities," *Commonwealth,* 17, no. 3 (1973): 59–61.

Nkoko, G. M. "Apartheid and Alienation: Mphahlele's *The Wanderers,*" *Africa Today,* 20, no. 4 (1973): 59–70.

Nkosi, Lewis. "Fiction by Black South Africans: Richard Rive, Bloke Modisane, Ezekiel Mphahlele, Alex La Guma," in *Introduction to African Literature: An Anthology of Critical Writing from "Black Orpheus."* Edited by Ulli Beier. London: Longman, 1967. Pp. 211–17.

Obuke, J. O. "The Structure of Commitment: A Study of Alex La Guma," *Ba Shiru,* 5, no. 1 (1973): 14–20.

Ogungbesan, Kolawole. "Autobiographies in Africa," *Savanna* (June 1973): 1–10.

———. "The Political Novels of Peter Abrahams," *Présence Africaine,* 83 (1972): 33–50.

———. "Politics and the African Writer," *African Studies Review,* 17 (1974): 43–53.

Olney, James. *Tell Me Africa: An Approach to African Literature.* Princeton, New Jersey: Princeton University Press, 1973.

Omotoso, Kole. "Interview," *African Book Publishing Record,* 2 (1976): 12–14.

Owomoyela, Oyekan. "Western Humanism and African Usage: A Critical Survey of Non-African Responses to African Literature," *Issue,* 4, no. 4 (1974): 9–14.

Paden, John N., and Edward W. Soja, eds. *The African Experience.* 3 vols. in 4. Evanston, Illinois: Northwestern University Press, 1970.

Palmer, Eustace. *An Introduction to the African Novel: A Critical Study of 12 Books by Chinua Achebe, James Ngugi, Camara Laye, Elechi Amadi, Ayi Kweh Armah, Mongo Beti and Gabriel Okara.* London: Heinemann, 1972.

"Panel on Literature and Commitment in South Africa: Proceedings of the First Symposium on Contemporary African Literature and First African Literature Association Conference," *Issue,* 6, no. 1 (1976): 34–46.

"Panel on South African Fiction and Autobiography: Proceedings of the First Symposium on Contemporary African Literature and First African Literature Association Conference," *Issue,* 6, no. 1 (1976): 14–24.

Panter-Brick, S. K. "Fiction and Politics: The African Writers' Abdication," *Journal of Commonwealth and Comparative Politics,* 13 (1975): 79–86.

Páricsy, Pál. "A Short Survey of the History of Black African Literature," in *Studies on Modern Black African Literature.* Edited by Pál Páricsy. Studies on Developing Countries, no. 43. Budapest: Center for Afro-Asian Research of the Hungarian Academy of Sciences, 1971. Pp. 1–11.

Paton, Alan. "Four Splendid Voices," in *Quartet: New Voices from Africa.* Edited by Richard Rive. New York: Crown Publishers, 1963. Pp. 11–14.

Perry-Widstrand, Rede. "Publishing in Africa." Paper prepared for the Seminar on African Literature Organised by the Finnish Unesco Commission, Helsinki, September 13–15, 1974 (Mimeographed).

Pieterse, Cosmo, and Donald Munro, eds. *Protest and Conflict in African Literature.* London: Heinemann, 1969.

Povey, John F. "African Literature and American Universities," *African Studies Bulletin,* 11, no. 2 (1966): 13–19.

―――. "Introduction," in *Black African Literature in English Since 1952, Works and Criticism.* Compiled by Barbara Abrash. New York: Johnson Reprint, 1967. Pp. i–xiv.

―――. " 'Non-European' Writing in South Africa," *Review of National Literatures,* 2, no. 2 (1971): 66–80.

―――. "Political Protest in the African Novel in English," in *Protest and Power in Black Africa.* Edited by R. Rotberg and A. Mazrui. New York: Oxford University Press, 1970. Pp. 823–53.

―――. "South Africa," in *Literatures of the World in English.* Edited by Bruce King. London: Routledge & Kegan Paul, 1974. Pp. 154–71.

Priebe, Richard K. "African Literature and the American University," *Issue,* 4, no. 4 (1974): 19–22.

"Prominent Bookshops in Africa," *African Book Publishing Record,* 2 (1976): 155, 165–69.

Quartermaine, Peter. "Library Specialization in Commonwealth Literature: Some Notes on the Role of the Provincial Library." Paper presented at the Conference on Library Holdings of Commonwealth Literature, Commonwealth Institute, London, 5 June 1970 (Mimeographed).

Rabkin, D. "La Guma and Reality in South Africa," *Journal of Commonwealth Literature,* 8, no. 1 (1973): 54–62.

Ramsaran, John A. *New Approaches to African Literature: A Guide to Negro-African Writing and Related Studies.* Second edition. Ibadan: Ibadan University Press, 1970.

Randall, Peter. " 'Minority' Publishing in South Africa," *African Book Publishing Record,* 1 (1975): 219–22.

Rea, Julian. "Aspects of African Publishing 1945–74," *African Book Publishing Record,* 1 (1975): 145–49.

"Report of Working Party on the Teaching of Commonwealth Literature," in *National Identity: Papers Delivered at the Commonwealth Literature Conference, University of Queensland, Brisbane, 9–15 August 1968.* Edited by K. L. Goodwin. London: Heinemann, 1970. Pp. 203–205.

Rubadiri, David. "Why African Literature?," in *African Writers on African Writing.* Edited by G. D. Killam. London: Heinemann, 1973. Pp. 140–47.

Rutherfoord, Anna. "Commonwealth Literature Studies Have Taken Hold of West European Universities," *Commonwealth,* 16, no. 6 (1972): 154–56.

Shorter, A. *African Culture and the Christian Church: An Introduction to Social and Pastoral Anthropology.* London: Geoffrey Chapman, 1973.

Simpson, Donald H. "The Working Party on Library Holdings of Commonwealth Literature," *Education Libraries Bulletin,* 18, 1, no. 52 (1975): 13–17.

Smith, Datus C., Jr. "The Bright Promise of Publishing in Developing Countries," *Annals of the American Academy of Political and Social Science,* no. 421 (1975): 130–39.

Smith, Keith. "Who Controls Book Publishing in Anglophone Middle Africa?," *Annals of the American Academy of Political and Social Science,* no. 421 (1975): 140–50.

Smith, Rowland. "The Johannesburg Genre," in *Exile and Tradition: Studies in African and Caribbean Literature.* Edited by Rowland Smith. Dalhousie African Studies 1; John Flint, editor. London: Longman, 1976. Pp. 116–31.

Snyder, Emil. "The Teaching of Modern African Literature Written in a Western Language," in *Proceedings of a Conference on African Languages and Literature Held at Northwestern University, April 28–30, 1966.* Edited by Jack Berry, Robert P. Armstrong and John Povey. Evanston, Illinois: Northwestern University Press, 1966.

Srinivasa, K. R. Iyengar. *Two Cheers for the Commonwealth: Talks on Literature and Education.* London: Asia Publishing House, 1970.

Steele, M. C. *"Children of Violence" and Rhodesia: A Study of Doris Lessing As Historical Observer.* Local Series Pamphlets 29. Salisbury, Rhodesia: Central Africa Historical Association, 1974.

Thompson, James. *The Librarian and English Literature.* London: Association of Assistant Librarians, 1968.

Tucker, Martin. *Africa in Modern Literature: A Survey of Contemporary Writing in English.* New York: Frederick Ungar, 1967.

Udoeyop, N. J., and Dan Izevbaye. *Themes and Patterns in Black Literature.* Ibadan: Ibadan University Press, 1975.

Varley, Douglas H. "Trends Abroad: South Africa," *Library Trends,* 19 (1970): 139–51.

von Hahmann, Gail, ed. *Directory of African Studies in the United States 1974–1975.* Fourth edition. Waltham, Massachusetts: Research Liaison Committee, African Studies Association, 1975.

Wade, Michael. "William Plomer, English Liberalism and the South African Novel," *Journal of Commonwealth Literature,* 8, no. 1 (1973): 20–32.

Wästberg, Per. "Themes in African Literature Today," *Daedalus* (Spring 1974): 135–50.

————, ed. *The Writer in Modern Africa: Scandinavian Writers Conference, Stockholm.* Uppsala, Sweden: Scandinavian Institute of African Studies, 1970.

Wake, Clive. "The Political and Cultural Revolution," in *Protest and Conflict in African Literature.* Edited by Cosmo Pieterse and Donald Munro. London: Heinemann, 1969. Pp. 43–55.

Wauthier, Claude. *The Literature and Thought of Modern Africa: A Survey.* Translated by Shirley Key. London: Pall Mall Press, 1966.

Wilhelm, Donald. "The Crisis in Area Programs: A Time for Innovation," *African Studies Review,* 14 (1971): 171–78.

Wilson, Gail, comp. *A Handbook of Library Holdings of Commonwealth Literature in the United Kingdom.* Reprint. London: Commonwealth Institute Working Party on Library Holdings of Commonwealth Literature, 1974 [1971].

Wilson, Monica, and Leonard Thompson, eds. *The Oxford History of South Africa.* 2 vols. Oxford: Clarendon Press, 1971.

Winegarten, Renee. *Writers and Revolution: The Fatal Lure of Action.* New York: Franklin Watts, 1974.

Winterbottom, Irina. "Towards a Bibliography of South African Literature in English," *English in Africa,* 3, no. 1 (1976): 49–52.

Witherell, Julian W. *Africana Acquisitions: Report of a Publications Survey Trip to Nigeria, South Africa and Europe, 1972.* Washington, D.C.: Library of Congress, African Section, 1973.

"Writers in Exile," *African Arts,* 1, no. 4 (1968): 19–25.

Yang, C. K. "A Conceptual Review of Area and Comparative Studies: Some Initial Reflections," in *The Comparative Approach in Area Studies and the Disciplines; Problems of Teaching and Research on Asia: Selected Papers Presented at the Conference on Asian Studies and Comparative Approaches Sponsored by the Comparative Studies Center, Dartmouth College, September 13–17, 1965.* Edited by Ward Morehouse. Occasional

Publication no. 4. New York: Foreign Area Materials Center, University of the State of New York, State Education Department, 1966. Pp. 46–54.

Zell, Hans M. "Publishing and Book Development in Africa: A Bibliography," *African Book Publishing Record,* 2 (1976): 95–103.

Biographical Data

Abrahams, Peter. *Tell Freedom: Memories of Africa.* London: Faber and Faber, 1954.

African Encyclopedia. London: Oxford University Press, 1974.

African Who's Who. Fourth edition. Johannesburg: Central News Agency, 1969.

Anderson, Susan. "Something in Me Died: Autobiographies of South African Writers in Exile," *Books Abroad,* 44 (1970): 398–403.

The Author's and Writer's Who's Who. Sixth edition. London: Burke's Peerage, 1972.

Biography Index: A Cumulative Index to Biographical Materials in Books and Magazines. New York: H. W. Wilson, 1946– .

Callan, Edward. *Alan Paton.* Twayne's World Authors Series, no. 40. New York: Twayne Publishers, 1968.

———. *Alan Paton.* Translated by Rolf Italiaander. Hamburger Bibliographien Band II. Hamburg, West Germany: Hans Christian Verlag, 1970.

Carpenter, F. I. *Laurens van der Post.* Twayne's World Authors Series, no. 68. New York: Twayne Publishers, 1970(?).

Current Biography. New York: H. W. Wilson, 1940– .

Daiches, David, ed. *The Penguin Companion to Literature: Britain and the Commonwealth.* Harmondsworth: Penguin, 1971.

de Kock, W. J., ed. *Dictionary of South African Biography.* Cape Town: Nasionale Boekhandel for the National Council for Social Research, Department of Higher Education, 1968– .

Dickie, John, and Alan Rake. *Who's Who in Africa: The Political, Military and Business Leaders of Africa.* London: African Development, 1973.

Dudley, D. R., and D. M. Lang, eds. *The Penguin Companion to Literature: Classical and Byzantine; Oriental and African.* Harmondsworth: Penguin, 1969.

Fleischmann, W. Bernard. *Encyclopaedia of World Literature in the Twentieth Century.* New York: Frederick Ungar, 1967–1968.

Friedrich-Ebert-Stiftung. *African Biographies.* Bonn-Bad Godesburg, West Germany: Verlag Neue Gesellschaft, 1971– .

Fung, Karen, comp. "Index to 'Portraits' in West Africa, 1948–1966," *African Studies Bulletin,* 9, no. 3 (1966): 103–20.

Herdeck, Donald E. *African Authors: A Companion to Black African Writing. Vol. I, 1300–1973.* Washington, D.C.: Black Orpheus Press, 1973.

Hutchinson, Alfred. *Road to Ghana.* London: Victor Gollancz, 1960.

The International Who's Who. Thirty-eighth edition. London: Europa, 1974.

Jabavu, Noni. *Drawn in Colour; African Contrasts.* London: Murray, 1960.

————. *The Ochre People; Scenes from a South African Life.* London: Murray, 1963.

Jahn, Janheinz, Ulla Schild and Almut Nordmann, eds. *Who's Who in African Literature: Biographies, Works, Commentaries.* Tübingen, West Germany: Horst Erdman Verlag for the German Africa Society, 1972.

Jacobson, Dan. "Settling in England," *Commentary,* 29 (1960): 23–24.

Kay, Ernest, comp. *Dictionary of African Biography.* Second edition. London: Melrose Press, 1971.

Kinsman, Clare D., ed. *Contemporary Authors: A Bio-Bibliographical Guide to Current Authors and Their Works.* Detroit, Michigan: Gale Research, 1962– .

Kronenberger, Louis, ed. *Brief Lives: A Biographical Guide to the Arts.* London: Allen Lane, 1972 [1965].

Larson, Charles R. "Review of Jahn, *Who's Who in African Literature,*" *Africana Library Journal,* 4, no. 4 (1973): 23.

Le Beau, Dennis, and Gary C. Tarbert, eds. *Biographical Dictionaries Master Index; First Edition, 1975–1976.* 3 vols. Detroit, Michigan: Gale, 1975.

Lessing, Doris. *Going Home.* St. Albans, Herts.: Panther Books, 1968 [1957].

Matshikiza, Todd. *Chocolates for My Wife; Slices from My Life.* London: Hodder and Stoughton, 1961.

Modisane, Bloke. *Blame Me on History.* London: Thames and Hudson, 1963.

Mphahlele, Ezekiel. *Down Second Avenue.* London: Faber and Faber, 1959.

Pollard, Arthur, ed. *Webster's New World Companion to English and American Literature.* London: Compton Russell, 1973.

"Portrait: Ezekiel Mphahlele," *West Africa,* no. 2390 (1963): 317.

Richardson, Kenneth, ed. *Twentieth Century Writing: A Reader's Guide to Contemporary Literature.* London: Newnes, 1969.

Rosenthal, Eric, ed. *Encyclopaedia of Southern Africa.* Sixth edition. London: Frederick Warne, 1973.

————, ed. *Southern African Dictionary of National Biography.* London: Frederick Warne, 1966.

Royal Commonwealth Society, comp. *Biography.* Vol. 7 of *Subject Catalogue of the Royal Commonwealth Society.* Boston: G. K. Hall, 1971.

Rutherfoord, Peggy. *African Voices: An Anthology of Native African Writing.* New York: Vanguard, 1961.

Seymour-Smith, Martin. *Guide to Modern World Literature.* London: Wolfe, 1973.

————. *Who's Who in Twentieth Century Literature.* London: Weidenfeld and Nicholson, 1976.

Simpson, Donald H., ed. *Biography Catalogue of the Library of the Royal Commonwealth Society.* London: Royal Commonwealth Society, 1961.

Standard Encyclopaedia of Southern Africa. 10 vols. Cape Town: Nasionale Opvoedkundige Uitgewery, 1970–1974.

Steinberg, S. H., ed. *Cassell's Encyclopaedia of World Literature.* Revised edition by J. Buchanan-Brown. 3 vols. London: Cassell, 1973.

Taylor, Sidney, ed. *The New Africans; A Guide to the Contemporary History of Emergent Africa and Its Leaders.* London: Paul Hamlyn, 1967.

Thorne, J. O., and T. C. Collocott, eds. *Chambers Biographical Dictionary.* Revised edition. London: W. and R. Chambers, 1974.

Tibble, Anne, ed. *African-English Literature: A Short Survey and Anthology of Prose and Poetry up to 1965.* London: Peter Owen, 1965.

Ushpol, Rowse, comp. *A Select Bibliography of South African Autobiographies.* Cape Town: University of Cape Town, School of Librarianship, 1958.

Vinson, James, ed. *Contemporary Novelists.* Second edition. Contemporary Writers of the English Language. London: St. James Press, 1976.

van Heyningen, C., and J. A. Berthoud. *Uys Krige.* Twayne's World Authors Series, no. 2. New York: Twayne Publishers, 1967(?).

Wade, Michael. *Peter Abrahams.* Modern African Writers, edited by Gerald Moore. London: Evans Brothers, 1972.

Wakeman, John, ed. *World Authors 1950–1970.* Wilson Author Series. New York: H. W. Wilson, 1975.

Webster's Biographical Dictionary. Springfield, Massachusetts: G. and C. Merriam, 1972.

Who's Who of Southern Africa; Including Mauritius and Incorporating South African Who's Who. Johannesburg: Combined Publishers, 1907– .

The Writer's Directory. London: St. James Press, 1973.

Zell, Hans M., and Helene Silver, eds. *A Reader's Guide to African Literature.* New York: Africana, 1971 (London: Heinemann, 1972).

General Bibliographical Guides

Avicenne, Paul. *Bibliographical Services Throughout the World 1960–1964.* Unesco Bibliographical Handbooks, no. 11. Paris: Unesco, 1969.

―――. *Bibliographical Services Throughout the World 1965–69.* Documentation, Libraries and Archives: Bibliographies and Reference Works, no. 1. Paris: Unesco, 1972.

Besterman, Theodore. *A World Bibliography of African Bibliographies.* Revised edition by J. D. Pearson. Totowa, New Jersey: Rowman and Littlefield, 1975.

―――. *A World Bibliography of Bibliographies and of Bibliographical Catalogues, Calendars, Abstracts, Digests, Indexes and the Like.* 5 vols. Lausanne, Switzerland: Societas Bibliographica, 1965–1966.

Bibliographic Index: A Cumulative Bibliography of Bibliographies. New York: H. W. Wilson, 1938– .

Bibliography, Documentation, Terminology. Paris: Unesco, 1961– .

Bogaert, Jozef. *Sciences Humaines en Afrique Noire: Guide Bibliographique (1945–1965).* Enquêtes Bibliographiques 15. Brussels: Centre de Documentation Economique Sociale Africaine, 1966.

Collison, Robert L. *Bibliographical Services Throughout the World 1950–59.* Unesco Bibliographical Manuals, no. 9. Paris: Unesco, 1961.

―――. *Bibliographies Subject and National: A Guide to Their Contents, Arrangement and Use.* Second edition. London: Crosby Lockwood, 1962.

Conover, Helen F. *Africa South of the Sahara.* Washington, D.C.: Library of Congress, 1961.

Duignan, Peter, ed. *Guide to Research and Reference Works on Sub-Saharan Africa.* Hoover Institution Bibliographical Series, no. 46. Stanford, California: Hoover Institution, 1971.

―――. "Review of Panofsky's *A Bibliography of Africana,*" *Africana Journal,* 4 (1975): 316–17.

Easterbrook, David L. "Bibliography of Africana Bibliographies, 1965–1975," *Africana Journal,* 7 (1976): 101–48.

Fontvieille, Jean-Roger, comp. *Bibliographic Guide to the Negro World: History, Literature, Ethnology.* 1 vol. in 2. Yaoundé, Cameroun: Ministry of Education, Culture and Vocational Training, Direction of Cultural Affairs, 1970.

Freer, Percy, and Douglas Varley, comps. *A Bibliography of African Bibliographies Covering Territories South of the Sahara.* Fourth edition revised by A. M. Lewin Robinson. Grey Bibliographies, no. 7. Cape Town: South African Public Library, 1961.

Garling, Anthea, comp. *Bibliography of African Bibliographies.* Occasional

Papers, no. 1. Cambridge, England: Cambridge University, African Studies Centre, 1968.

Gibson, Gordon D. "A Bibliography of Anthropology Bibliographies: Africa," *Current Anthropology*, 10 (1969): 527–66.

Gray, Richard A., ed. *Serial Bibliographies in the Humanities and Social Sciences.* Ann Arbor, Michigan: Pierian Press, 1969.

Hartwig, Gerald W., and William M. O'Barr. *The Student Africanist's Handbook: A Guide to Resources.* Cambridge, Massachusetts: Schenkman, 1974.

Matthews, Daniel. "African Bibliography Today: Selected and Current Bibliographical Tools for African Studies, 1967–68," *A Current Bibliography on African Affairs,* 1, no. 11 (1968): 4–17.

Musiker, Reuben. "Bibliographical Notes: Southern Africa," *African Studies Bulletin,* 10, no. 2 (1967): 83.

———. "Bibliographical Progress," *South African Library Association Newsletter,* 22, no. 8 (1971): 144–47; 23, no. 8 (1972): 250–56; 26, no. 9 (1975): 144–47; 26, no. 11 (1975): 171–72.

———. "Bibliographical Progress in South Africa," *African Studies Bulletin,* 11, no. 2 (1968): 221–24; 12, no. 3 (1969): 305–14.

———. "Bibliographical Progress in South Africa, January 1971," *Africana Library Journal,* 2, no. 1 (1971): 10–11.

———. "Bibliographical Progress in South Africa, January 1972," *Africana Library Journal,* 3, no. 2 (1972): 21–23.

———. *Guide to South African Reference Books.* Fifth edition. Cape Town: A. A. Balkema, 1971.

———. *Guide to South African Reference Books: Third Cumulative Supplement 1970–1974.* Johannesburg: University of the Witwatersrand, 1975.

———. "South African Bibliographical Notes and News," *African Research and Documentation,* 11 (1977): 28–32.

———. "South African Bibliographical Progress," *African Studies Bulletin,* 10, no. 2 (1967): 103–106; 10, no. 3 (1967): 117–19.

———. *South African Bibliography: A Survey of Bibliographies and Bibliographical Work.* London: Crosby Lockwood, 1971.

———. *South African Bibliography: A Survey of Bibliographies and Bibliographical Work. Supplement 1970–1974.* Johannesburg: University of Witwatersrand Library, 1975.

Panofsky, Hans E. *A Bibliography of Africa.* Contributions in Librarianship and Information Science, no. 11; Paul Wasserman, general editor. Westport, Connecticut: Greenwood Press, 1975.

Patterson, Margaret C. *Literary Research Guide.* Detroit, Michigan: Gale, 1976.

Reitz, Conrad H. *South African Bibliography.* Occasional Papers, no. 90. Urbana: University of Illinois, Graduate School of Library Science, 1967.

Staatsbibliothek Preussischer Kulturbesitz, ed. *Bibliographische Bericht.* Frankfurt am Main, West Germany: Verlag Vittorio Klostermann, 1959– .

Taylor, Alan R. *African Studies Research; A Brief Guide to Selected Bibliographies and Other Sources for African Studies.* Preliminary edition. Bloomington: Indiana University, African Studies Program, 1964.

———. *Bibliographical and Archival Resources for African Studies.* Bloomington: Indiana University, 1972(?) (Mimeographed).

———. "Introduction to the Bibliography of Sub-Saharan Africa at Indiana University," *African Studies Bulletin,* 8, no. 2 (1965): 97–99.

Selective, Non-Serial Bibliographies

Abramova, S. Yu, comp. *African Studies in the U.S.S.R.: List of Annotations on Major Works Published in 1952–First Half of 1962.* Moscow: U.S.S.R. Academy of Sciences, Institute of Africa, 1962.

African Bibliographic Center, comp. *African Affairs for the General Reader: A Selected and Introductory Bibliographical Guide 1960–67.* Edited by Daniel G. Matthews. Special Bibliographic Series. Vol. 5, no. 4. Washington, D.C.: African Bibliographic Center, 1967.

———. *African Affairs for the General Reader, 1968.* Special Bibliographic Series. Vol. 6, no. 3. Washington, D.C.: African Bibliographic Center, 1968.

Alexander, H. P., comp. "Supplement to the Catalogue of the African Collection in the Moorland Foundation of the Howard University Library." Unpublished M.L.S. thesis, Catholic University of America, 1963.

Altick, Richard D., and Andrew Wright. *Selective Bibliography for the Study of English and American Literature.* Fifth edition. London: Collier Macmillan, 1975.

American Universities Field Staff, Inc. *A Select Bibliography: Asia, Africa, Eastern Europe, Latin America.* New York: American Universities Field Staff, Inc., 1960.

Beyer, Barry K. *Africa South of the Sahara: A Resource and Curriculum Guide.* New York: Thomas Y. Crowell, 1969.

"Bibliography of Books and Key Articles on Africa Published in Polish, English and other Languages in Poland Since 1960, with an Introductory Essay on African Studies in Eastern Europe and the Soviet Union," *Munger Africana Library Notes,* no. 33 (1976).

Brown, J. Cudd, and Kraig A. Schwartz, comps. *Africa: A Selective, Working*

Bibliography. University Park: Pennsylvania State University Libraries, 1970(?).

Central Asian Research Centre, comp. *Soviet Writing on Africa, 1959–61: An Annotated Bibliography.* London: Royal Institute of International Affairs, 1963.

The Combined Book Exhibit, Inc. *A Bibliography of African Studies.* Scarborough Park, Briarcliff Manor, New York: The Combined Book Exhibit, Inc., 1971(?).

Conover, Helen F., comp. *Africa South of the Sahara: A Selected, Annotated List of Writings.* Washington, D.C.: Library of Congress, General Reference and Bibliography Division, Reference Department, 1963.

Dargitz, Robert E., comp. *A Selected Bibliography of Books and Articles in the Disciples of Christ Research Library in Mbandaka, Democratic Republic of the Congo and the Department of Africa and Jamaica of the United Christian Missionary Society in Indianapolis, Indiana.* Indianapolis, Indiana: The United Christian Missionary Society, Division of World Mission, Department of Africa and Jamaica, n.d.

Duignan, Peter. *Guide to Research and Reference Works on Sub-Saharan Africa.* Hoover Institution Bibliographical Series, no. 46. Stanford, California: Hoover Institution, 1971.

————, et al., eds. *Africa South of the Sahara: A Bibliography for Undergraduate Libraries.* Occasional Publication no. 12, Foreign Area Materials Center, University of the State of New York, State Education Department and National Council of Associations for International Studies. Williamsport, Pennsylvania: Bro-Dart, 1971.

Ehrman, Edith, and Ward Morehouse, eds. *Preliminary Bibliography on Africa South of the Sahara for Undergraduate Libraries.* New York: University of the State of New York, State Education Department, Center for International Programs and Services, Foreign Area Materials Center, 1967.

Fontvieille, Jean-Roger, comp. *Bibliographic Guide to the Negro World: History, Literature, Ethnology.* 1 vol. in 2. Yaoundé, Cameroun: Ministry of Education, Culture and Vocational Training, Direction of Cultural Affairs, 1970.

Forde, Daryll, comp. *Select Annotated Bibliography of Tropical Africa.* New York: The Twentieth Century Fund, 1956 (New York: Kraus Reprint, 1969).

Geoffrion, Charles A. *Africa: A Study Guide to Better Understanding.* Bloomington: Indiana University, African Studies Program, 1970.

Glazier, Kenneth M. *Africa South of the Sahara: A Select and Annotated Bibliography, 1958–1963.* Hoover Institution Bibliographical Series, no. 16. Stanford, California: Hoover Institution, 1964.

————. *Africa South of the Sahara: A Select and Annotated Bibliography, 1964–1968*. Hoover Institution Bibliographical Series, no. 42. Stanford, California: Hoover Institution, 1969.

Gutkind, Peter C. W., and John B. Webster. *A Selected Bibliography on Traditional and Modern Africa*. Occasional Bibliography, no. 8. Syracuse, New York: Syracuse University, Program of Eastern African Studies, 1968.

Hartwig, Gerald W., and William M. O'Barr. *The Student Africanist's Handbook: A Guide to Resources*. Cambridge, Massachusetts: Schenkman, 1974.

Harvard University Library. *Africa: Classification Schedule, Classified Listing by Call Number, Alphabetical Listing by Author or Title, Chronological Listing*. Widener Library Shelflist, no. 2. Cambridge, Massachusetts: Harvard University Library, 1965.

Holdsworth, Mary. *Soviet African Studies, 1918–59: An Annotated Bibliography*. London: Royal Institute of International Affairs, 1961.

Ibadan University Library. *Africana Catalogue of the Ibadan University Library*. 2 vols. Boston: G. K. Hall, 1973.

International African Institute. *Cumulative Bibliography of African Studies*. 5 vols. Boston: G. K. Hall, 1973.

Lehman, Robert L., comp., and Frank W. Price, ed. *Africa South of the Sahara: A Selected and Annotated Bibliography of Books in the Missionary Research Library on Africa and African Countries South of the Sahara*. New York: Missionary Research Library, 1969(?).

McGill University, McLennan Library, Reference Department. *Africa South of the Sahara: A Student's Guide to Selected Reference Sources for African Studies*. Montreal: McGill University, 1973.

Missionary Research Library. *Dictionary Catalog of the Missionary Research Library*. 17 vols. Boston: G. K. Hall, 1967.

Musée de l'Homme, Bibliothèque. *Catalogue Systématique de la Section Afrique*. 2 vols. Boston: G. K. Hall, 1970.

Musiker, Reuben. *South African Bibliography: A Survey of Bibliographies and Bibliographical Work*. London: Crosby Lockwood, 1971.

————. *South African Bibliography: A Survey of Bibliographies and Bibliographical Work. Supplement 1970–1974*. Johannesburg: University of Witwatersrand Library, 1975.

National Book League and the Commonwealth Institute. *The Commonwealth in Africa: An Annotated List 1969*. London: National Book League, 1969.

New York Public Library. *Dictionary Catalog of the Schomburg Collection of Negro Literature and History*. 9 vols. Boston: G. K. Hall, 1962.

————. *Dictionary Catalog of the Schomburg Collection of Negro Literature and History. First Supplement*. 2 vols. Boston: G. K. Hall, 1967.

————. *Dictionary Catalog of the Schomburg Collection of Negro Literature and History. Second Supplement.* 4 vols. Boston: G. K. Hall, 1972.

Northwestern University Library. *Catalogue of the Melville J. Herskovits Library of African Studies, Northwestern University Library and Africana in Selected Libraries.* 8 vols. Boston: G. K. Hall, 1972.

Paden, John N., and Edward W. Soja, eds. *The African Experience. Vol. IIIA, Bibliography.* Evanston, Illinois: Northwestern University Press, 1970.

————. *The African Experience. Vol. IIIB, Guide to Resources.* Evanston, Illinois: Northwestern University Press, 1970.

Panofsky, Hans E. *A Bibliography of Africana.* Contributions in Librarianship and Information Science, no. 11; Paul Wasserman, general editor. Westport, Connecticut: Greenwood Press, 1975.

Patterson, Margaret C. *Literary Research Guide.* Detroit, Michigan: Gale, 1976.

Porter, Dorothy B., ed. *A Catalogue of the African Collection in the Moorland Foundation, Howard University Library.* Washington, D.C.: Howard University Press, 1958.

Robinson, Harland D. *Africa, Sub-Sahara: A Selected Functional and Country Bibliography.* Washington, D.C.: U.S. Department of State, 1974.

Royal Commonwealth Society. *Subject Catalogue of the Royal Commonwealth Society.* 7 vols. Boston: G. K. Hall, 1971.

Simmons, Wendy. "A Bibliography of Recent Africanist Bibliographies in Journals," *A Current Bibliography on African Affairs,* 9 (1976/77): 317–24.

U.S., Foreign Service Institute, Center for Area and Country Studies. *Africa, Sub-Sahara: A Selected Functional Bibliography.* Washington, D.C.: U.S. Foreign Service Institute, 1967.

U.S., Library of Congress. *National Union Catalog.* Washington, D.C.: Library of Congress, Resources Committee of the Resources and Technical Services Division, 1956– .

————. *National Union Catalog: Pre-1956 Imprints.* London: Mansell, 1968– .

————, European Affairs Division. *Introduction to Africa: A Selective Guide to Background Reading.* Washington, D.C.: University Press of Washington, 1952 (New York: Negro Universities Press, 1969).

University of Ife Bookshop, Ltd. *"Printed and Published in Africa": Catalogue of an Exhibition of Outstanding African Published Materials.* Ile-Ife, Nigeria: University of Ife Bookshop, 1974(?) (Mimeographed).

University of London, School of Oriental and African Studies. *Library Catalogue.* 21 vols. Boston: G. K. Hall, 1963.

————. *Library Catalogue. First Supplement.* 13 vols. Boston: G. K. Hall, 1968.

————. *Library Catalogue. Second Supplement.* 13 vols. Boston: G. K. Hall, 1973.

————. *Library Catalogue: Author Index.* 8 vols. Boston: G. K. Hall, 1963.

————. *Library Catalogue: Author Index. First Supplement.* 3 vols. Boston: G. K. Hall, 1968.

————. *Library Catalogue: Author Index. Second Supplement.* 3 vols. Boston: G. K. Hall, 1973.

University of Nigeria. *Institute of African Studies Research Library Classified List 1.* Nsukka, Nigeria: University of Nigeria, 1973.

National Bibliographies and Selected Serial Bibliographies

African Bibliographic Center. *A Current Bibliography on African Affairs.* Farmingdale, New York: Baywood, 1962–1967; n.s. 1968– .

African Book Publishing Record. Oxford, England: Hans Zell (Publishers), 1975– .

Africana Journal: A Bibliographic and Review Quarterly. New York: Africana, 1970– .

American Book Publishing Record. New York: R. R. Bowker, 1960– .

American Library Association et al. *Choice.* Middletown, Connecticut: American Library Association, 1964– .

Bibliographic Guide to Black Studies. Boston: G. K. Hall, 1976– .

Books Abroad; An International Library Quarterly. Norman: University of Oklahoma Press, 1927– .

Books in Print. New York: R. R. Bowker, 1948– .

Books in Print. Subject Guide. New York: R. R. Bowker, 1957– .

Bookseller. London: J. Whitaker, 1858– .

British Book News. London: British Council, 1940– .

British Books in Print. 2 vols. London: J. Whitaker, 1974– .

British National Bibliography. London: Council of the British National Bibliography for the British Library, 1950– .

Bulletin of Bibliography and Magazine Notes. Westwood, Massachusetts: F. W. Faxon, 1897– .

Catalogue Général de la Libraire Française. Paris: Champion, 1840– .

Centre d'Analyse et de Recherche Documentaires pour Afrique Noire. "Bibliographie Française sur l'Afrique au Sud du Sahara," *Bulletin d'Information et de Liaison.* Paris: CARDAN, 1969– .

Cercle de la Libraire. *Bibliographie de la France; Journal Officiel de l'Imprimerie et de la Libraire.* Paris: Cercle de la Libraire, 1811– .

Collison, Robert L. *Bibliographies Subject and National: A Guide to Their Contents, Arrangement and Use.* Second edition. London: Crosby Lockwood, 1962.

Cumulative Book Index; A World List of Books in the English Language. New York: H. W. Wilson, 1898– .

de Benko, Eugene. "A Select Bibliography of Africana, 1973–74." *ASA Review of Books,* 1 (1975): 162–84.

———. "A Select Bibliography of Africana, 1974–75," *ASA Review of Books,* 2 (1976): 207–26.

Deutsche Bibliographie: Wöhentliches Verzeichnis. Frankfurt am Main, West Germany: Buchhandler-Vereinigung GmbH., 1947– .

Deutsche Bucherei, comp. *Deutsche Nationalbibliographie.* Leipzig, East Germany: VEB Verlag für Buch-und Bibliothekswesen, 1931– .

English Association. *The Year's Work in English Studies.* London: Murray, 1919– .

Essay and General Literature Index. New York: H. W. Wilson, 1900– .

Fiction Catalog. Eighth edition. New York: H. W. Wilson, 1971.

Forthcoming Books. New York: R. R. Bowker, 1966– .

Hoover Institution on War, Revolution and Peace. *United States and Canadian Publications and Theses on Africa.* Hoover Institution Bibliographical Series. Stanford, California: Stanford University, Hoover Institution, 1962– .

International African Bibliography: Current Books, Articles and Papers in African Studies. London: Mansell Information/Publishing, 1971– .

Modern Humanities Research Association. *Annual Bibliography of English Language and Literature.* Cambridge, England: Modern Humanities Research Association, 1920– .

Modern Language Association of America. *MLA International Bibliography of Books and Articles on the Modern Languages and Literatures.* New York: Modern Language Association of America, 1921– .

Northwestern University, Melville J. Herskovits Library of African Studies, comp. *Joint Acquisitions List of Africana.* Evanston, Illinois: Northwestern University Library, 1962– .

Overseas Books. London: Publishing and Distributing, 1964– .

Paperbound Books in Print. New York: R. R. Bowker, 1955– .

The Publishers' Trade List Annual. New York: R. R. Bowker, 1873– .

Publishers' Weekly: The Book Industry Journal. New York: R. R. Bowker, 1877– .

Scandinavian Institute of African Studies. *Africana in Scandinavian Research Libraries.* Uppsala, Sweden: Scandinavian Institute of African Studies, 1963– .

South Africa, State Library. *Bibliography of Overseas Publications about South Africa.* Pretoria: State Library, 1973– .

————. *South African National Bibliography.* Pretoria: State Library, 1959– .

South African Public Library. *Africana Nova: A Quarterly Bibliography of Books Currently Published in and about the Republic of South Africa, Based on the Accessions to the Africana Department . . . and Including Material Received on Legal Deposit.* Cape Town: South African Public Library, 1958–1969.

Standing Conference on Library Materials on Africa. *United Kingdom Publications and Theses on Africa.* Cambridge, England: W. Heffer, 1966–1973 (publisher varies).

Ulrich's International Periodicals Directory: A Classified Guide to Current Periodicals, Foreign and Domestic. Sixteenth edition. New York: R. R. Bowker, 1975–1976.

U.S., Library of Congress. *National Union Catalog.* Washington, D.C.: Library of Congress, Resources Committee of the Resources and Technical Services Division, 1956– .

————. *National Union Catalog: Pre-1956 Imprints.* London: Mansell Information/Publishing, 1968– .

Whitaker's Cumulative Booklist. London: J. Whitaker, 1926– .

Zell, Hans M., ed. *African Books in Print: An Index by Author, Title and Subject. Part I: English Language and African Languages.* London: Mansell Information/Publishing, 1975.

————. "Publishing Progress in Africa 1975–76: Problems in Securing Information and the Role of the *African Book Publishing Record.*" Unpublished paper presented at the SCOLMA Conference on Progress in African Bibliography, Commonwealth Institute, London, March 17–18, 1977.

Periodical Lists and Indices

(This section does not list individual periodical titles which include South African literature in their coverage, as these may be found in the appendix on pages 125–42 above).

African Bibliographic Center. *Periodicals for Pan-African Studies: A Selected and Current Guide to Resources.* Current Reading List Series, vol. 8, no. 1. Washington, D.C.: African Bibliographic Center, 1971.

African Book Publishing Record. Oxford, England: Hans Zell (Publishers), 1975– .

Asamani, J. O. *Index Africanus*. Hoover Institution Bibliographies, 53. Stanford, California: Stanford University, Hoover Institution, 1975.

Birkos, Alexander S., and Lewis A. Tambs, eds. *African and Black American Studies*. Vol. 3 of Academic Writer's Guide to Periodicals. Littleton, Colorado: Libraries Unlimited, 1975.

British Humanities Index. London: Library Association, 1962– .

Conover, Helen, comp. *Serials for African Studies*. Washington, D.C.: Library of Congress, General Reference and Bibliography Division, Reference Department, 1961.

de Benko, Eugene, and Patricia L. Butts. *Research Sources for African Studies: A Checklist of Relevant Serial Publications Based on Library Collections at Michigan State University*. East Lansing: Michigan State University, African Studies Center, 1969.

Dickman, Daryl, comp. *Abstract/Index to A.S.A. Annual Meeting Papers, 1960–1974*. Waltham, Massachusetts: African Studies Association, 1976.

Duignan, Peter, and Kenneth M. Glazier. *A Checklist of Serials for African Studies Based on the Libraries of the Hoover Institution and Stanford University*. Hoover Institution Bibliographical Series, 13. Stanford, California: Hoover Institution, 1963.

Freer, Percy, ed. *Catalogue of Union Periodicals*. Johannesburg: National Research Council and National Research Board, 1943–1952.

Gorman, G. E., and M. H. Rogers. "Review of SCOLMA, *Periodicals from Africa: A Bibliography and Union List of Periodicals Published in Africa*," *African Research and Documentation* (forthcoming).

Hamner, R. D., comp. "Literary Periodicals in World-English (Commonwealth and Former Commonwealth Countries): A Selective Checklist," *W.L.W.E. Newsletter*, 14 (1968), supplement.

Humanities Index. New York: H. W. Wilson, 1967– .

Internationale Bibliographie der Zeitschriften Literatur aus Allen Gebeiten des Wissens. Osnabrück, West Germany: Felix Dietrich Verlag, n.s. 1965– .

Johannesburg Public Library. *Index to South African Periodicals*. Johannesburg: Johannesburg Public Library, 1940– .

Lever, Rachelle, comp. *Little Magazines in South Africa Since 1945: A Bibliography*. Johannesburg: University of the Witwatersrand, Department of Bibliography, Librarianship and Typography, 1973.

Maison des Sciences de l'Homme, Service d'Echange d'Informations Scientifiques. *World List of Specialized Periodicals: African Studies*. Publications Serie C: Catalogues et Inventaires III. Paris: Mouton, 1969.

Panofsky, Hans, and Robert Koester. "African Newspapers and Periodicals," in *The African Experience. Vol. IIB, Guide to Resources.* Edited by John N. Paden and Edward Soja. Evanston, Illinois: Northwestern University Press, 1970. Pp. 33–55.

Parry, V. T. H. *African Periodicals in the Library of the British Museum (Natural History).* London: SCOLMA, 1974.

Readers' Guide to Periodical Literature: An Author Subject Index to Selected General Interest Periodicals of Reference Value in Libraries. New York: H. W. Wilson, 1900– .

Scheven, Yvette. "Africana in the Indexes," *History in Africa*, 4 (1977): 207–27.

Simpson, Donald H. "Commonwealth Literary Periodicals." Unpublished paper presented at the Conference on Library Holdings of Commonwealth Literature, Commonwealth Institute, London, 5 June 1970.

South Africa, South African Council for Scientific and Industrial Research. *Periodicals in South African Libraries: A Revised Edition of the Catalogue of Union Periodicals.* Pretoria: South African Council for Scientific and Industrial Research, 1961– .

South Africa, State Library. *Current South African Periodicals: A Classified List, July, 1965.* Pretoria: State Library, 1966.

Spohr, O. H. *Indexes to African Books.* Cape Town: the author, 1967.

———. "Recent Indexes to Africana Books," *South African Libraries*, 37 (1969): 29–31.

Standing Conference on Library Materials on Africa. *Periodicals from Africa: A Bibliography and Union List of Periodicals Published in Africa.* Compiled by Carole Travis and Miriam Alman; edited by Carole Travis. Bibliographies and Guides in African Studies; James C. Armstrong, advisory editor. Boston: G. K. Hall, 1977.

———. "Periodicals Published in Africa, Parts 1–10," *Library Materials on Africa*, Vols. 3–7, 1965–1970.

Syracuse University Libraries, Area Studies Department. *Serials and Newspapers for African Studies: A Checklist.* Syracuse, New York: Syracuse University Libraries, 1970.

Travis, Carole. "Recording African Periodicals." Unpublished paper presented at the SCOLMA Conference on Progress in African Bibliography, Commonwealth Institute, London, March 17–18, 1977.

U.S., Library of Congress, African Section. *Sub-Saharan Africa: A Guide to Serials.* Washington, D.C.: Library of Congress, 1970.

———, Reference Department, General Reference and Bibliography Division, African Section, comp. *Africa South of the Sahara: Index to Periodical Literature, 1900–1970.* 4 vols. Boston: G. K. Hall, 1971.

———. *Africa South of the Sahara: Index to Periodical Literature. First Supplement, 1973.* Boston: G. K. Hall, 1974.

Warwick, Ronald. "Literary Periodicals of the Commonwealth," *Royal Commonwealth Society Library Notes,* n.s. no. 219: 1–2.

Zell, Hans M., and Helene Silver, eds. *A Reader's Guide to African Literature.* New York: Africana, 1971 (London: Heinemann, 1972).

Dissertations, Theses and Research in Progress
(This section does not include individual theses on South African literature, as these may be found in the appendix on pages 155–60 above.)

African Studies Association. *Research in Progress 1972–1974: A Selected Listing of Current Research on Africa.* Waltham, Massachusetts: African Studies Association, 1974.

African Studies Research Committee. *Register of Research.* Pietermaritzburg, South Africa: African Studies Research Committee, 1974.

American Doctoral Dissertations. Ann Arbor, Michigan: University Microfilms, 1965– .

ASLIB. *Index to Theses Accepted for Higher Degrees by the Universities of Great Britain and Ireland and the Council for National Academic Awards.* London: ASLIB, 1953– .

Association des Universités Partiellement ou Entièrement de Langue Française. *Repertoire des Thèses de Doctorat Soutenues devant les Universités de Langue Française.* Quebec: Université Laval, Centre de Documentation de la Bibliothèque, 1970.

Bratton, Michael, and Anne Schneller, comps. *American Doctoral Dissertations on Africa, 1886–1972.* Waltham, Massachusetts: African Studies Association, Research Liaison Committee, 1973.

Centre d'Analyse et de Recherche Documentaires pour l'Afrique Noire. "Inventaire de Thèses et Mémoires Africanistes de Langue Française en Cours," *Bulletin d'Information et de Liaison: Etudes Africaines.* Paris: CARDAN, 1969– .

———. "Inventaire de Thèses et Mémoires Africanistes de Langue Française: Soutenances," *Bulletin d'Information et de Liaison: Etudes Africaines.* Paris: CARDAN, 1969– .

Colman, James S. "Research on Africa in European Centres: Appendix B; Ph.D. Dissertations on African Subjects Completed at British Universities, 1950–1956," *African Studies Bulletin,* 2, no. 3 (1959): 18–22.

Cruger, Doris M. *A List of American Doctoral Dissertations on Africa, Covering 1961/62 through 1964/65; France, Covering 1933/34 through*

1964/65; Italy, Covering 1933/34 through 1964/65. Ann Arbor, Michigan: University Microfilms Library Services, 1967.

Deutsche Bucherei, comp. *Jahresverzeichnis der Deutschen Hochschulschriften.* Leipzig, East Germany: Verlag für Buch- und Bibliothekswesen, 1887– .

Deutsche Nationalbibliographie; Reihe C: Dissertationen und Habilitationsschrift. Leipzig, East Germany: VEB Verlag für Buch- und Bibliothekswesen, 1968– .

de Villiers, André. "South African Research Since 1969 in the Literatures of the Republic: Some Notes and a Checklist," *Research in African Literatures,* 6 (1975): 237–46.

Dinstel, Marion. *List of French Doctoral Dissertations on Africa.* Boston: G. K. Hall, 1966.

Dissertation Abstracts; A: The Humanities and Social Sciences. Ann Arbor, Michigan: University Microfilms, 1966–1969.

Dissertation Abstracts: Abstracts of Dissertations and Monographs Available in Microfilm. Ann Arbor, Michigan: University Microfilms, 1938–1966 (title varies).

Dissertation Abstracts International; A: The Humanities and Social Sciences. Ann Arbor, Michigan and High Wycombe, Bucks: University Microfilms International, 1969– .

Dissertation Abstracts International; Retrospective Index. 29 vols. Ann Arbor, Michigan: Xerox University Microfilms, 1970.

"Dissertations on Africa," *African Studies Newsletter,* 7, no. 3 (1974): 14; 7, no. 4 (1974): 2; 7, no. 6 (1974): 18.

Doctoral Dissertations Accepted by American Universities. New York: H. W. Wilson, 1934–1956.

Duignan, Peter, comp. *United States and Canadian Doctoral Dissertations on Africa.* Ann Arbor, Michigan: University Microfilms, 1973.

France, Direction des Bibliothèques de France. *Catalogue des Thèses de Doctorat Soutenues devant les Universités Françaises.* Paris: Direction des Bibliothèques de France, 1885–1959.

———. *Catalogue des Thèses de Doctorat Soutenues devant les Universités Françaises, Nouvelle Serie.* Paris: Cercle de la Librairie, 1960– .

Frey, Mitsue Miyata, comp. "Research in Progress, 1975–76," *African Studies Newsletter,* 9, no. 2 (1976), special insert.

Garlick, Peter C. "Theses on Africa Accepted by Howard University, Washington, D.C.," *African Studies Bulletin,* 11 (1968): 259–68.

Hoehn, R. Philip, and Jean Judson. "Theses on Sub-Saharan Africa Accepted by the University of California at Berkeley," *African Studies Bulletin,* 12 (1969): 157–66.

Hoover Institution on War, Revolution and Peace. *United States and Canadian Publications on Africa.* Hoover Institution Bibliographical Series. Stanford, California: Stanford University, Hoover Institution, 1962– .

Indiana University, African Studies Program. *Dissertations on Africa: A List of Titles of Dissertations on Africa That Were Completed at Indiana University From 1938 to the Present.* Bloomington: Indiana University, African Studies Program, 1976(?).

Index to American Doctoral Dissertations. Ann Arbor, Michigan: University Microfilms, 1957–1964.

International African Institute. *International Guide to African Studies Research; An Enlarged and Revised Edition (1974) of the "International Register of Organisations Undertaking Africanist Research in the Social Sciences and Humanities," Together with "Current Africanist Research" Number 4.* London: International African Institute, 1975.

————, Research Information Liaison Unit. *Current Africanist Research: International Bulletin.* London: International African Institute, 1971– .

————. *International Register of Organisations Undertaking Africanist Research in the Social Sciences and Humanities.* London: International African Institute, Research Information Liaison Unit, 1971.

McCartney, Barney C., and Rae G. McCartney. "Work in Progress in African Literatures," *Research in African Literatures,* 4 (1973): 209–15.

Makerere College Library. *Annotated List of Theses Submitted to University of East Africa and Held by Makerere College Library.* Kampala, Uganda: Makerere College Library, 1970.

Malan, S. I., comp. *Union Catalogue of Theses and Dissertations of the South African Universities, 1942–1958.* Potchefstroom, South Africa: Potchefstroom University, Department of Librarianship, 1959.

"Master's Theses on Africa," *African Studies Newsletter,* 6 (1973)– .

Modern Lanuage Association. "Research in Progress in the Modern Languages and Literatures," *Modern Language Association Publications.* New York: Modern Language Association, 1948–1960.

Munro, Ian. "Work in Progress in African Literatures," *Research in African Literatures,* 2 (1971): 28–38.

National Library of Canada. *Canadian Theses/Thèses Canadiennes.* Ottawa: National Library of Canada, 1962– .

————. *Canadian Theses/Thèses Canadiennes, 1947–1960.* 2 vols. Ottawa: National Library of Canada, 1973.

Pollak, Oliver B., and Karen Pollak. *Theses and Dissertations on Southern Africa: An International Bibliography.* Boston: G. K. Hall, 1976.

Potchefstroom University, F. Potsma Library. *Union Catalogue of Theses and Dissertations of the South African Universities: Supplement.* Potchefstroom, South Africa: Potchefstroom University, 1959.

Reynolds, Michael M. *A Guide to Theses and Dissertations: An Annotated, International Bibliography of Bibliographies.* Detroit, Michigan: Gale, 1975.

"Research in Progress," *African Research and Documentation* no. 1 (1973)– .

Rial, Jacques. *Inventaire des Thèses Suisses Consacrées à l'Afrique au Sud au Sahara, à l'Ethiopie et à Madagascar, 1897–1970.* Berne: Commission Nationale Suisse pour l'Unesco, 1972.

Robinson, Harland D. *Africa, Sub-Sahara: A Selected Functional and Country Bibliography.* Washington, D.C.: Department of State, 1974.

Sackett, S. J. "Master's Theses in Literature Presented at American Colleges and Universities, July 1, 1964–June 30, 1965," *Fort Hays Kansas State College Language and Literature Series,* no. 7 (1966): 89–165.

Sander, Reinhold. "Work in Progress in African Literatures," *Research in African Literatures,* 3 (1972): 54–59.

Scheven, Yvette, comp. *Africa-Related Theses and Dissertations at the University of Illinois at Urbana-Champaign, 1921–1974.* Urbana-Champaign: University of Illinois, African Studies Program, 1976.

Schmidt, Nancy J. "A Bibliography of American Dissertations and Theses on African Literature," *Research in African Literatures,* 5 (1974): 89–92.

––––––. "Bibliography of American Doctoral Dissertations on African Literature," *Research in African Literatures,* 1 (1970): 62–65.

Sims, Michael, and Alfred Kagan, comps. *American and Canadian Doctoral Dissertations and Master's Theses on Africa, 1886–1974.* Waltham, Massachusetts: African Studies Association, 1976.

South Africa, Human Sciences Research Council. *Register of Current Research in the Humanities at the Universities.* Pretoria, South Africa: Human Sciences Research Council, 1949– .

Standing Conference on Library Materials on Africa. *Theses on Africa Accepted by Universities in the United Kingdom and Ireland.* Cambridge, England: W. Heffer, 1964.

––––––. *United Kingdom Publications and Theses on Africa 1963.* Cambridge, England: W. Heffer, 1966.

––––––. *United Kingdom Publications and Theses on Africa 1964.* Cambridge, England: W. Heffer, 1967.

––––––. *United Kingdom Publications and Theses on Africa 1965.* Cambridge, England: W. Heffer, 1968.

––––––. *United Kingdom Publications and Theses on Africa 1966.* Cambridge, England: W. Heffer, 1969.

————. *United Kingdom Publications and Theses on Africa 1967–1968.* Edited by Miriam Alman. London: F. Cass, 1973.

Sullivan, Sally L. "Work in Progress in African Literatures," *Research in African Literatures,* 5 (1974): 213–14.

"Thèses . . . ," *Bibliographie de la France.* Paris: Cercle de la Librairie, 1932– .

U.S., Library of Congress, African Section, comp. *A List of American Doctoral Dissertations on Africa.* Washington, D.C.: U.S. Government Printing Office for the Library of Congress, General Reference and Bibliography Division, Reference Department, 1962.

University Microfilms. *Comprehensive Dissertation Index 1861–1972.* 34 vols. Ann Arbor, Michigan: University Microfilms, 1973.

University Microfilms International. *Doctoral Dissertations on Africa.* London and Ann Arbor, Michigan: University Microfilms International, 1976(?).

University of London, Institute of Commonwealth Studies. *Theses in Progress in Commonwealth Studies: A Cumulative List.* London: University of London, Institute of Commonwealth Studies, 1976.

University of Wisconsin—Madison, African Studies Program. *Africa-Related Doctoral Dissertations and Master's Theses Completed at University of Wisconsin—Madison through 1973.* Madison: University of Wisconsin—Madison, African Studies Program, 1974.

Bibliographies of African and South African Literature

Accra Central Library. *Guide to Writing by Africans in English.* Accra, Ghana: Accra Central Library, 1973.

Abrash, Barbara, comp. *Black African Literature in English Since 1952: Works and Criticism.* New York: Johnson Reprint, 1967.

Amosu, Margaret, comp. *Creative African Writing in the European Languages: A Preliminary Bibliography.* Ibadan: University of Ibadan, Institute of African Studies, 1964.

————. "Selected Bibliography of Critical Writing," in *Introduction to African Literature: An Anthology of Critical Writing from "Black Orpheus."* Edited by Ulli Beier. London: Longman, 1967. Pp. 265–70.

"Appendix: South Africa," *Journal of Commonwealth Literature,* no. 10 (1970): 123–31; 6, no. 2 (1971): 110–19; 7, no. 2 (1972): 136–47; 8, no. 2 (1973): 147–57; 9, no. 2 (1974): 140–48.

Astrinsky, Aviva, comp. *A Bibliography of South African English Novels, 1930–1960.* Cape Town: University of Cape Town, School of Librarianship, 1965.

Beeton, D. R., ed. *A Pilot Bibliography of South African English Literature (from the Beginnings to 1971).* Documenta 14. Pretoria: University of South Africa, 1976.

Beinash, Judith, comp. *Books and Pamphlets by South African Jewish Writers.* Johannesburg: University of the Witwatersrand, Department of Bibliography, Librarianship and Typography, 1965.

Bentel, Lea, comp. *Alan Paton: A Bibliography.* Johannesburg: University of the Witwatersrand, Department of Bibliography, Librarianship and Typography, 1969.

Bishop, Rand. "A Bibliography of African Literary Criticism, 1947–1966," *Africana Library Journal,* 4, no. 2 (1973): 2–31.

Bol, Vincent P., and Jean Allary. *Littératures et Poètes Noirs.* Léopoldville, Congo: Bibliothèque de l'Etoile, 1964.

Brady, Sister Mary William, comp. *A Selective Bibliography of Literature Written in Africa, Australia, Canada, New Zealand, West Indies.* St. Paul, Minnesota: College of St. Catherine, 1975.

Burkom, Selma P. *Doris Lessing; a Checklist of Primary and Secondary Sources.* Troy, New York: Whitston, 1973.

Callan, Edward. *Alan Paton.* Translated by Rolf Italiaander. Hamburger Bibliographien Band II. Hamburg, West Germany: Hans Christian Verlag, 1970. Pp. 35–80.

Camberg, Helen, comp. *Daphne Rooke; Her Works and Selected Literary Criticism: A Bibliography.* Johannesburg: University of the Witwatersrand, Department of Bibliography, Librarianship and Typography, 1969.

Crooke, Arthur, ed. *British and Commonwealth Fiction Since 1950.* London: National Book League, 1966.

Davidson, Elizabeth, comp. *Some Writings by Non-European South Africans (1928–1971): A Bibliography.* Johannesburg: University of the Witwatersrand, Department of Bibliography, Librarianship and Typography, 1972.

Davis, Valerie Margaret, comp. *Bibliography of the Works of Ignatius Roy Dunnachie Campbell.* Cape Town: University of Cape Town, School of Librarianship, 1954.

de Saxe, Shora Gertrude, comp. *Herman Charles Bosman: A Bibliography.* Johannesburg: University of the Witwatersrand, Department of Bibliography, Librarianship and Typography, 1971.

Gérard, Albert. "Bibliographical Problems in Creative African Literature," *Journal of General Education,* 19, no. 1 (1965): 25–43.

Gorman, G. E. "Review of Beeton's *A Pilot Bibliography of South African English Literature,*" *African Book Publishing Record,* 3 (1977): 91.

Gray, Stephen. "Review of Beeton's *A Pilot Bibliography of South African English Literature,*" *South African Libraries,* 44 (1977): 170–71.

Herdeck, Donald E. *African Authors: A Companion to Black African Writing. Vol. 1: 1300–1973.* Washington, D.C.: Black Orpheus Press, 1973.

Holson, M. B., comp. *A Select Bibliography of South African Novels in English, 1870–1950.* Cape Town: University of Cape Town, School of Librarianship, 1952.

Ipp, Catherina, comp. *Doris Lessing: A Bibliography.* Johannesburg: University of the Witwatersrand, Department of Bibliography, Librarianship and Typography, 1967.

Jahn, Janheinz. *A Bibliography of Neo-African Literature from Africa, America and the Caribbean.* London: André Deutsch, 1965.

————, and Claus Peter Dressler. *Bibliography of Creative African Writing.* Nedeln, Liechtenstein: Kraus-Thomson, 1971.

————, and John A. Ramsaran. *Approaches to African Literature.* Ibadan: University of Ibadan Press, 1959.

Kiersen, S., comp. *English and Afrikaans Novels on South African History: A Bibliography.* Cape Town: University of Cape Town, School of Librarianship, 1958.

Killam, G. D. "Modern Black African Writing in English: A Selected Bibliography," *Canadian Journal of African Studies,* 9 (1975): 537–66.

————. "Modern Black African Writing in English: Selected Bibliography," *Twentieth Century Literature,* 17 (1971): 37–47.

————. "Recent African Fiction," *Bulletin of the Association for African Literature in English,* 2 (1965): 1–10.

Laredo, Ursula. "Bibliography of South African Literature in English, 1964–1968," *Journal of Commonwealth Literature,* no. 9 (1970): 1–27.

————. "Supplement to Bibliography of South African Literature in English," *Journal of Commonwealth Literature,* 6 (1971): 1–5.

Levy, Fanelle, comp. *The Works of Sarah Gertrude Millin, 1952–1968: A Bibliography.* Johannesburg: University of the Witwatersrand, Department of Bibliography, Librarianship and Typography, 1969.

Lindfors, Bernth. "Additions and Corrections to Janheinz Jahn's *Bibliography of Neo-African Literature* (1965)," *African Studies Bulletin,* 11 (1968): 129–48.

————. "Africana Bibliomania," *Africana Journal,* 4, no. 1 (1973): 21–24.

————. "A Preliminary Checklist of English Short Fiction by Non-Europeans in South Africa, 1940–1964," *African Studies Bulletin,* 12 (1969): 272–91.

————. "Reviews of African Literature in Nigerian Periodicals," *Africana Journal,* 6 (1975): 195–231.

Musiker, Reuben. "South African English Literature: Bibliographic and

Biographical Resources and Problems," *English Studies in Africa*, 13 (1970): 265–73.

Mutiso, Gideon-Cyrus M. *Messages: An Annotated Bibliography of African Literature for Schools.* Upper Montclair, New Jersey: Montclair State College Press, 1970.

National Book League. *Creative Writing from Black Africa, Sub-Sahara; a Checklist.* London: National Book League, 1971.

Nell, Racilia Jilian, comp. *Nadine Gordimer, Novelist and Short Story Writer: A Bibliography of Her Works and Selected Literary Criticism.* Johannesburg: University of the Witwatersrand, Department of Bibliography, Librarianship and Typography, 1964.

New, William H. *Critical Writings on Commonwealth Literatures: A Selective Bibliography to 1970, with a List of Theses and Dissertations.* University Park: Pennsylvania State University Press, 1975.

Páricsy, Pál, comp. "The History of Black African Literature (A Select Bibliography of Criticism)," *Studies on Modern Black African Literature.* Edited by Pál Páricsy. Studies on Developing Countries, no. 43. Budapest: Center for Afro-Asian Research of the Hungarian Academy of Sciences, 1971. Pp. 99–121.

————. *A New Bibliography of African Literature.* Studies on Developing Countries, no. 24. Budapest: Center for Afro-Asian Research of the Hungarian Academy of Sciences, 1969.

————. "A Supplementary Bibliography to J. Jahn's *Bibliography of Neo-African Literature from Africa, America and the Caribbean*," *Journal of the New African Literature and the Arts*, 4 (1967): 70–82.

"Peter Abrahams: A Selected Bibliography," *World Literature Written in English,* 13, no. 2 (1974): 184–90.

Porter, Dorothy B. "African and Caribbean Writings: A Bibliographic Survey," *African Forum*, 1, no. 4 (1966): 107–11.

————. "Fiction by African Authors: A Preliminary Checklist," *African Studies Bulletin*, 5, no. 2 (1966): 54–66.

————. "Notes on Some African Writers," in *Africa and the United States: Images and Realities.* African Series 26, Department of State Publication 7332. Washington, D.C.: Department of State, 1961. Pp. 165–73.

Priebe, Richard K., comp. *Letters and Manuscripts from Southern Africa: A Survey of the Holdings of the Humanities Research Centre, the University of Texas at Austin.* African and Afro-American Research Institute Occasional Publication, no. 6. Austin: University of Texas at Austin, African and Afro-American Research Institute, 1972.

Ramsaran, John A. *New Approaches to African Literature: A Guide to Negro-African Writing and Related Studies.* Second edition. Ibadan: University of Ibadan Press, 1970.

Raum, O. F. "Some Recent African Novels in English," *New South African Writing,* n.s. no. 5 (n.d.): 30–49.

Snyman, J. P. L. *A Bibliography of South African Novels in English Published between 1880 and 1930.* Potchefstroom, South Africa: Potchefstroom University, 1951.

South African Centre of the International P. E. N. Club. "Fifty Years of the South African Novel," *South African P.E.N. Yearbook 1960.* Cape Town: Timmins, 1960(?).

————. "Selected Bibliography (of Works by South African Writers) 1945–1954," *South African P.E.N. Yearbook 1954.* Johannesburg: Central News Agency, 1954. Pp. 81–92.

————. "Selected Bibliography of Works by South African Writers 1954–55," *South African P.E.N. Yearbook 1955.* Johannesburg: Central News Agency, 1955. Pp. 124–27.

————. "Selected Bibliography of Works by South African Writers 1955–57," *South African P.E.N. Yearbook 1957.* Cape Town: Timmins, 1957. Pp. 116–20.

Stern, Maureen J., comp. *South African Jewish Biography, 1900–1966: A Bibliography.* Cape Town: University of Cape Town, School of Librarianship, 1972.

Tucker, Martin. "Selected Reading List of Modern African Literature throuh 1966," in *Africa in Modern Literature: A Survey of Contemporary Writing in English.* New York: Frederick Ungar, 1967. Pp. 265–309.

Ushpol, Rowse, comp. *A Select Bibliography of South African Autobiographies.* Cape Town: University of Cape Town, School of Librarianship, 1958.

Weinstock, D. J., comp. *The Boer War in the Novel in English, 1884–1966: A Descriptive and Critical Bibliography.* Cape Town: University of Cape Town, School of Librarianship, 1968.

Whyte, Morag, comp. *The Works of Sarah Gertrude Millin: Bibliography.* Cape Town: University of Cape Town, School of Librarianship, 1952.

Wilkov, A., comp. *Some English Writings by Non-Europeans in South Africa, 1944–1960.* Johannesburg: University of the Witwatersrand, Department of Bibliography, Librarianship and Typography, 1962.

Wilson, Richard Middlewood. *A Working Index to African Literature, with Selected Bibliographies in the Novel and Theater in America.* Evanston, Illinois: EPDA, Institute for College Teachers, Program of African Studies, 1970.

Winterbottom, Irina. "Towards a Bibliography of South African Literature in English," *English in Africa,* 3, no. 1 (1976): 49–52.

Yudelman, Myra, comp. *Dan Jacobson: A Bibliography.* Johannesburg:

University of the Witwatersrand, Department of Bibliography, Librarianship and Typography, 1967.

Zell, Hans M. "African Literature 1971–1972: A Checklist," *Africana Library Journal*, 4, no. 4 (1973): 7–16.

————, and Helene Silver, eds. *A Reader's Guide to African Literature.* New York: Africana, 1971 (London: Heinemann, 1972).

Selected Publishers and Scholarly Societies

Altbach, Philip G. "Publishing in Developing Countries: A Select Bibliography," *Scholarly Publishing,* 6 (1975): 267–79.

————. " 'Third World' Publishing: Problems and Prospects," *Scholarly Publishing,* 5 (1973): 247–53.

Anyakoha, Maduka W. "Publishing in Africa: A Bibliography," *A Current Bibliography on African Affairs*, 8 (1975): 296–319.

Armstrong, Robert P. "The University Press in a Developing Country," *Scholarly Publishing,* 5 (1973): 35–40.

Clark, Alden H. "Publishing in Sub-Saharan Africa," *Scholarly Publishing,* 2 (1970): 67–74.

Dipeolu, J. O. "Problems of Acquiring African Published Materials: The Experience of African Universities," in *Publishing in Africa in the Seventies: Proceedings of an International Conference on Publishing and Book Development Held at the University of Ile-Ife, Nigeria, 16–20 December 1973.* Edited by E. Oluwasanmi *et al.* Ile-Ife, Nigeria: University of Ife Press, 1975. Pp. 134–42.

Hale, Thomas. "Establishment of African Literature Association," *Research in African Literatures*, 6 (1975): 60–63.

Jahn, Janheinz, ed. *The Black Experience I: 400 Years of Black Literature from Africa and the Americas.* Nedeln, Liechtenstein: Kraus Reprint, 1970(?).

Kraus Bibliographical Bulletin 16 (1977).

"Proceedings of the Symposium on Contemporary African Literature and First African Literature Association Conference," *Issue*, 6, no. 1 (1976): 3–63.

Randall, Peter. " 'Minority' Publishing in South Africa," *African Book Publishing Record*, 1 (1975): 219–22.

Taubert, Sigfred, ed. *African Book Trade Directory 1971.* Munich: Verlag Dokumentation; New York: R. R. Bowker; London: André Deutsch, 1971.

University Microfilms International. *Doctoral Dissertations on Africa.* London and Ann Arbor, Michigan: University Microfilms International, 1976(?).

Zell, Hans M., ed. *The African Book World and Press—a Directory*. Compiled by *African Book Publishing Record*. Oxford: Hans Zell (Publishers), 1977.

————. "Publishing and Book Development in Africa: A Bibliography," *African Book Publishing Record*, 2 (1976): 95–103.

Subject Index

Acquisitions lists, *see* Bibliographies, acquisitions lists as

Ad. Donker (Pty.) Ltd., 107, 168, 176

African Bibliographic Center, 105

African Imprint Library Services, 39, 50n8

African Literature Association, 27, 44, 180, 182n6

African Literature Commission/Committee [ASA, U.S.], 4, 11n3, 180

African Literature Group [MLA], 4, 11n3

African Studies Association [U.K.], 178, 179

African Studies Association [U.S.], 4, 11n3, 44, 178–79, 180, 181

African studies centers, 34n7

Africana bibliographies, *see* Bibliographies

Africana Publishing Company, 176–77

Allan Lane Ltd., 177

Area studies: and humanities, 28–29; interdisciplinary approach in, 10; and literature, 27–30

Association for African Literature in English, 181

Association for Commonwealth Literature and Language Studies, 4, 11n3, 26, 44, 180–81

Authors: affected by political oppression, 7–8; published worldwide, x; socially committed, 16–20

Autobiographies, 20; as sources of biographical data, 64

Bateleur Press, 107, 176

Bibliographical center: British proposal, 47–48; proposal for 43–49, 184; proposal for guide to periodicals by, 118; proposal for ongoing bibliography by, 170

Bibliographical improvements, need for, 42–49, 109–10

Bibliographical problems, 37–42

Bibliographical resources: guide to, xii–xiii, 48–49; improvements in, 42–49, 109–10

Bibliographies: acquisitions lists as, 108–09; of Africana bibliographies, 71–76; of African literature, 162–66, 169–70; of bibliographies, 70–71; of bibliographies, essential titles, 77–78; of biography, 55–68; of biography, essential titles, 65; black exclusiveness in, 40–41; comprehensive, need for, ix, 184; general, 69–81; library catalogues as, 84–89; library catalogues, essential titles, 88–89; of literary bibliographies, 76–77; national, 100–03; selective, Africana, 89–93; selective, literary, 90; selective non-serial, 83–98; selective non-serial, essential titles, 93–94; serial, Africana, 104–09; serial, essential titles, 109–10; serial, improvements in, 109–10; serial, literary, 103–04; of South African literature, 38, 43–49, 78, 166–73; trade publication as, 100–03; *see also* Encyclopedias, Literature, Periodicals, Research in progress, Theses

Biography, 55–68

BLAC Publishing House, 176

Booksellers, 4

Boston University, 45

Canadian Association for Commonwealth Language and Literary Studies, 26, 33-n3, 181

Canadian Association for Commonwealth Literature and Language Studies, *see* Canadian Association for Commonwealth Language and Literary Studies

Censorship, x, 7, 12n14

Censorship Act, 7

Commonwealth Literature, *see* Literature, Commonwealth

221

Conference on British Commonwealth Literature, 180
Conference on Commonwealth Literature, 1971, 103
Current bibliographies, *see* Bibliographies, serial

David Philip Publisher (Pty.) Ltd., 176
Davis-Poynter Publishers, 176
Dictionaries of biography, 58–61, 62–64
Dissertations, *see* Theses
Division on English Literature Other Than British and American, *see* English Literature Other Than British and American

Encyclopedias of literature, 58–61
English Group 12—World Literature Written in English [MLA], 180
English Literature Other Than British and American, 27, 180
Evans Brothers Ltd., 51n16, 177
Exhibition catalogues, 89

Festschriften, index to, 106
Fiction, *see* Literature
First International Exhibition of African Books, 72, 89

G. K. Hall and Company, 83, 84–87, 178
Gale Research Company, 178
General Law Amendment Act, 7
Government, *see* Political situation

H. W. Wilson Company, 56, 70
Heinemann Educational Books Ltd., 176-77
Hoover Institution, 57, 66n6, 114, 123n3
Howard Timmins (Pty.) Ltd., 107, 176
Howard University, 163
Human and Rousseau (Pty.) Ltd., 176

Indices, *see* Periodicals, indices to
Institute for the Study of English in Africa, 43, 45, 49n4, 118, 150, 169, 181, 184
International African Institute, 105

Journals, *see* Periodicals

Kraus-Thomson Organization, 178, 182n5

Library catalogues, *see* Bibliographies, library catalogues as
Library of Congress, *see* U.S., Library of Congress
Literary bibliographies, *see* Bibliographies
Literary criticism, *see* Literature, criticism
Literature: academic context of, 9–11, 29;

activity in increasing, x–xi, 4, 6–8; associations for the study of, 4, 11n3. *See also* Societies, scholarly; artistic merit of, 13–16; black exclusiveness of, 40–41; collection of, by libraries, 9–10; Commonwealth, study of, 26–27; criticism of, 8, 13–16; development of, 3–8, 14–16, 21–22; encyclopedias of, *see* Encyclopedias of literature; English, as a discipline, 25–26, 41–42; form and content of, 14–16; functional value of, 30–31; history of, 5–6; multidisciplinary value of, 30–33; and propaganda, 19–20; quality of, improving, 5; research on, increasing, 4; self-identity of Africa in, 5; as social commentary, 16–20, 21–22; social opinions expressed in, 18–19; and social sciences, 31–33; study of, 25–36, 39–40; themes in, 20–22; university curricula for, 25–30; *see also* Bibliographies, Encyclopedias, Periodicals, Research in progress, Theses
Longman Group, 51n16, 177
Longman Penguin Southern Africa Ltd., 51n16
Longman Rhodesia Ltd., 51n16

Macmillan South Africa (Pty.) Ltd., 177
Maskew Miller Ltd., 107
Michigan State University, 114, 123n4
Modern Language Association of America, 4, 11n3, 27, 179–80, 181

National Bibliographies, *see* Bibliographies, national
National Documentation Centre for Afrikaans Language and Literature, 150
National English Documentation Centre, 42, 150
Non-serial bibliographies, *see* Bibliographies, non-serial
Northwestern University, 28, 45, 92
Novel, *see* Literature
Novelists, *see* Authors

Oxford University Press, 177
Oxford University Press Southern Africa, 51n16

Penguin Books, 177
Periodicals: growth of, 4; guide to, as proposed project, 118; guides to Africana, 113–18; indices, general, 119–20; indices to Africana, 105–07, 119–25; indices to literary, 103–04, 119–25; list of Africana, 113–19, 125–42; as serial bibliographies of Africana, 105–09
Perskor-Boeke, 50n7, 107, 176

Political situation, ix–x; government control of, 6–7, 11–12n11; *see also* titles of individual Acts
Publishers: of African Literature, 175–78; directories of, 175
Publishing, 42–43; data on, 38–39; increase in, 4

R. R. Bowker Company, 178
Racial discrimination, as literary concern, 17–20
Ravan Press, 107, 176
Regional studies, *see* Area studies
Research in progress: Africanist, essential titles, 151; guides to, 149–55; guides to Africanist, 150–51
Rhodes University, 49n4
Rocky Mountain Southwest African Studies Association, 179
Royal Commonwealth Society, 45, 56

Scholarly societies, *see* Societies, scholarly
School of Oriental and African Studies, *see* University of London, School of Oriental and African Studies
Second World Black and African Festival of Arts and Culture, 89
Serial bibliographies, *see* Bibliographies, serial
Social conditions expressed in literature, 15, 16–20
Social sciences, and area studies, 10
Societies: African literature, best sources of information on, 181–82; scholarly and professional, 178–82; *see also* Literature, associations for the study of
Society, as influence on creativity, 14–16
South African bibliographies, *see* Bibliographies
South African Literature, *see* Literature
Southern African Research Association, 179
Southern Association of Africanists, 179
Standing Conference on Library Materials on Africa, 39, 40, 43, 44, 45, 47–48, 179
Stanford University, 114, 123n3
Suppression of Communism Act, 7

Tafelberg Publishers Ltd., 176
Theses: bibliographies of, 143–49; bibliographies of African literature, essential titles, 149; bibliographies of Africanist, 147–49; list of South African Literature, 155–60
Trade publications, 100–103, 175
Twayne Publishers, 177

U.S., Library of Congress, 163
Union of Writers of African Peoples, 41
University Microfilms, 178, 182n4
University of Birmingham, 34n7
University of Cambridge, African Studies Centre, 86
University of Cape Town, 73; School of Librarianship, 166, 167, 172n23
University of East Anglia, 33n1
University of Edinburgh, 33n1
University of Exeter, 33n1
University of Hull, 33n1
University of Kent, 33n1
University of Lancaster, 34n7
University of Leeds, 26, 33n1, 34n7, 45
University of London, School of Oriental and African Studies, 28, 34n7, 105, 121
University of Oxford, 34n7
University of Sussex, 26, 34n7
University of Texas at Austin, 45
University of the Witwatersrand, 73; Department of Bibliography, Librarianship and Typography, 166, 167, 172n20
University of York, 34n7

Western Association of Africanists, 179
William Collins Sons, 177
Working Party on Library Holdings of Commonwealth Literature, 27, 40, 50-n10
Writers, *see* Authors
Writing, *see* Literature

Yale University, 45, 78, 184

Zell, Hans, 105

Author/Title Index

This index includes all authors, corporate and personal, mentioned in the preceding pages as well as the titles of books and articles by them. In the case of titles short forms have been used wherever feasible, although in many cases it has been necessary to include full citations in order to avoid confusion. The entries also include the titles of journals and series discussed in the text. The only items not entered in this author/title index are theses (pages 155–60) and citations in the bibliography (pages 185–219).

ACLALS Bulletin, 180
ASA Review of Books, 131, 178, 179
ASLIB, 146, 152n9
Abbia, 126–27
Abrahams, Lionel, 176
Abrahams, Peter, 5, 18, 21, 26, 33, 57, 61, 64, 67n30, 68n39, 85, 88, 92, 101, 162, 164, 168
Abramova, S. Yu, 96n18
Abrash, Barbara, 29, 35n14, 87, 162, 163, 164, 170n4
Abstract/Index to A.S.A. Annual Meeting Papers, 122, 125n29
Academic Writer's Guide to Periodicals, 115, 123n8
Accessions List of Pretoria State Library, 102
Achebe, Chinua, 41–42, 51n15
"Acquisition of African Published Materials," 50n7
Acquisitions from the Third World, 51–52n19
"Additions and Corrections to Janheinz Jahn's *Bibliography of Neo-African Literature*," 165, 171n16
Adloff, Virginia, 57, 66n7
Africa, 79n7, 88, 124n22
Africa: A Handbook, xivn2
Africa: A Selective, Working Bibliography, 87, 95n5
Africa: Classification Schedule, Classified Listing [Harvard University Library], 87, 94–95n4
Africa Current, 127

Africa Digest, 127
Africa in Modern Literature, 22n6, 23-n20, 91, 164, 171n9
Africa-Related Doctoral Dissertations and Masters Theses Completed at University of Wisconsin-Madison, 154n26
Africa-Related Theses and Dissertations at the University of Illinois at Urbana-Champaign, 154n26
Africa Report, 88, 90, 127
Africa South, 182n5
Africa South in Exile, 182n5
Africa South of the Sahara [Conover], 74, 80n19
Africa South of the Sahara: A Bibliography for Undergraduate Libraries, 91, 96n11
Africa South of the Sahara: A Resource and Curriculum Guide, 92–93, 96n17
Africa South of the Sahara: A Select and Annotated Bibliography, 91, 94, 96n13
Africa South of the Sahara: A Selected and Annotated Bibliography [Missionary Research Library], 87, 88, 95n5
Africa South of the Sahara: A Selected, Annotated List of Writings, 91–92, 94, 96n14
Africa South of the Sahara: A Student's Guide to Selected Reference Sources, 96n17
Africa South of the Sahara: Index to Periodical Literature, 120–21, 122, 125-n25, 125n30
Africa Today, 88, 127, 128

"African Acquisitions Trip Report–1975," 51–52n19
African Affairs, 124n22, 128, 182n5
Africa and Black American Studies, 115, 116, 123, 123n8
"Africa and Caribbean Writings: A Bibliographic Survey," 163, 170n6
African Arts, 128
African Authors: A Companion to Black African Writing, 63, 68n34, 166, 172n19
African Bibliographic Center, 115, 123n7
"African Bibliography Today: Selected and Current Bibliographical Tools for African Studies, 1967–68," 74, 80n19
African Biographies, 59, 67n19
African Book Publishing Record, 41, 42, 51n16, 106–07, 112n20, 116–17, 124-n13, 128, 175, 182n2
African Book Trade Directory, 175, 182n1
African Book World and Press – a Directory, 175, 182n2
African Books in Print, 105, 106–07, 112n20, 112n21
African Creative Writing Series [Longman], 4, 177
"African Critics on African Literature," 129
African Culture and the Christian Church, 35n19
African Encyclopedia, 58, 65, 66n10
African-English Literature: A Short Survey and Anthology of Prose and Poetry Up to 1965, 61
African Experience, 23n22, 92, 96n16, 114, 123n5
African History and Literatures: Classification Schedule, Classified Listing [Harvard University Library], 87, 94, 95n4
"African Literary Themes," 134
"African Literature and American Universities," 33n2, 34n9, 35n23, 50n6
"African Literature and Its Western Critics," 127
African Literature and the Universities, 34n6, 91, 92
African Literature Association Newsletter, 180
African Literature in English, 77, 81n27
"African Literature in University Education," 34n6
"African Literature 1971–1972: A Checklist," 165, 172n18
"African Literature Revisited: A Search for African Critical Standards," 141
African Literature Today, 4, 11n4, 124-n21, 128–29, 134, 181
"African Literature: What Does It Take to Be Its Critic?" 129

African Periodicals in the Library of the British Museum, 116, 123–24n12
African Research and Documentation, 45, 46, 80n17, 129, 148–49, 150–51, 154-n22, 179
"African Socio-Political Process: A Model from Literature," 35n17
African Studies: A Quarterly Journal, 129
African Studies Association [U.S.], 150, 155n30
African Studies Association [U.K.], 150
African Studies Bulletin, 80n16, 130
African Studies in the U.S.S.R., 96n18
"African Studies in the United States: 1955–1975," 34n9, 35n13
African Studies Newsletter, 76, 148, 153-n16, 178, 179
African Studies Research: A Brief Guide to Selected Bibliographies, 72, 74, 80n19
African Studies Research Committee [South Africa], 151, 155n36
African Studies Review, 122, 125n28, 129–30, 132, 135, 178, 179
African Voices, 61, 67–68n31
African Who's Who, 67n25
African Writers on African Writing, 12-n13, 23n19, 24n24, 176
African Writers Series [Heinemann], 4, 84, 114, 176
African Writing Today, 109
Africana Acquisitions: Report of a Publication Survey Trip, 51n19
"Africana Bibliomania," 170n2
Africana Catalogue of the Ibadan University Library, 86, 84n3
Africana in Scandinavian Research Libraries, 108, 109, 112n23
"Africana in the Indexes," 125n30
Africana Journal, 45, 76, 106, 112n18, 130, 132
Africana Library Journal, 80n16, 130
Africana Nova, 91, 108, 112n22
Afriscope, 117
Afro-American Studies, 130
Alan Paton, 68n37, 168, 169, 173n29, 177
Alan Paton: A Bibliography, 169, 172n20
"Alex La Guma and Responsibilities of the South African Writer," 137
Alexander, H. P., 97n5
Allary, Jean, 171n11
Alman, Miriam, 116, 123n9, 153–54n21
Altbach, Philip G., 38, 50n7, 51n18
Altick, Richard D., 90, 94, 95n9
American and Canadian Doctoral Dissertations and Master's Theses on Africa, 1888–1974, 147–48, 153n15
American Book Publishing Record, 101, 102, 110n5

American Doctoral Dissertations, 145–46, 147, 152n6, 153n14
"American Image in African Literature," 133
American Library Association, 102, 111-n12
American Literature, English Literature and World Literatures in English: An Information Guide Series [Gale], 178
American Universities Field Staff, 90, 91, 96n12
"American University and Research Library Holdings in African Literature," 52n20
Amosu, Margaret, 76, 92, 162, 170n3
Anderson, Susan, 57, 66n9, 68n39
Annotated List of Theses Submitted to University of East Africa, 154n26
Annual Bibliography of English Language and Literature, 103, 104, 111n13, 120
Anyakoha, Maduka W., 38, 50n7, 134
Apartheid: Its Effects on Education, Science, Culture and Information, 23n20
"Apollo, Dionysius and Other Performers in Dan Jacobson's South African Circus," 142
Approaches to African Literature, 162, 170n5
"Area Studies and Library Resources," 12n20
Ariel, 119, 124n21, 125n28, 130–31
Armstrong, James C., 51–52n19
Armstrong, Robert P., 13, 22n1, 35n13, 51n14, 51n18
"Artist As a Creative Force in Education and Society," 139
"Arts in Human Culture," 22n1
Asamani, J. O., 120, 121, 125n25
"Aspects of African Publishing 1945–1974," 51n17
Association des Universités Partiellement ou Entièrement de Langue Française, 145, 152n4
Astrinsky, Aviva, 41, 51n14, 92, 167, 172n22
Author's and Writer's Who's Who, 59, 60, 65, 67n26
"Autobiographies in Africa," 23n21
Aviecenne, Paul, 70, 79n2

Ba Shiru, 115, 131
Bantock, G. H., 31, 35n19
Bantu Studies, 129
Beeton, D. R., 23n20, 108, 168–69, 173n30
Beier, Ulli, 22n2, 162n3
Beinash, Judith, 172n20
Bennett, Jack, 14–15
Bentel, Lea, 169, 172n20

Berry, Jack, 35n13, 51n14
Berthoud, J. A., 68n37
Besterman, Theodore, 70, 72, 78n1, 80n14
Beyer, Barry, 92–93 96n17, 164
Bibliographic Guide to Black Studies, 94-n2, 108, 109, 112n23
Bibliographic Guide to the Negro World, 78, 79n13, 89, 94, 95n7
Bibliographic Index, 70–71, 78, 79n4
"Bibliographical and Archival Resources for African Studies," 80n20
"Bibliographical Notes: Southern Africa," 80n16
"Bibliographical Problems in Creative African Literature," 35n15, 49n3, 161, 170n1
"Bibliographical Progress" [Musiker], 80-n16
"Bibliographical Progress in South Africa," 80n16
Bibliographical Series [University of Cape Town], 92
Bibliographical Services Throughout the World, 70, 79n2
Bibliographie de la France, 100, 110n2, 146, 152n10
"Bibliographie Française sur l'Afrique au Sud du Sahara," 15, 111n16
Bibliographies Subject and National, 71, 79n8, 110n2
Bibliographische Bericht, 70–71, 78, 79n5
Bibliography, Documentation, Terminology, 79n2
Bibliography of African Bibliographies, 72, 79n11
Bibliography of African Bibliographies Covering Territories South of the Sahara, 71–72, 79n10
"A Bibliography of African Literary Criticism, 1947–1966," 163–64, 171n8
Bibliography of African Studies, 89, 95n6
Bibliography of Africana, 76, 79n9, 81-n24, 90, 95n8
"Bibliography of Africana Bibliographies 1965–1975," 76, 81n25
"Bibliography of American Dissertations and Theses on African Literature," 148, 153n17
"Bibliography of American Doctoral Dissertations on African Literature," 148, 153n17
"Bibliography of Anthropology Bibliographies: Africa," 75, 81n22
"Bibliography of Books and Key Articles on Africa Published in . . . Poland," 96n18
Bibliography of Commonwealth Literature, 164, 171n14

Bibliography of Creative African Writing, 49n5, 165, 171n15, 182n5
Bibliography of Criticism on African Literature in English, 49n5
Bibliography of Neo-African Literature, 171n15
Bibliography of Overseas Publications about South Africa, 80n18, 108, 112n22
"Bibliography of Recent Africanist Bibliographies in Journals," 81n25
Bibliography of South African English Literature, 169, 173n33
Bibliography of South African English Novels, 51n14, 167, 172n22
Bibliography of South African Literature in English, 49n4
"Bibliography of South African Literature in English, 1964–1968," 167, 172n24
Bibliography of the Works of Ignatius Roy Dunnachie Campbell, 172n23
Biographical Dictionaries Master Index, 57, 66n4
Biography [Royal Commonwealth Society], 56, 66n1, 66n2
Biography Index, 56, 66n3
Birkos, Alexander S., 115, 116, 118, 123, 123n8
Bishop, Rand, 163–64, 171n8
Bite of Hunger, 14
Black Academy Review, 130
Black Aesthetics: Papers from a Colloquium, 35n17
Black African Literature: An Introduction, 23n16, 23n20
Black African Literature in English, 29, 35n15, 162, 170n4
Black Creation, 130
Black Experience I: 400 Years of Black Literature, 182n5
Black Images, 130
Black Interpreters, 12n16, 22n9, 23n20, 107, 136, 176
Black Mind, 134
Black Orpheus, 117, 121, 125n28, 131
Black Review, 132
Blair, Dorothy, 34n6
Blame Me on History, 21, 68n39
Blanket Boy's Moon, 63
"Blanket Order Supplier: A Resumé of the Work of the African Imprint Library Services," 50n8
Bloom, Harry, 40
Bloomfield, Valerie, 49n1
Blotner, Joseph, 31–32, 35n21
The Boer War in the Novel in English, 1884–1966, 172n23
Bogaert, Jozef, 72, 78, 79n12
Bol, Vincent P., 171n11

Bolt, 116
Book Trade of the World, 175, 182n1
Books Abroad, 102, 111n12, 124n21, 132
Books and Pamphlets by South African Jewish Writers, 172n20
"Books and Publishing in Selected African Countries," 51–52n19
Books in Print, 101, 110n6
Bookseller, 102, 111n10
Brady, Sister Mary William, 164, 171n13
Bratton, Michael, 147, 153n14
Brief Lives: A Biographical Guide to the Arts, 61, 67n28
"Bright Promise of Publishing in Developing Countries," 51n18
Brink, André, 140
British and Commonwealth Fiction Since 1950, 164, 171n12
British Book News, 102, 111n9
British Books in Print, 102, 111n9
British Humanities Index, 119, 120, 122, 124n20, 124–25n22
British National Bibliography, 101–02, 106, 111n7, 111n8
Brown, J. Cudd, 87, 95n5
Brown, Lloyd W., 133, 142
Brutus, Dennis, 14, 22n4, 40
Bulletin d'Information et de Liaison: Études Africaines, 149, 151, 154n24, 155n35
Bulletin of Bibliography and Magazine Notes, 104, 111n14
Bulletin of Information on Current Research on the Human Sciences Concerning Africa, 79n7
Bulletin of the Association for African Literature in English, 114, 128, 181
Burkom, Selma P., 168, 173n29
Butts, Patricia L., 114, 123n4

CBCL Newsletter, 180
Callan, Edward, 68n37, 168, 169, 173n29, 177
Camberg, Helen, 172n20
Canadian Journal of African Studies, 132, 163
Canadian Theses, 146, 152n8
Carnes, Valerie, 142
Carpenter, F. I., 68n37
Carter, Gwendolen, 22n1, 29, 34n9, 35n13
Cartey, Wilfred, 23n20, 23n22
Cassell's Encyclopaedia of World Literature, 58, 66n14
Castaways, 15, 177
Catalogue des Thèses de Doctorat Soutenues devant les Universités Française, 146, 152n10

Catalogue Général de la Libraire Fran-çaise, 100, 110n2

Catalogue of the African Collection in the Moorland Foundation, 87–88, 95n5

Catalogue of the Melville J. Herskovits Library of African Studies, 84, 85–86, 93, 94n2

Catalogue of Union Periodicals, 116, 124-n14

Catalogue Systématique de la Section Afrique [Musée de l'Homme], 86, 87, 94n3

"Censorship and the Primary Homeland," 140

Central Asian Research Centre, 93, 96n18

Centre d'Analyse et de Recherche Documentaires pour l'Afrique Noire, 105, 111n16, 120, 149, 150, 151, 154n24, 155n35

Cercle de la Libraire, 100, 110n2

Chambers Biographical Dictionary, 58, 67n18

" 'Chaos, That's the Point': Art as Metaphor in Doris Lessing's *The Golden Notebook,*" 142

Checklist of Serials for African Studies, 114, 123n3

Children of Violence, 33, 64

Ch'indaba, 117, 132–33

Chocolates for My Wife; Slices From My Life, 68n39

Choice, 90, 102, 111n12

Chosen Tongue; English Writing in the Tropical World, 12n15

Clark, Alden H., 51n18

Clarke, D. A., 37, 49n1, 51–52n19

Classic, 115, 120, 139

Cloete, Stuart, 67n30

Coetzee, J. M., 137

Collison, Robert, 52n22, 70, 71, 79n2, 79n8, 110n2

Collocott, T. C., 67n18

Colman, James S., 148, 153n19

Combined Book Exhibit, Inc., 89, 95n6

Commonwealth in Africa, 89, 95n6

Commonwealth Institute, 89, 95n6

"Commonwealth Literary Periodicals," 124n18

"Commonwealth Literature: Its Study and Sources," 33n2

"Commonwealth Literature 1974–1975: A Guide to Resources," 126

Commonwealth Newsletter, 180

"Company Profiles," 51n16

Comparative Approach in Area Studies and the Disciplines, 34n12

Comparative Literature, 124n21

Comparative Literature Studies, 124n21

Comprehensive Dissertation Index, 146, 152n7

"Conceptual Review of Area and Comparative Studies," 34n12

Conch, 115, 133

Conch Review of Books, 133

Conference on the Acquisition of Material from Africa, 49n1

Congress of Africanists, 41

Conover, Helen F., 74, 80n19, 90, 91–92, 94, 96n14, 114, 123n2

"Contemporary African Literature," 23n22

Contemporary Authors: A Bio-Bibliographical Guide, 57, 60, 65, 67n27

Contemporary Novelists, 61, 67n29

Contrast, 114, 115, 117, 125n28, 133

Cook, Mercer, 35n21, 109

Cope, Jack, 56, 57, 58, 60, 85

Couzens, Tim, 168

Creative African Writing in the European Languages, 162, 170n3

Creative Writing from Black Africa, Sub-Sahara, 164, 171n12

"Crisis in Area Programs: A Time for Innovation," 34–35n12

"Crisis of Consciousness in Modern African Literature," 132

Critical Writings on Commonwealth Literature: A Selective Bibliography, 164, 171n13

Criticism, 124n21

Criticism on African Literature in English, 77, 81n28, 164, 171n14

Critique, 124n21, 125n28, 134

Critique: Revue Générale, 133–34

Crooke, Arthur, 164, 171n12

Cruger, Doris M., 147, 153n13

Crux, 116

Cry the Beloved Country, 5–6, 18

Cullinan, Patrick, 176

"Cultural Formalism and the Criticism of Modern African Literature," 136

Cumulative Bibliography of African Studies, 86–87, 94n2

Cumulative Book Index, 101, 110n4

Current Africanist Research: International Bulletin, 150, 154n28, 154n29

Current Bibliography on African Affairs, 76, 79n7, 105, 106, 111n17, 121–22, 134

Current Biography, 56, 57, 65, 66n3

Current South African Periodicals, 117, 123, 124n15

Daedalus, 124n21

Daiches, David, 60, 67n27

Dan Jacobson: A Bibliography, 172n20

Daphne Rooke; Her Works and Selected Literary Criticism, 172n20
Dargitz, Robert L., 87, 88, 95n5
Dathorne, O. R., 134
Davidson, Elizabeth, 87, 162, 166, 167, 172n21
Davis, Valerie Margaret, 172n23
de Benko, Eugene, 51–52n19, 106, 112n18, 114, 123, 123n4
"Declaration of African Writers," 51n13
de Kock, W. J., 59, 67n23
de Saxe, Shora Gertrude, 172n20
Deutsche Bibliographie: Wöhentliches Verzeichnis, 100, 110n2
Deutsche Bucherei, 100, 110n2, 146–47, 152–53n11
Deutsche Nationalbibliographie, 100, 110-n2
Deutsche Nationalbibliographie; Reihe C: Dissertationen und Habilitationsschrift, 146, 147, 152–53n11
Development Studies: Register of Research in the United Kingdom 1975/76, 151, 155n34
de Villiers, André, 38, 43, 49n4, 151, 155-n38, 169
Dickie, John, 59, 67n21
Dickman, Daryl, 122, 125n29
Dictionary Catalog of the Missionary Research Library, 95n5
Dictionary Catalog of the Schomburg Collection, 84, 85, 86, 88–89, 93, 94n2, 109
Dictionary of African Biography, 58, 59, 67n22
Dictionary of National Biography, 59
Dictionary of South African Biography, 59, 67n23
Dikobe, Modikwe, 15, 176
Dinstel, Marion, 152n10
Direction des Bibliothèques de France, *see* France, Direction des Bibliothèques de France
Directory of African and Afro-American Studies in United States, 34n7
Directory of African Studies in the United States 1974–75, 34n11
Disciples of Christ Research Library, 87, 88, 95n5
Dissertation Abstracts, 144, 152n2
Dissertation Abstracts International, 144–45, 146, 147, 152n2, 152n3
"Dissertations on Africa" [*African Studies Newsletter*], 148, 153n16
Dissertations on Africa: A List of Titles of Dissertations on Africa That Were Completed at Indiana University, 154n26
Doctoral Dissertations Accepted by American Universities, 147, 152n6

Doctoral Dissertations on Africa, 178, 182n4
Dodson, Don, 23n20
Doris Lessing: A Bibliography, 172n20
Doris Lessing: A Checklist of Primary and Secondary Sources, 168, 173n29
Down Second Avenue, 32, 68n39
Downey, J. A., 39, 50n8
Drawn in Colour, 68n39
"Dream and Action in Lessing's *Summer Before the Dark*," 134
Dressler, Claus Peter, 38, 49n5, 165, 166, 168, 171n15, 171n17, 182n5
Drum, 5, 6, 167, 134–35
Dudley, D. R., 67n27
Duignan, Peter, 57, 66n6, 71, 72, 74, 75-76, 77, 78, 81n23, 81n24, 90, 91, 94, 95n8, 96n11, 114, 123n3, 147, 153n14

Easterbrook, David L., 76, 81n25
Ehrman, Edith, 90–91, 95–96n10, 96n11
Emenyonu, Ernest, 129, 141
The Emergence of African Fiction, 12n17, 23n20
Encyclopaedia Africana, 58
Encyclopaedia of Southern Africa, 58, 66n11
Encyclopaedia of World Literature in the Twentieth Century, 58, 66n15
English and Afrikaans Novels on South African History: A Bibliography, 172n23
"English and the African Writer," 51n15
English Association, 104, 111n14
English in Africa, 135, 181
"English-Language Literature and Politics in South Africa," 137
English Literature in Transition, 124n21
English Studies in Africa, 11n4, 45, 103, 115, 117, 120, 121, 135, 167–68
"Establishment of African Literature Association," 182n6
Essay and General Literature Index, 104, 111n14
Essays in Criticism, 124n21, 124–25n22
Exile and Tradition, 23n20
Expanding Horizons in African Studies, 22n1

Fanon, Franz, 28
"Fiction and Politics: The African Writers Abdication," 23n17
"Fiction by African Authors: A Preliminary Checklist," 163, 170n6
"Fiction by Black South Africans," 22n2
Fiction Catalog, 104, 111n14
"Fifty Years of the South African Novel," 167, 172–73n26
Fleischmann, W. Bernard, 58, 66n15

Fontana Modern African Novels [Collins], 177
Fontvieille, Jean-Roger, 72, 78, 79n13, 89, 94, 95n7
Forde, Daryll, 93, 96n18
"Form and Technique in the Novels of Richard Rive and Alex La Guma," 137
Forthcoming Books, 110n6
"Four Modes of *Drum,*" 23n20
"Four Splendid Voices," 23n18
France, Direction des Bibliothèques de France, 146, 152n10
Freer, Percy, 71–72, 79n10, 116, 124n14
Frey, Mitsue Miyata, 34n7, 34n11, 150, 155n31
Friedrich-Ebert-Stiftung, 59, 67n19
Fugard, Sheila, 15, 177
Fung, Karen, 57, 66n5

Gardner, Colin, 140
Garlick, Peter C., 154n26
Garling, Anthea, 72, 79n11
Gérard, Albert, 35n15, 38, 49n3, 140, 161, 170n1
Gibson, Gordon D., 75, 81n22
Glazier, Kenneth M., 90, 91, 94, 96n13, 114, 123n3
Going Home, 22n13, 64, 68n41, 169
Goodwin, K. L., 52n23
Gordimer, Nadine, 8, 12n16, 15, 18–19, 21, 22n9, 22n13, 23n20, 24n24, 32, 40, 56, 57, 58, 59, 60, 67n30, 85, 101, 107, 137, 140, 176
Gorman, G. E., 173n30
Grass Is Singing, 176
Gray, Richard A., 71, 79n6, 79n7, 107
Gray, Stephen, 138, 173n30
Greider, Theodore, 77, 81n27, 178
Guest of Honour, 15, 19, 32
Guide to Modern World Literature, 67n28
Guide to Research and Reference Works on Sub-Saharan Africa, 75–76, 81n23, 90, 94, 95n8
Guide to South African Reference Books, 73, 80n18
Guide to Theses and Dissertations: An Annotated, International Bibliography of Bibliographies, 144, 146, 152n1
Gurr, Andrew, 35n17
Gutkind, Peter C. W., 92, 94, 96n15

H. W. Wilson Company, 78
Hale, Thomas, 182n6
Hamner, R. D., 117, 124n16
Handbook of Library Holdings of Commonwealth Literature in the United Kingdom, 33–34n4, 52n22
Haresnape, Geoffrey, 177

Harris, Chauncey D., 10, 12n20
Hartwig, Gerald W., 74–75, 77, 81n21, 90, 95n8
Harvard University Library, 87, 94–95n4
Hawk Alone, 15
Head, Bessie, 15, 67n30, 87, 176
Herbstein, Denis, 35n24
Herman Charles Bosman: A Bibliography, 172n20
Henderson, Stephen E., 35n21, 109
Herdeck, Donald E., 63, 65, 68n34, 166, 172n19
"History of Black African Literature (A Select Bibliography of Criticism)," 165, 171n17
History of Neo-African Literature, 91
Hoehn, R. Philip, 154n26
Holdsworth, Mary, 93, 96n18
Holson, M. B., 167, 172n23
Hoover Institution, 105, 111n15, 148, 153n18
Horne, A. J., 33n1
Howard University Library, 87–88, 95n5
Human Sciences Research Council, *see* South Africa, Human Sciences Research Council
Humanities Index, 119, 120, 122, 124n20, 124n21
Hutchinson, Alfred, 60, 61, 64, 68n39, 87, 168

Ibadan University Library, 86, 94n3
Index Africanus, 105, 120, 121, 125n25
Index to American Doctoral Dissertations, 152n6
Index to American Literature, English Literature and World Literatures in English, 77, 81n27
Index to Commonwealth Little Magazines, 79n7
Index to South African Periodicals, 121, 122, 125n25
Index to Theses Accepted for Higher Degrees by the Universities of Great Britain and Ireland, 146, 152n9
Indexes to African Books, 125n29
Indiana University, African Studies Program, 154n26
Institute of African Studies Research Classified List 1, 87, 95n5
Institute of Commonwealth Studies [London], *see* University of London, Institute of Commonwealth Studies
International African Bibliography, 45, 76, 105–06, 111n17, 121–22, 123
International African Institute, 34n7, 86, 93, 94n3, 96n18, 120, 150, 154n28, 154n29

International Bibliography of Books and Articles on the Modern Languages and Literatures, 103, 104, 111n13, 120, 122
International Guide to African Studies Research, 34n7, 150, 154n29
International Register of Organisations Undertaking Africanist Research, 150, 154–55n29
International Who's Who, 59, 67n26
Internationale Bibliographie der Zeitschriftenliteratur, 119–20, 125n23
"Interview" [Kole Omotoso], 51n13
"Introduction" [*Black African Literature in English*], 35n14
Introduction to African Literature, 22n2, 162n3
Introduction to the African Novel, 176
"Introduction to the Bibliography of Sub-Saharan Africa at Indiana University," 80n20
"Inventaire de Thèses et Mémoires Africanistes de Langue Française en Cours," 151, 155n35
"Inventaire de Thèses et Mémoires Africanistes de Langue Française: Soutenances," 149, 154n24
Inventaire des Thèses Suisses Consacrées à l'Afrique an Sud du Sahara, 149, 154n25
Ipp, Catherina, 172n20
Issue, 122, 178, 179
Iyasere, Solomon Ogbede, 129, 136
Izevbaye, D. S., 129

Jabavu, Noni, 60, 61, 64, 68n39, 87, 168
Jacobson, Dan, 40, 56, 60, 64, 67n30, 68n40, 85
Jahn, Janheinz, 38, 49n5, 62, 65, 68n33, 91, 92, 162, 165, 166, 168, 170n5, 171n15, 171n17, 182n5
Jahresverzeichnis der Deutschen Hochschulschriften, 146–47, 152–53n11
Jeanpierre, W., 32, 35n23
Jeffares, A. Norman, 35n14, 61
"Johannesburg Genre," 23n20
Johannesburg Public Library, 121, 125n25
Joint Acquisitions List of Africana, 76, 86, 89, 106, 108–09, 112n23
Journal of African Studies, 122
Journal of Commonwealth Literature, 4, 11n4, 38, 45, 50n6, 56, 79n7, 103, 110, 115, 119, 120, 122, 124–25n22, 136, 167–68, 169, 173n28, 180, 181
Journal of Modern African Studies, 122, 124–25n22, 136
Journal of Modern Literature, 124n21
Journal of Southern African Affairs, 136–37, 179

Journal of Southern African Studies, 124–25n22, 137
Journal of the New African Literature and the Arts, 120, 137
Judson, Jean, 154n26

Kagan, Alfred, 147–48, 153n15
Kallish, Steven, 134
Kay, Ernest, 67n22
Keane, Christiane, 126
Kettle, M. R., 50n9
Killam, G. D., 23n19, 24n24, 40–41, 50–n11, 163, 164, 170n7, 176
Kiersen, S., 172n23
Kinsman, Clare D., 60, 65, 67n27
Klima, Vladimir, 12n11, 93, 107
Knoke, Susan, 38, 49n2
Koester, Robert, 114, 123n5
Kraus Bibliographical Bulletin, 182n5
Krige, Uys, 67n30
Kronenberger, Louis, 61, 67n28
Kuper, Hilda, 14–15
Kuse, Wandile F., 122

La Guma, Alex, 15, 19, 21, 40, 60, 61, 62, 67n30, 85, 89, 92, 101, 163, 164
Lang, D. M., 67n27
Laredo, Ursula, 167, 172n24
Larson, Charles R., 8, 12n17, 23n20, 63, 68n36, 142
Laurens van der Post, 68n37
Lawal, Babatunde, 139
Le Beau, Dennis, 66n4
Lefcowitz, Barbara F., 134
Legum, Colin, x, xivn2
Lehman, Robert L., 87, 88, 95n5
Lessing, Doris, 8, 17, 22n13, 32, 33, 40, 64, 67n30, 68n41, 85, 142, 168, 169, 176
Lever, Rachelle, 118, 124n19
Levy, Fanelle, 172n20
Lewin Robinson, A. M., 71–72, 74
Librarian and English Literature, 12n18
Library Catalogue [SOAS], 84–85, 86, 94n2
Library of Congress, *see* U.S., Library of Congress
Lindfors, Bernth, 38, 46, 47, 49n5, 52n20, 61, 77, 81n27, 81n28, 127, 130, 137, 161, 163–64, 165, 167, 170n2, 171n8, 171n14, 171n16, 172n25, 178
List of American Doctoral Dissertations on Africa, 147, 153n13
List of Commonwealth Periodicals of Literary Interest, 50n10
List of French Doctoral Dissertations on Africa, 152n10

"Literary Periodicals in World English," 117, 124n16

"Literary Periodicals of the Commonwealth," 124n18

Literary Research Guide, 76, 81n26, 90, 94, 95n9

Literary Review, 124n21, 137–38

"Literature and Politics in South Africa," 12n13

"Literature and the Social Sciences," 35-n19

Literature and Thought of Modern Africa: A Survey, 4, 11n2, 91

Literature East and West, 138

Littératures et Poètes Noirs, 171n11

Little Magazines in South Africa, 118, 124n19

Living and the Dead, 21

Local Colour, 107

Lotus: Afro-Asian Writings, 138

Lytton, David, 40

McCartney, Barney C., 151, 155n37

McCartney, Rae G., 151, 155n37

McGill University, McLennan Library, Reference Department, 96n17

McIlwaine, John H. St. J., 148

MacRae, Donald, 3–4, 5, 8, 11n1

Maison des Sciences de l'Homme, Service d'Echange d'Informations Scientifiques, 116, 123–24n12

Makerere College Library, 154n26

Makouta-Mboukou, J. P., 19, 23n16, 23n20

Malan, S. I., 147, 153n12

"Man with the Golden Typewriter," 35n24

Marabi Dance, 176

Martha Quest, 32

Masters, Brian, 22n12

"Master's Theses in Literature Presented at American Colleges and Universities," 148, 153n17

"Master's Theses on Africa" [*African Studies Newsletter*], 153n16

Matshikiza, Todd, 60, 64, 68n39, 168

Matthews, Daniel, 74, 80n19

May, Rollo, 34n10

Mazrui, A., 23n17

Messages, 164, 171n11

Microfilm Abstracts, 144, 152n2

Militant Black Writer in Africa and the United States, 35n21

"'Minority' Publishing in South Africa," xivn3, 51n17, 128

Missionary Research Library, 87, 88, 95n5

Mizan Newsletter, 93

Modern African Writers [Evans], 64, 177

Modern American Political Novel, 35n21

"Modern Black African Writing in English: A Selected Bibliography," 50n11, 163–64, 170n7

Modern Fiction Studies, 124n21, 138

Modern Humanities Research Association, 103, 104, 111n13

Modern Language Association of America, 103, 104, 111n13, 149–50, 154n27, 164, 171n14

Modisane, Bloke, 21, 60, 61, 64, 68n39, 85

Moore, Gerald, 8, 11n15, 34n6, 35n23, 61, 91, 92, 140

Morehouse, Ward, 34n12, 90–91, 95–96-n10, 96n11

Moss, R. P., 39, 50n9

Moko, 181

Mphahlele, Ezekiel, 15, 18, 19, 21, 23n17, 23n20, 24n25, 26, 32, 40, 58, 60, 61, 64, 67n30, 68n39, 85, 89, 107, 109, 131, 162, 163, 164, 168

Munger Africana Library Notes, 138

Munro, Donald, 36n25

Munro, Ian, 151, 155n37, 176

Musée de l'Homme, Bibliothèque, 86, 87, 94n3

Musiker, Reuben, ix, xivn1, 38, 41, 43, 49n3, 49n4, 51n14, 70, 71, 73, 75, 76, 78, 79n3, 80n15, 80n16, 80n17, 80n18, 90, 94, 95n8, 129, 161, 169, 170n1

Mutiso, Gideon-Cyrus M., 4–5, 11n5, 16, 22n11, 30–31, 35n17, 35n18, 164, 171-n11

"Myth, Truth and the South African Reality in the Fiction of Sarah Gertrude Millin," 137

Nadine Gordimer, Novelist and Short Story Writer: A Bibliography, 172n20

"Nadine Gordimer: The Solitude of a White Writer," 22–23n13

"Nadine's World of Strangers," 140

National Book League, 89, 95n6, 164, 171n12

National Identity, 52n23

National Library of Canada, 146, 152n8

National Union Catalog, 84, 88, 94n1, 100–01, 110n3

"Negritude and Its Enemies," 35n23

Nell, Racilia Jilian, 172n20

New, William H., 164, 171n13

New Africans: A Guide to the Contemporary History . . . , 59, 67n20

New Approaches to African Literature, 23n20, 35n16, 162–63, 170n5

New Bibliography of African Literature, 165, 171n17

New Classic, 117, 139, 141

New Coin, 115

New Literary History, 124n21

New Nation, 139
New South African Writing, 114
New Writing from South Africa [Donker], 176
New York Public Library, 84, 85, 86, 93, 94n2, 109
Nkosi, Lewis, 13–14, 15, 18, 22n2, 58, 61, 86, 131
" 'Non-European' Writing in South Africa," 24n23
Nordmann, Almut, 68n33
Northwestern University, 84, 85–86, 88–89, 93, 94n2
Northwestern University, Melville J. Herskovits Library of African Studies, 108–09, 112n23
"Notes on Some African Writers," 163, 170n6
Novel, 124n21
"Novel and the Nation in South Africa," 12n13, 24n24

O'Barr, William M., 74–75, 77, 81n21, 90, 95n8
Obuke, J. Okpure, 131
Ochre People; Scenes from a South African Life, 68n39
Ofuso-Appiah, L. H., 66n13
Ogungbesan, Kolawole, 23n17, 23n21
Omotoso, Kole, 41, 51n13
Onge, Omafume F., 132
"Outline of U.K. Library Holdings of Commonwealth Imaginative Literature: Statistics," 33n1
Overseas Books, 102, 111n12
Oxford History of South Africa, 11n7

Paden, Ann, 22n1
Paden, John N., 23n22, 92, 96n16, 114, 123n5
Palmer, Eustace, 176
Panafrica, 114
Panofsky, Hans E., 71, 74, 75–76, 77, 79n9, 81n22, 90, 95n8, 114, 123n5
Panter-Brick, E. K., 23n17, 106
Paperbound Books in Print, 110n6
Páricsy, Pál, 6, 9, 11n9, 22n4, 93, 165, 171n16, 171n17
Parry, V. T. H., 116, 123–24n12
Paton, Alan, 5–6, 18, 19, 21, 23n18, 26, 33, 40, 58, 59, 67n30, 85, 88, 168, 177
Patterson, Margaret C., 76–77, 81n26, 90, 94, 95n9
Pauline Smith, 177
Pearson, J. D., 70, 71, 73, 78, 80n14, 105
Penguin Companion to Literature, 60, 65, 67n27
Pennsylvania State University, 87, 95n5

Periodicals for Pan-African Studies, 115, 123n7
Periodicals from Africa, 115–16, 123n9, 123n11
Periodicals in South African Libraries, 116, 117, 124n13
"Periodicals Published in Africa," 116, 123–24n12
Perry-Widstrand, Rede, 34n8
Peter Abrahams, 68n38, 168, 173n29, 177
"Peter Abrahams: A Selected Bibliography," 168, 173n29
Phylon, 120, 139
Pieterse, Cosmo, 36n25, 60, 176
Pilot Bibliography of South African English Literature, 108, 168–69, 173n30
"Political and Cultural Revolution," 36n25
"Political Theme in South and West African Novels," 122
"Politics and the African Writer," 23n17
Pollak, Karen, 145, 152n1, 152n5
Pollak, Oliver B., 145, 152n1, 152n5
Pollard, Arthur, 61, 67n28
"Popular Literature in English in Black South Africa," 137
Porter, Dorothy B., 87–88, 92, 95n5, 163, 170n6
"Portrait: Ezekiel Mphahlele," 66n5
"Position of the Afrikaans Writer," 140
Potchefstroom University, 74
Potchefstroom University, F. Potsma Library, 147, 153n12
Povey, John, 23n17, 24n23, 29, 34n9, 35n13, 35n14, 50n6, 51n14, 122, 137
Power and Innocence, 34n10
Preliminary Bibliography on Africa South of the Sahara, 90–91, 95–96n10
"Preliminary Checklist of English Short Fictions by Non-Europeans in South Africa," 167, 172n25
Présence Africaine, 5, 6, 105, 121, 133, 139
Price, Frank W., 87, 88, 95n5
Priebe, Richard K., 33n2, 34n7, 163
"Printed and Published in Africa," 89, 95n7
Proceedings of a Conference on African Languages and Literatures, 35n13, 51-n14
"Profile of an African Artist: Dennis Brutus," 137
"Prominent Bookshops in Africa," 51n16
Proper Marriage, 32
Protest and Conflict in African Literature, 36n25, 176
"Protest and Power in Black Africa," 23n17
"Protest—the South African Way," 142

Publishers' International Directory, 182n1
The Publishers' Trade List Annual, 101, 110n6
Publishers' Weekly, 101, 110n5
"Publishing and Book Development in Africa: A Bibliography," 50n7, 175, 182n3
"Publishing in Africa: A Bibliography," 50n7, 134
"Publishing in Africa: A Paper for the Seminar on African Literature," 34n8
"Publishing in Developing Countries: A Select Bibliography," 50n7
"Publishing in Sub-Saharan Africa," 51n18
"Publishing Progress in Africa 1975–76," 112n21

Quartet, 23n18
Question of Power, 176

Rake, Alan, 59, 67n21
Ramsaran, John A., 23n20, 35n16, 92, 162–63, 170n5
Randall, Peter, x–xi, xivn3, 51n17, 128, 176
Raum, O. F., 172n24
Rea, Julian, 51n17
Reader's Guide to African Literature, 62, 68n32, 117, 123, 124n17, 165–66, 172-n18
Readers' Guide to Periodical Literature, 119, 124n20
Reality, 140, 141
"Recent African Fiction," 163, 170n7
"Recent Indexes to Africana Books," 125-n29
"Recording African Periodicals," 123n1
Register of Current Research in the Humanities at the Universities [South Africa], 151, 155n36
" 'Reintegration with the Lost Self': A Theme in Contemporary African Literature," 140–41
Reitz, Conrad H., 74, 80n19
"Remembering William Plomer," 139
Répertoire des Thèses de Doctorat Soutenues Devant les Universités de Langue Française, 145, 152n4
"Report of Working Party on the Teaching of Commonwealth Literature," 52-n23
"Report on a Library Acquisitions Trip to Africa," 49n2
Research Bulletin [South Africa], 151, 155n36
Research in African Literatures, 4, 11n4, 45, 114, 115, 119, 120, 124n21, 136, 140, 142, 151, 180, 182

Research in Education, 76
"Research in Progress" [*African Research and Documentation*], 148–49, 154n22
"Research in Progress in the Modern Languages and Literatures," 149–50, 154n27
Research in Progress 1972–1974: A Selected Listing of Current Research on Africa, 150, 155n30
"Research in Progress, 1975–76" [*African Studies Newsletter*], 150, 155n31
"Research on Africa in European Centres," 148, 153n19
Research Sources for African Studies, 114, 123n4
Review of English Literature, 131
Review of English Studies, 124n21, 124–25n22
"Reviews of African Literature in Nigerian Periodicals," 130, 163–64, 171n8
Review of National Literatures, 140
Revue de Littérature Comparée, 105, 140–41
Reynolds, Michael M., 144, 152n1
Rial, Jacques, 149, 154n25
Richardson, Kenneth, 60, 67n27
Rive, Richard, 15, 19, 21, 23n19, 40
Road to Ghana, 68n39
Robben Island, 176
Rosenthal, Eric, 59, 66n11, 67n24
Rotberg, R., 23n17
Royal Commonwealth Society, 84, 85, 93, 94n2
Rubadiri, David, 20, 23n19, 23n20
Rubenstein, Roberta, 142
Rutherfoord, Anna, 61, 65, 67–68n31, 103

SCOLMA Directory of Libraries and Special Collections on Africa, 52n22
Sackett, S. J., 148, 153n17
Sartre, Jean Paul, 16–17, 30
Sartre: A Study, 22n12
Scandinavian Institute of African Studies, 108, 109, 112n23
Scheven, Yvette, 125n30, 154n26
Schild, Ulla, 68n33
Schmidt, Nancy J., 130, 133, 148, 153n17
Schneller, Anne, 147, 153n14
Scholarly Publishing, 43, 51n18
School of Oriental and African Studies, *see* University of London, School of Oriental and African Studies
Schwartz, Kraig A., 87, 95n5
Sciences Humaines en Afrique Noire: Guide Bibliographique, 72, 78, 79n12
Select Annotated Bibliography of Tropical Africa, 93, 91n18
Select Bibliography: Asia, Africa, 91, 96-n12

"Select Bibliography: Books and Articles on English Language and Literature Published in South Africa," 135

"Select Bibliography of Africana," 106, 112n19

Select Bibliography of South African Autobiographies, 66n8, 172n23

Select Bibliography of South African Novels in English, 167, 172n23

Select Bibliography on Traditional and Modern Africa, 92, 94, 96n15

Selected Bibliography of Books and Articles in the Disciples of Christ Research Library, 87, 88, 95n5

"Selected Bibliography of Critical Writing," 170n3

"Selected Bibliography (of Works by South African Writers)," 167, 172–73-n26

'Selected Reading List of Modern African Literature," 164, 171n9

Selective Bibliography for the Study of English and American Literature, 90, 94, 95n9

Selective Bibliography of Literature Written in English in Africa, Australia . . . , 164, 171n13

"Selective Introductions to African Literature," 133

Serial Bibliographies in the Humanities and Social Sciences, 71, 79n6

Serials for African Studies, 114, 123n2

Serowe, Village of the Rain Wind, 176

"Settling in England," 68n40

Seymour-Smith, Martin, 61, 67n28

"Shape of Things: Sexual Images and the Sense of Form in Doris Lessing's Fiction," 142

"Short Survey of the History of Black African Literature," 11n9

Shorter, A., 35n19

Silver, Helene, 106, 117, 124n17, 165–66, 168, 172n18

Simmons, Wendy, 81n25

Simpson, Donald, 56, 66n1, 124n18

Sims, Michael, 34n7, 34n11, 147–48, 153-n15

Smith, Datus C., Jr., 51n18

Smith, Keith, 43, 51n18

Smith, Rowland, 23n20, 106

Smith, Wilbur, 32, 36n24, 107

Snarl, 117, 141

Snyder, Emile, 51n14

Social and Political World of Alan Paton, 109

"Social Relevance of the South African Novel," 122

Social Sciences and Humanities Index, 124n20

Socio-Political Thought in African Literature, 5, 11n5, 22n11, 35n17

Soja, Edward W., 23n22, 92, 96n16, 114, 123n5

Some English Writings by Non-Europeans in South Africa, 172n20

"Some Recent African Novels in English," 172n24

Some Writings by Non-European South Africans, 166, 167, 172n21

"Something in Me Died: Autobiographies of South African Writers in Exile," 66n9

"Something Old, Something New: Recent Studies of African Literature," 130

"Sources of the First Black South African Novel in English," 138

South Africa, Human Sciences Research Council, 151, 155n36

South Africa, South African Council for Scientific and Industrial Research, 116, 117, 124n13

South Africa, State Library, 102, 108, 111n11, 112n22, 117, 124n15

"South Africa: Politics and Economics," 49n1

"South Africa: The Renaissance That Failed," 136

"South Africa: The Tortoise Literature," 22n4

"South African Bibliographical Notes and News," 80n17, 129

"South African Bibliographical Progress," 80n16

South African Bibliography: A Survey, 73, 78, 79n3, 80n15, 90, 94, 95n8

South African Bibliography [Reitz], 74, 80n19

"South African Black Writing," 131

South African Centre of the International Pen Club, 167, 172–73n26

South African Council for Scientific and Industrial Research, *see* South Africa, South African Council for Scientific and Industrial Research

"South African English Literature: Bibliographic and Bibliographical Resources and Problems," xivn1, 49n3, 51n14, 161, 170n1

"South African English Literature from the Perspective of the Seventies," 23n20

South African Jewish Biography, 172n23

South African Libraries, 73, 80n16

South African Library Association Newsletter, 73, 80n16

South African National Bibliography, 102, 111n11

South African P.E.N. Yearbook, 167, 172–73n26

South African Prose Writing in English, 12n11, 108

"South African Research Since 1969 in the Literatures of the Republic," 151, 155n38

Southern African Dictionary of National Biography, 59, 67n24

Southern African Studies: Report . . . , 39, 50n9

Southern Literary Journal, 124n21

Southern Review, 124n21

Soviet African Studies, 93, 96n18

Soviet Writing on Africa, 93, 96n18

Spohr, O. H., 125n29

Staatsbibliothek Preussischer Kulturbesitz, 71, 79n5

Standard Encyclopaedia of Southern Africa, 58, 66n12

Standing Conference on Library Materials on Africa, 105, 111n15, 116, 123n9, 123–24n12, 148, 153n20, 153–54n21

Standpunte, 126

State Library [Pretoria], *see* South Africa, State Library

"State of Criticism in African Literature," 129

Steinberg, S. H., 66n14

Stern, Maureen J., 172n23

"Structure of Commitment: A Study of Alex La Guma," 131

Student Africanist's Handbook, 90, 95n8

Studies in African Literature [Heinemann], 176

Studies in Black Literature, 124n21

Studies in English Literature, 124n21

Studies in the Novel, 124n21, 141

Studies on Modern Black African Literature, 9, 22n4, 171n17

"Study of Commonwealth Literature," 35n14

Subject Catalogue of the Royal Commonwealth Society, 84, 85, 93, 94n2

Subject Catalogue of the Royal Empire Society, 85

Subject Guide [Books in Print], 101, 110-n6

Sub-Saharan Africa: A Guide to Serials, 114–15, 123n6

Sullivan, Sally L., 151, 155n37

"Supplement to Bibliography of South African Literature in English," 167, 172n24

"Supplementary Bibliography to J. Jahn's

Bibliography of Neo-African Literature," 165, 171n16

Symposium, 124n21

Tambs, Lewis A., 115, 116, 118, 123n8

Tanna, Laura, 127

Tarbert, Gary C., 66n4

Taubert, Sigfred, 175, 182n1

Taylor, Alan R., 72, 74, 75, 77–78, 80-n19, 80n20, 89

Taylor, Sidney, 59, 67n20

"Teaching of Modern African Literature Written in a Western Language," 51n14

Tell Freedom, 68n39

Themba, Can, 15, 61

"Themes in African Literature Today," 23n20

Theoria, 117, 125n28, 141

"Thèses" [France], 146, 152n10

Theses and Dissertations on Southern Africa: An International Bibliography, 145, 152n1, 152n5

Theses in Progress in Commonwealth Studies, 149, 150, 154n23

"Theses on Africa Accepted by Howard University," 154n26

Theses on Africa Accepted by Universities in the United Kingdom and Ireland, 148, 153n20

"Theses on Sub-Saharan Africa Accepted by the University of California at Berkeley," 154n26

" 'Third World' Publishing: Problems and Prospects," 51n18

Thompson, James, 9, 12n18

Thompson, Leonard, 6, 11n7

Thorne, J. O., 67n18

Three Crown Books [Oxford University Press], 177

Threefold Cord, 21

Tibble, Anne, 61, 65, 67n31

"Towards a Bibliography of South African Literature in English," 49n4, 135, 169, 173n33

Tradition and Exile, 106

Transition, 117, 121, 122, 131, 132

Travis, Carole, 116, 123n1, 123n9

Trek, 115, 126

"Trends Abroad: South Africa," 12n11

Tucker, Martin, 14, 15, 18, 22n6, 23n20, 91, 92, 164, 171n9

Turn to the Dark, 63

Twayne's World Authors Series, 63, 64, 68n37, 177

Twentieth Century Literature, 119, 124-n21, 141, 163

Twentieth Century Writing: A Reader's Guide, 60, 67n27

Ulrich's International Periodicals Directory, 99–100, 110n1
Union Catalogue of Theses and Dissertations of the South African Universities,
147, 153n12
UNISA, 142
UNISA English Studies, 116, 141–42
United Kingdom Publications and Theses
on Africa, 105, 111n15, 148, 149, 153–
54n21
United States and Canadian Publications
and Theses on Africa, 105, 111n15, 147,
148, 153n14, 153n18
U.S., Library of Congress, 84, 94n1, 100,
101, 110n3, 114–15, 120–21, 123n6,
125n25, 147, 153n13
University of Ife Bookshop Ltd., 89, 95n7
University of London, Institute of Com-
monwealth Studies, 49, 150, 154n23
University of London, School of Oriental
and African Studies, 28, 34n7, 45, 84–
85, 86, 94n2
University of Nigeria, 87, 95n5
University of Wisconsin-Madison, African
Studies Program, 154n26
"University Press in a Developing Coun-
try," 51n18
Ushpol, R., 57, 66n8, 172n23
Uys Krige, 68n37

van der Post, Laurens, 67n30, 85
van Heyningen, C., 68n37
Varley, Douglas H., 12n11, 71–72, 79-
n10, 80n16
Vinson, James, 61, 65, 67n29
Visser, N. W., 136
Voices in the Whirlwind, 23n17, 107
von Hahmann, Gail, 34n11

Wade, Michael, 64, 68n38, 137, 142, 177
Wästberg, Per, 23n20, 109
Wake, Clive, 36n25
Wakeman, John, 60, 67n27
Walk in the Night, 21
Wanderers, 21
Warwick, Ronald, 124n18
Wauthier, Claude, 4, 91
Webster, John B., 92, 94, 96n15
Webster's Biographical Dictionary, 58,
66n17
Webster's New World Companion to Eng-
lish and American Literature, 61, 67n28
Weinstock, D. J., 172n23
Whispers from a Black Continent, 23n20
Whitaker's Cumulative Booklist, 102, 111-
n9
"Who Controls Book Publishing in Anglo-
phone Middle Africa?" 43, 51n18
Who's Who in Africa, 59, 67n21

Who's Who in African Literature, 62, 63,
68n33
Who's Who in Twentieth Century Liter-
ature, 61, 67n28
Who's Who of Southern Africa, 59, 67n25
"Why African Literature?" 23n19, 23n20
Whyte, Morag, 172n23
Wilhelm, Donald, 34n12
Wilhelm, Peter, 139
Wilkov, A., 87, 167, 172n20
Wilson, Gail, 33n4, 52n22
Wilson, Monica, 6, 11n7
Wilson, Richard Middlewood, 163, 164,
171n10
Winegarten, Renee, 32, 35n22
Winterbottom, Irina, 49n3, 135, 169, 173-
n33
Witherell, Julian W., 43, 51n19, 122, 125-
n30
"Work in Progress in African Literatures,"
151, 155n37
Working Index to African Literature, 164,
171n10
Working Party on Library Holdings of
Commonwealth Literature, 117–18, 124-
n18
Works of Sarah Gertrude Millin, 172n20,
172n23
World Authors, 60, 67n27
World Bibliography of African Bibliog-
raphies, 72–73, 78, 80n14
World Bibliography of Bibliographies, 70,
78n1
World List of Specialized Periodicals, 116,
123–24n12
"World Literature in Review," 132
World Literature Written in English, 27,
142, 180, 182
Wreath for Udomo, 18
Wright, Andrew, 90, 94, 95n9
Writer in Modern Africa, 109
Writers and Revolution: The Fatal Lure
of Action, 35n22
Writer's Directory, 59, 60, 67n26
"Writers in Exile: South Africans in Lon-
don," 128

Yang, C. K., 34n12
Year's Work in English Studies, 104, 111-
n14
Yudelman, Myra, 172n20

Zell, Hans M., 38, 50n7, 62, 65, 68n32,
106, 107, 112n20, 112n21, 117, 123,
124n17, 129, 165–66, 168, 172n18, 175,
182n2, 182n3
Zirimu, Pio, 35n17
Zonk, 126
Zwelonke, D. M., 176